WILLIAM III AND THE RESPECTABLE REVOLUTION

William III
and the Respectable Revolution

The Part Played by William of Orange
in the Revolution of 1688

by Lucile Pinkham

Archon Books   1969

SBN: 208 00724 5
Library of Congress Catalog Card Number: 69-12422
Printed in the United States of America

FOR
VICTOR

Acknowledgments

I wish first of all to express my thanks to the Social Science Research Council for the grant which made it possible for me to begin the research necessary for this study, and to the President and the Trustees of Carleton College for giving me the leave of absence necessary for bringing it to completion. The librarians of Carleton College, especially Mrs. David Bryn Jones, have been very helpful in securing for me on inter-library loan material which we did not have ourselves. Mr. Ralph Henry, director of the Publications Office at Carleton, has been very generous in answering questions and giving suggestions about the preparation of the manuscript and the correction of the proof.

There remain those more personal acknowledgments of which only a few can be stated publicly. First, not only in point of time but also in the value of his contribution, should be placed the late Professor Wilbur C. Abbott who not only encouraged me to pursue leads that had attracted my attention when I was a graduate student at Radcliffe, but also gave me the benefit of his wise and sane teaching in the methods of historical research. Nor should I fail to mention those generations of classes in History 204 at Carleton who have been so patient with their instructor's preoccupation with the Revolution of 1688 and so generous with the amount of class time they have let her devote to it. To one of those former students, especially, Dr. Helen Nutting now on the faculty of Wells College, I am grateful not only for reading and making suggestions about parts of the work while it was in progress, but also for the number of hours during which she listened to me expound my ideas. My mother and my husband, in addition to providing moral support, have given invaluable assistance, first in helping me to prepare the manuscript and later, in sharing with me the task of correcting the proof. The interest that my only sister Helena took in my work, and her belief, in the face of many discouraging interruptions, that I could and would complete this study, are debts that are, in more ways than one, beyond acknowledgment.

Lucile Pinkham

Carleton College
Northfield, Minnesota
March 23, 1954

Contents

WILLIAM III AND THE RESPECTABLE REVOLUTION

CHAPTER 1

The Long Prologue

Sometime in the afternoon of February 6, 1685, James II, King of England, sat in his private closet writing a letter. He was very tired. He had spent the last four days in almost constant attendance at his brother Charles II's bedside until, a few hours before, there had come an end to the need for vigil. But the inexorable period placed to one phase of his life had not meant rest for James. There had been countless duties to perform, statements to issue, councilors to meet. Now he had come to this quiet place to do still one more task. His pen scratched a few lines:

For my sonne and nephew, the Prince of Orange:
I have only time to tell you that it has pleased God Almighty to take out of this world the King, my brother. You will from others have an account of what distemper he died of, and that all the usual ceremonies were performed this day in proclaiming me king in the City and other parts. I must end, which I do, with assuring you that you shall find me as kind as you can expect.[1]

He paused for a moment, looked back over what he had written, and then signed his name: James R.

It was the first letter which he had ended with that signature.

✳   ✳

A few days later the man to whom the letter had been addressed, William III, Prince of Orange, in his turn sent a note, to his cousin, the Prince of Nassau Dietz:

I have great obligation to you for the grace you have done me the honor of showing how well you understand the loss I have made by the death of the King of England and the joy I have had to see the present king mount the throne with such tranquility. God grant that his reign be happy! [2]

"God grant that his reign be happy!" That prayer, if sincere, was certainly not answered. Four years from the day it was uttered James was a refugee in France and William himself was making ready to mount the throne of England. How the strange reversal came about is the theme of this study.

✷   ✷

William, Prince of Orange, bore a name and a title that were a part of the glorious past of his home, the United Provinces of the Netherlands. By birth and by deeds he could well be identified with that country, where he lived the first thirty-eight years of his life and where, as Stadholder Prince, he achieved a position of note in European politics. Nevertheless, as Stadholder Prince he might have been forgotten or have become, at best, a "minor character" in the *dramatis personnae* of the late seventeenth century. It is as William III, King of England, that he is remembered. Names are symbols. Often they tell us not only who individuals are, but also something of what others think of them. The people of that nation where this man once reigned have, throughout the centuries, shown a disinclination to refer to him as William III, a title which would place him firmly in the roster of their accepted monarchs, but have chosen rather to use the patronymic "Orange" or the definitely foreign-sounding designation of "the Dutchman." Why is it that the English have thus refused to take this man to themselves, have considered him an outsider, whose place in their history was almost accidental?

Can it be that he has been rejected because through his mother, Mary, the daughter of Charles I, he was one of the Stuarts, that always-alien family that thought to find in England the goal of their hopes and ambitions but never realized their dreams? Not likely, for the Stuarts were either loved or hated, and to arouse those emotions is in itself a form of acceptance, one that William never achieved. A more plausible answer to our question lies elsewhere. William III came to the throne of England through a revolution that is called "glorious." Cherished in all the nation's annals, from folklore and ballad to political essay and scholarly monograph, this revolution is the proud capstone of a national tradition. Insomuch as William's contribution is recognized, by just so much must that of the English themselves be diminished. If the revolution is to remain "glorious," William must remain forever an outsider, an alien prince whose interest in what happened on the island was as incidental to his personal goals as those goals were to England.

That was not the case. When this man was crowned king he was realizing an ambition which had influenced him since his boyhood. No sudden decision nor immediate need had led him across the North Sea and down the length of the Channel to accept the "invitation" of his English friends to help them submit their troubles to "a free parliament." On the contrary, his expedition was the result of plans laid carefully over many years. The setting, both in England and on the Continent, had been judiciously arranged. Public opinion had been subtly molded in his favor. Even his chosen adherents had been selected carefully for the weight they would carry for him in his struggle to win the crown. That hangers-on and potential political opponents not of his choosing found their way into his camp before the revolution was over in no way diminishes the importance of the above fact.

His significant position in English politics had been recognized for almost twenty years. The only male heir to the throne who was a Protestant, in 1677 he had married the one person whose claims seriously rivaled his own: his cousin Mary, the Protestant daughter of the Roman Catholic Duke of York. Although he married her, in part at least, because he did not wish to see her become the wife of some man who might champion her rights in opposition to his own, by this deed William accomplished a great deal more than the mere elimination of possible future disputes. He established himself throughout Europe as well as in the British Isles as the man who would one day rule England either in his own right or as consort of the Queen.

Prior to 1685 he had made three visits to England in the course of which he had made several friends and a few enemies in court circles. The latter were negligible. Of the friends, closest and dearest had been the gentle Ossory, son and heir of the Duke of Ormonde. Passionately loyal alike to his sovereign and to the Prince, so long as he lived Ossory had had a moderating influence on his friend. When he died in 1680 William's grief was deep and sincere. He may have realized that he had lost the only one in England whose affection for him was always disinterested; whose counsel was always wise. Yet Ossory, for all the shining beauty of his character, or perhaps because of it, was not of outstanding importance in politics. Others whom William could call his friends carried greater weight. Sir William Temple had known and liked him for many years. The Earl of Danby vied with Temple for the honor of having been principally responsible for arranging the all-important marriage. The Marquis of Halifax thought well of the Prince. These men, along with all but one or two of the others who knew and were well-disposed toward William, were politically moderate in that, although they disapproved of unrestricted absolutism, they disliked still more the suggestion that Parliament had the right to regulate and change what seemed to them to be the fundamental laws of the realm.

With his mother's brothers, the King and the Duke of York, William was on terms that usually, to all appearances, were fairly friendly. Differences of disposition and background probably prevented the growth of any truly warm feeling, for the cold and proper Prince, unsympathetic toward the lax standards of the English court, put up a wall of reserve that annoyed Charles and baffled York. To the former William gave a good measure of reluctant and grudging respect, having discovered, as many others had done, that the superficially nonchalant King was a clever and dangerous opponent and that it was better, if possible, to have him as a friend. Charles, on his side, was equally willing to respect his nephew, but he would stand no nonsense from him. To determine the nature of William's attitude toward York is much more difficult. He seems to have had a sort of contemptuous affection for this uncle. One of the few occasions of his life when he yielded publicly to his emotions came, as we shall see later, at the height of the Revolution, when a letter from James brought home to him just how irrevocably he had broken the personal ties between them.

As one of the heirs to the throne William could not but be concerned with English political affairs for they were as important to him as he was to them. During the reign of Charles II the principal issue had been nothing less than the succession itself. James, Duke of York, stood first in line, with unquestionable precedence if the only criterion were indefeasible hereditary right. He was, however, a Roman Catholic, and there were a number of people who, unable to stomach the prospect of a king of that faith, looked for means of supplanting him by another. Had William so desired he could have won a large following in this group. That he did not wish to do so does not mean that he had any compunctions about breach of family loyalty. Two other considerations were of more importance. He had enough political acumen to know that the weight and stability of the malcontent faction, which made up the most active and vociferous element of those who opposed James's succession, were not commensurate to its size. Moreover, and therein lies the real basis of his decision, the Exclusion Bill, the means by which the end was to be achieved, was objectionable to him. There is a difference, subtle, it is true, but of great consequence in constitutional development, between declaring that a man cannot be an heir and in making a law to that effect. William had no wish to see his uncle disqualified by act of Parliament. No more than any other Stuart was he willing to admit, even tacitly, that that body was the highest power in England. Nevertheless he could not afford to display his sentiments too plainly for, distasteful though the outright support of the malcontents might be to him, their opposition might be dangerous. Fortunately for him, the King's strong policy during the Exclusion Controversy and thereafter made it unnecessary for William to take a positive stand.

He arrived, then, at the end of the reign of Charles II with a position in England that drew much of its strength from its ambiguous nature. Those opponents of the Crown who would ultimately be called Whigs assumed that his strong Protestantism indicated a more thoroughgoing sympathy with their views than was actually the case. The nascent Tories, for their part, and with more justification, accepted him as one of themselves, believing that it was to his interest that the royal prerogative should be upheld.

Strong though William's position in England might be there was little to presage any immediate movement in his favor. On that February day when the weary Charles II embarked upon the last of his travels he could, with some justification, have believed that he had done his work well, and that the reign of his younger brother, of whose ability he had had such grave doubts, might after all be successful. The Duke, for all the noisy opposition of the Exclusionists, had never entirely lost his share of the popularity which had been bestowed upon the whole Stuart family at the time of the Restoration. "The glory of the Stuart line, Old Jamie's come again" sang the crowds when he returned to London from semi-exile in Scotland in 1682, and they had meant it. The very excesses of the Popish Plot and the Exclusion Controversy had rebounded to the favor of the man for whose injury they had been intended. Now, three years after that occasion, far from questioning his succession, most of the people cheered it. The Church of England hastened to assure him of its loyalty. A few weeks later the country sent him a House of Commons which has been called "exuberantly loyal." [3]

The penetrating observer, however, especially one who can be wise after the event, could have discerned some cause for alarm. In spite of all he could do or say to reassure his people, the new King was still of a religion which most of them hated, and this hatred could be played upon by his opponents. His entry into his heritage was uncontested not so much because his subjects wished to accept him as because they feared a return to the strife and instability of the Civil Wars and the Commonwealth. The favorable Commons had been obtained less through the exertion of popular will than through royal pressure and as a result of the reorganization of the corporations that had been carried out in the last years of the preceding reign. Hungry for power and office, the Shaftesbury Whigs looked upon James as the personification of those forces which had led to their downfall. And across the North Sea the Prince of Orange watched carefully for any sign of weakness he could use to his own advantage.

Writing his memoirs several years later, James accused William of intriguing against him from the very moment that Charles II died.[4] Filled, at the time he wrote those accusations, with bitterness and grief over what seemed to him to be an unnatural betrayal by his own children, James's after-impressions do not correspond with the opinion he held throughout his brief reign, or, in fact, for many years before that. Although he recognized temperamental as well as religious incompatibility, although he probably disliked his nephew personally, although he was frequently annoyed with him, James was never, until he knew that William was actually on the way to England, able to believe that the younger man was hostile and willing to carry that hostility to the length of taking up arms against him. True, James realized that William had been sought after in the past and might be in the future as a leader of those who were politically opposed to the Crown, but it was the people who made up this group whom James distrusted, not William. He was convinced that the only legitimate grandson of Charles I would hew to the family line. There was much in his past to contribute to that conviction, for during the Commonwealth the little band of exiled Stuarts had had good reason to develop a strong sense of unity and mutual responsibility, and they had retained that attitude after the Restoration. In Charles it had taken the form of protecting family interest sometimes even at the expense of his own. In James, unfortunately, it expressed itself in the belief that all other members of the family would immediately and without question subordinate their own concerns to what he thought best for the dynasty. To the very end it was difficult for him to believe that his sister's only son and his own elder daughter would reject his patriarchal authority.

Whether or not this trust was justified is another matter. One thing at least is certain, and that is that for the first six to eight months after James became king William made great efforts to be friendly. As we shall see later, however, the reason for his compliant attitude derived less from policy toward James than from domestic problems in the United Provinces. With respect to England the chief point at issue during the first year of James's reign is the nature and extent of William's connection with the Monmouth rebellion. Unfortunately this is a subject about which no positive statement can be made. Comte d'Avaux, the French ambassador at The Hague, was sure that William gave Monmouth secret encouragement and support.[5] Monmouth, however, went out of his way to absolve the Prince of complicity.[6] As far as any active participation by William is concerned, two points should be remembered. One is that while the Monmouth-Argyle expedition needed money and a good deal of it, there is no evidence that William supplied any funds to his cousin. Rather he is reported to have accused the French of doing so.[7] The only fact clear here is that regardless of who helped him Monmouth was inadequately financed. The second point is of greater significance. Proof of William's complicity has been argued from the very fact that the rebels were allowed to leave the Netherlands for Great Britain. The responsibility, and even the authority for curbing their activities, however, lay not in the Prince but in the States General, in the provincial Estates of Holland, and in the local government of the city of Amsterdam. Not only did William's position as Stadholder give him little actual control over any of these bodies, but also political opposition to him was so strong in all three that they were as likely as not to disregard his wishes. Even James, who often found it difficult to understand that his nephew did not have sovereign powers, recognized this and made his stiffest representations through the English ambassador, Bevil Skelton, directly to the States General. There Skelton discovered that the complicated federalism of the Netherlands government offered boundless opportunity for evading responsibility. The States General turned the complaints over to the provincial Estates of Holland who in turn passed them to Amsterdam where they were ignored while city officials blandly allowed the conspirators to fit out ships and sail away.[8]

The probability is that, reasonably certain of Monmouth's ultimate failure, and not unwilling to have him out of the way, William neither helped nor hindered his cousin. On the other hand, he did give positive assistance to his uncle. Not only did he send home immediately the British regiments in the service of the United Provinces, but he offered to come over himself, and sent his closest friend, Hans Willem Bentinck, to carry that offer in person. It was refused, a little testily. James felt that he could take care of the situation himself without calling in his nephew. There is nothing to indicate that the refusal was based on anything more than self-assurance. From Bentinck, one of the most reliable observers of the time, we have the statement that James, far from suspecting William, agreed with him in believing that it was the French who were supporting Monmouth and providing funds for the rebellion.[9]

This incident over, William returned to an attitude of superficial disregard of English affairs, although he watched them with interest. All seemed well on the island; the coolness with which Monmouth was greeted and the disastrous end of his uprising seemed to be good omens for James. Yet the whole affair was, in a way, the beginning of his downfall. The rebels had to be punished and to that end Jeffreys and Kirke were sent on their infamous journey to the Southwest. Whether or not it is true, as has been contended since, that they went a good deal further in their prosecutions than James had either ordered or intended* it has always been the lot of the administrator to have to bear the onus for the excesses of his subordinates, and James could be no exception. Rumors, given a favorable start and some foundation, spread rapidly under the guidance of that small group in whose eyes nothing that James could do was good, and the fears created by them had much to do with strengthening the conviction among the common people that England, under a Catholic king, would find scenes of slaughter and oppression becoming everyday affairs.

The rebellion was also partly responsible for the changed relations between James and his Parliament when it reassembled in November. The incident had both frightened James and encouraged him. The former reaction led him, in his speech from the throne, to ask for an increase in the standing army; the latter, to announce, on the same occasion, that he had defied the Test

*For an excellent summary of this problem see F. C. Turner *James II* (New York: The Macmillan Company, 1948), 280–284.

Act by giving commissions to Catholic officers. Those two acts are typical of James. One might call them "ill-advised" and then ask who did the advising. We do not know. Whether the result of counsel or of James's own inspiration they could not have been more badly timed. Only a few weeks before this, Louis XIV had revoked the Edict of Nantes, and Huguenot refugees were beginning to stream out of France. The English, in whom the very word Papist conjured up nightmares, looked upon the Test and Penal laws as safeguards against a similar situation in their own land. The days of peaceful relations between James and his Parliament were over.

Two points should be mentioned about this Parliament before it is prorogued into oblivion. The Crown is said to have packed it carefully.[10] To the extent that this is true one has here evidence that not even the most carefully hand-picked body would have been subservient in matters of religion. Indeed, the very means by which James was able to exercise influence were such as to bring together a group of men who would be unyielding on this very point, for they were those which had been devised only a few years before by Charles and the Tories to assure the ascendency of the Church party and the defeat of the Whigs. To expect these men to submit to a relaxation of the Test Act which would expose them to the free competition of their rivals was to expect from them a political maturity far beyond the grasp of seventeenth-century England. That in itself should be enough to explain why a House of Commons did not love James in November as it had in May.

Still another explanation has, however, been advanced: that in the interval since the first session many of the members had been taken into the pay of William of Orange.[11] Although this assertion cannot be proven, neither can it be repudiated on purely moral grounds for William had bribed members of Parliament before, notably during the diplomatic crises of the late seventies, and he would scarcely have scrupled to do so again had it seemed desirable. On the other hand, the Pensionary Fagel, who was one of William's closest advisors, was most anxious, for reasons that will be developed more fully later,* that the members of

*See infra, pp. 85, 89.

Parliament should coöperate with the King.[12] William could easily have been acting without his friend's knowledge or even counter to his advice, but it is hard to see why this would have been necessary if the objective was, as it must have been, to create dissension and to stimulate opposition to James. The members of Parliament, if they had accepted bribes, would have been taking them for doing that which they would have done in any event. Angrily they refused to grant either of the royal requests, and James, just as angrily, ordered a prorogation.

Whether or not William had done anything to bring it about, or whether he even realized its significance at the time, the prorogation of Parliament was an indication that affairs in Great Britain were moving in a direction that would make it possible for him to join forces with the opponents of the occupant of the throne without giving in too freely to those who opposed royal authority as such. The party in power at the accession of James, the men who held the high offices in England and Scotland alike, were Tories and Anglicans who were thoroughly in accord with a royal prerogative which had been used to place and maintain them in power against all the assaults of their enemies: the Shaftesbury Whigs, the Presbyterians, and the more rabid Republicans and Covenanters. These Tory Anglicans were the group with whom James must deal if he wished to place Roman Catholics in office. Willing to condone discreet and occasional exercise of the royal dispensing power, agreeable to the maintenance of a standing army, not in opposition to the relaxation of the penal laws, they were implacably opposed to the open and legal nullification of the Test Act which had helped to give them their strangle hold upon the lucrative offices of government in the three kingdoms. Even before Parliament met for its second session the imminence of trouble had been apparent. Lord Halifax, who had been "kicked upstairs" to the Lord Presidency of the Council shortly after the death of Charles II, was removed in October for refusing to approve the King's proposal to bring the Roman Catholic peers back to the House of Lords. In the army the Duke of Albemarle, son of the famous Monck, had surrendered his command rather than serve under the Roman Catholic Earl of Feversham. Other officials held their positions, but noted uneasily that on the death of the Lord Keeper Guilford, his office was filled by Jeffreys who, although a Protestant, was known to favor policies almost more extreme than those of the King, and who, in addition to the place just mentioned, was given also the still more important post of Lord Chancellor. The brief session of Parliament merely brought out into the open a tension that already existed.

Before we explore any further the consequences of this tension and more specifically the way in which it led ultimately to the intervention of William of Orange, a word needs to be said about James's motives and objectives. He was firmly convinced of the right, and, one might even say, the *duty* of a king to exercise wide powers of government. He shared with his mother the opinion that the disasters of his father's reign had come from laxity and mistaken generosity rather than from arbitrary authority. He believed that his brother's greatest success had come through taking a stand against those who questioned the royal prerogative. What he had never understood was that, in the great struggle of the late 1670's and early 1680's, Charles had won because he had been clever enough to throw the weight of the royal prerogative on the side of those who wanted to use it for ends of their own which temporarily coincided with his.

James should not be condemned too harshly for his views and certainly least of all on the ground that they were out of keeping with his time. The trend of later developments has led to overemphasis on certain aspects of the seventeenth century. Republicanism and the more moderate Parliamentarianism were indeed popular with some people of England, but for a great many of the inhabitants of the country they evoked uncomfortable memories of the Commonwealth and of later disturbances. Good government meant strong government, one that could keep the peace at home and maintain or improve England's position in world trade. Political thought had as yet discovered no means more effective to achieve that desired end than absolute monarchy. Thus it was that many of his subjects believed as firmly as James in the principles of Divine Right, and felt with him that obedience to their king was a moral obligation. Perhaps nothing sums up their views so well as the Oxford Index of 1685 which anathematized, among other propositions, the assertions that civil authority was derived from the people; that there was a contract, tacit or expressed, between the Prince and his people; and that the sovereignty of England was in King, Lords, and Parliament.[13]

Nevertheless, powerful as the beliefs just mentioned undoubtedly were, equally powerful was the conviction that England must be kept Protestant and Episcopalian, and it was against this conviction that James had to fight when he tried to introduce religious toleration. His desire for toleration was probably even greater than his desire freely to exercise his kingly power. He attempted to realize the one through use of the other, thus posing for the modern evaluator of his reign the problem of how to condemn the one objective, which the twentieth century rejects, without disapproving of the other, which it claims to uphold. In short, it is the old problem of whether or not the ends justify the means. The solution would be easier if one could accept the claim, so often made, that James was trying to force the people of England to become Roman Catholic. That accusation, however, can be validated only on the assumption that every one of his own assertions to the contrary was a deliberate lie, for he himself insisted that his aim was religious toleration for those of all faiths, including Protestant Dissenters no less than Roman Catholics. Although among his followers were a number of Jesuit zealots who may have hoped for the exclusive victory of their own Church, at no point is it possible to find unquestionable proof that James agreed with them. Like most people of his own time and a good many of our own, he believed in the theory of the Œcumenical Church and hoped that the schisms of the Reformation might be healed, but he wanted this to come about through conviction or conversion rather than through force. Appalled by the Revocation of the Edict of Nantes, he believed that Louis XIV had injured the cause of Roman Catholicism by this rash act.[14] Perhaps one of the best pieces of evidence to his tolerance is the fact that one of his most wholehearted supporters was the Quaker William Penn, surely astute enough to know whether or not his master's policies were a mere mask.

Even Burnet, in the unrevised manuscript of his *History* says of James while he was still Duke of York: "yet when I knew him he seemed very positive in his opinion against all persecution for conscience sake" and goes on to marvel that "he left his daughters so entirely in the hands of the divines of the Church of England and that he never made any attempt to persuade them to change." [15]

For all of that, James's objectives were unpopular. Among the English masses, especially in London, fear of Popery was still hysterical, and the French excesses which accompanied the revocation of the Edict of Nantes did nothing to soothe it. The average Englishman of the larger cities hated and feared Popery, knew little about it, but was absolutely certain that if it were allowed free practice there would be an end to his personal safety and to the hope for the salvation of his immortal soul. In rural areas the sentiment was somewhat different, for there Papist and Protestant had lived side by side for more than a century in relative peace; but in times of crisis it was the urban attitude that was important.

In spite of unmistakable expressions of opposition James moved to achieve his purpose. Parliament, so suddenly dismissed in November, was prorogued first to February, then to May, and then to November of 1686 in the hope that during the interval a sufficient number of members could be induced to change their views to give formal approval to the royal policies. In the meantime other steps were taken. In April of that year four judges who were known to oppose the exercise of the dispensing power were removed. The test case of Hales, which came up in June with the decision in favor of the King, seemed to indicate that the drastic step had been wise. It might not be amiss here to point out that sound legal opinion contributed at least as much as servility to the judgment. As the debates on the Bill of Rights so plainly brought out a few years later, to deny the existence of the dispensing power entirely would lead to serious complications. Still later in the summer James formed the Court of Ecclesiastical Commission. The very creation of this court brought disapproval which was heightened by the fact that its first step, for which, indeed, it had been organized, was the suspension of the Bishop of London for refusing to obey the King's order that he should stop controversial preaching in his diocese. Yet even as it is significant that the decision in Hales's case cannot be entirely attributed to judicial servility, so it is noteworthy that of the three members of the clergy appointed to sit on this court, only the Archbishop of Canterbury refused. Whether he did so because of ill-health or because of objections to the fact that Jeffreys, a layman, was to be chairman [16] is not clear, but certainly he did not demur at the idea of the court itself. His place was easily filled by the Bishop of Chester.

The Tory Anglicans, already disturbed by the events of the preceding autumn, were now faced with a dilemma. As can be seen from what has already been said, the King's actions did not go against their theoretical views. Nevertheless, jealous to retain their control of the principal offices and to keep undiminished the political supremacy of the Anglican Church, they found that the King's program threatened their position on every side. To begin with there was some danger that the removal of the Tests might expose them to the rivalry of the Catholic nobles. As far as civil offices were concerned this was relatively unimportant as the Roman Catholics who might aspire to them were few in number and, because of the disqualifications under which they had suffered for many years, politically inexperienced. Their advantage lay in military affairs, mainly because, for lack of opportunity at home, many of them had taken commissions in armies abroad where the training they had obtained in active service justified to some extent James's eagerness to make use of them in his own forces. Few of the Protestant leaders, however, were interested in the army or the navy. It was the great and highly lucrative civil posts that they cherished. In this area, much more important than any Catholic challenge was the fact that no one expected James's reign to be long. Whether or not the nominal title of ruler after his death went to his elder daughter Mary, the effective rule would surely go to William. Those who yielded to James might retain their places so long as he lived, but his successor would almost surely turn all such persons out of office. A short term view might well advocate compliance to the reigning king. The long term view pronounced such action disastrous. Yet for the moment the Tory Anglicans were not strong enough to stay in power without royal support. If they were deprived of that prop about the only thing they could do was to try for some compromise with their bitter enemies, the Whigs and the Dissenters, opponents of Anglican supremacy and champions of the rights of Parliament against the King, who were on common ground with the Tories only in their opposition to Popery. Such a course of action was not only distasteful to the Tories but even dangerous to them. On the secular side concessions or advances would not only violate political convictions but it would also mean the loss of the advantage gained through the recent *Quo Warranto* proceedings. In religious matters, the Test and Penal laws had been directed just as much against the Dissenters as against the Papists, and indeed the former, being more numerous, were far the greater threat. There was the added factor that James, promising toleration, might win the Dissenters to his side. The task of the Tories boiled down to this: they must soft-pedal political affairs and make the King's religion the principal issue.

The dilemma which faced the Tories was also before the Prince of Orange. Let it be understood here that William wanted the English crown for its own sake much more than for the advantages it would give him in diplomatic maneuverings on the Continent. These last play their part, but a close scrutiny of them, especially of the time element, will reveal, as we shall see later, that they were more a support for the expedition of 1688 than a cause thereof, and undue emphasis upon them has obscured the significance of William's personal ambition and its relation to the outcome of the Revolution. We must not lose sight ever of the man with whom we are dealing. We must remember constantly the fact, often overlooked, that William was the grandson of Charles I and that Stuart influence had been stronger in his early life than that of his father's family. Ambitious with the zeal of an able man who *knows* that he can do better than his fellows, he had so far been given free reign in his native country only during a few terrible months in 1672. A youth of twenty-one, untrained and inexperienced alike in warfare, statecraft, and diplomacy, he had taken charge at a time when the United Provinces seemed doomed, and, relying only on himself and the magic appeal of his name to the masses of the Dutch people, he had saved the land. For thanks he won the opposition of the States General. Yet on the three occasions when he visited England he had been cheered. There he had been the darling of the Court, the sought-after companion of great politicians. England had no States General made up of proud merchants who felt themselves superior to kings and princes. In England, William could be the king he wanted to be — or so he thought in those days of the reign of James II when so many Englishmen hastened to tell him how thoroughly they were committed to his service.

Two possible courses were open to him. He could maintain the policy he had adopted in the closing years of Charles II: to wait for the natural run of events to bring him his — and his wife's — inheritance. Like almost everyone else he did not expect the interval to be long. As James was not particularly robust there was reason for thinking he would not long survive his brother. The possibility that a rival heir might be born was slight. Even more unlikely was it that James might try to divert the succession either to Anne, if she could be persuaded to apostatize, or to one of his bastard sons. Frequent warnings that this might happen were sent to William, but he was too well aware of his father-in-law's views on indefeasible hereditary right to be particularly disturbed by them. Against this policy of passivity stood William's own impatience and the imperative necessity of taking a stand. James's life expectancy might not be good, but neither was his own, for he was already in his middle thirties and his always-frail constitution did not hold out promise for too long a future. Moreover he was beginning to receive indications from England that people there, confident that he would oppose James's policies, were expecting him to do so immediately and openly.[17] Finally, as will be seen later on, his relations with England were inextricably bound in with his diplomatic connections on the Continent which were reaching a stage where specific plans had to be made. If a passive policy was neither tenable nor desirable, the alternative was, of course, direct action. Yet should William choose this course he had to be sure he would win, for the dangers inherent in the failure of an outright assault upon the English throne were too grave to warrant the contemplation of anything but success. In addition to making as sure of victory as was humanly possible, William had to plan a campaign, in both the military and political senses of the term, which would bring him the crown without damaging too severely those very attributes which made it so attractive to him. That is, he did not want a struggle based on purely constitutional issues. Therefore his best means of accomplishing his end in this respect lay in joining forces with the discontented Tories. But like them he would have to compromise with the Whigs, with the Dissenters, and with the malcontents. He must scheme to uphold the Church of England without antagonizing the Dissenters and to protect the prerogative without losing the support of the Whigs. He must pose as the savior of the Protestant religion while he maintained his friendly associations with Catholic Europe: Spain, the Empire, and the Papacy itself.

By the summer of 1686 affairs had reached a stage where William could no longer pretend a lack of interest in what was going on in England but must make up his mind whether to support James's policies or to oppose them. It so happened that this choice also involved the much larger decision to take direct action. News of growing dissatisfaction among the Tories had been reaching the Netherlands in ever-larger proportions as the spring advanced into summer. Its significance and the forewarning of the part he would have to play were laid squarely before William by Gilbert Burnet who arrived at that time in The Hague. Their meeting was that of two men, each of whom had a pretty good idea of what was in the other's mind, warily approaching a subject that was highly dangerous. The invitation to an audience was apparently unsolicited by Burnet, but seems to have come as the result of word sent to the Prince from England that here was a man whom he could take into his confidence.[18] Yet it can be assumed with reasonable certainty that if William had not called Burnet to his presence the latter would have sought to come there for he, too, was in communication with men back home who were eager to know what was going on in the mind of the inscrutable Prince.

The discoveries each made were of utmost value to them in determining their subsequent courses. Burnet learned that William was ready to accept the leadership of the Anglican party in its opposition to James, and William was made aware of the conditions under which he could accept that leadership. Those conditions were twofold. Religious toleration, which William as a Calvinist was assumed to favor, could go only so far that it did not endanger the hierarchy of the Tories in both Church and State. The form of the constitution which protected that hierarchy must be maintained. Without actually committing himself, William led Burnet to believe he would accept the conditions. Whether he could or would do so was another matter which depended, among other things, on the relative value to him of the Tories and on the necessity of making concessions to other groups.

The contention that in this conference we have the immediate inception of the Revolution of 1688 has formed the basis for a certain amount of discussion which, as it can be based on nothing but conjecture, need not concern us deeply here. The chief importance of the meeting lies in the fact that it is, so far as can be proven, the first direct contact in the reign of James II between William and the essentially conservative group who were so valuable to him later on and who gave the English government the character it was to maintain for a century and a half. Nevertheless, while the account in Burnet's *History* makes no mention of plans for direct action, one statement hints strongly that it was either tacitly understood or openly discussed. The narrative draws to a close with the statement by Burnet, "I told him it was necessary for his services to put the fleet of Holland in good condition." If a military expedition was not being considered that remark becomes irrelevant to the point of absurdity. It is significant that a little while later William, who up to this time had been interested almost exclusively in land forces, made a request to the States General for funds to be used for the improvement of the navy.*

One other outcome of the interview deserves some attention as background for what was to follow. Burnet, who was a bit of a busybody, had noticed the strained relations between William and Mary and had taken William to task for his coolness. Breaking through what may have been the bitterness of years, William confessed that the prospect of intervening in English politics only to end up in the humiliating position of the queen's husband had so colored his attitude toward his wife that he could hardly stand to look at her. As soon as he heard this Burnet hurried off to Mary. To his question as to the position she expected William to occupy when she inherited the crown she made the astonished reply that she had never thought that he would be anything less than king. After hearing further explanation of the laws of succession in England she announced her determination that when she became queen her husband must be invested for life with full regal rights. A touching scene followed, delightfully and anachronistically Victorian in all aspects but its likeness to the queen who gave that age its name. Burnet brought the two together and heard the infatuated Princess declare to her husband that "she did not know that the laws of England were so contrary to the laws of God" and that he should always be the ruler. The only command she wanted him to obey was "husbands, love your wives" so that she could obey "wives, be obedient to your husbands in all things." Not to Burnet nor to William nor to Mary does it appear to have occurred that the people of England might have something to say about the apparent discrepancy between the laws of England

---

*Von Ranke places the "immediate inception" of the expedition in a meeting that took place between William and the Great Elector at about this same time. This meeting is important in its relation to the diplomatic arrangements which made it possible for William to collect an army for his assault on Great Britain, and he may have mentioned his plans to the Elector, with whom he was always on terms of confidence. To put the inception here, however, is to disregard the significance of the interview with Burnet and to give primary importance to continental rather than to English affairs. For a fuller account of the conference with the Great Elector see *infra*, pp. 104–106.

and the laws of God. The incident, as related by Burnet, cannot but evoke a smile from the modern reader. It is so sentimental, so melodramatic. But history, being a record of living, is frequently melodramatic. If Mary had not been outrageously infatuated with her husband, William's course during the next two years would have been much more difficult. He had to know that she identified her interests completely with his own.

Because the discussions with Burnet could not, by their very nature, be highly publicized, they were therefore of only slight value in making William's position known to the people of England. Two other events during that year gave him an opportunity to declare himself more openly. The first came in August when James proposed to fill the command of the British regiments by appointing a Catholic, Lord Carlingford, to the position. Prompted perhaps more by Henry Sidney who had just come to The Hague, than by the remembrance of his conference with Burnet,[19] William refused to accept him. His refusal was favorably noted in England and his reputation as the champion of Protestantism grew.

About two months later William was able to state his views to still greater advantage. In November, William Penn arrived in The Hague to sound out the Prince on religious toleration. He had no official status, but his position in the English court was well known and the probability that he might be acting without the King's knowledge was negligible even if he were not under express orders. As a member of a dissenting group that believed in complete separation of Church and State he was opposed to Anglican supremacy which he hoped to end through the establishment of complete toleration. Although, to his way of thinking, the state should have nothing whatever to do with religious affairs, concessions to political necessity could be made through a division of the public offices so that one third of them should be reserved to the Anglicans and the remainder be divided equally between the Roman Catholics and the Protestant dissenters. Penn wanted William to express approval of this plan, giving him to understand that he had been commissioned by the King to make the request.[20]

Even if Penn's proposals had been workable William could

not have agreed with them without abandoning the support of the Anglican party against which they were directed. Neither could he afford to oppose the suggestions outright. The situation was delicate. William, himself a Calvinist, was well aware that he drew part of his strength in England, especially among the Dissenters, from that fact. Moreover, the first forerumblings of the Enlightenment were beginning to undermine the bases of intolerance. The Prince met the problem astutely. He told Penn, and Burnet saw to it that the right people in England knew the nature of his answer, that he was in favor of religious toleration even for Roman Catholics, but that he looked upon the Test Act as a political safeguard of Protestantism and that nothing could induce him to take a different stand.[21] Penn's visit, therefore, hurt James instead of giving him the help that he had hoped for, in that it supplied William with the chance to pronounce views that would attract Dissenters and even those Catholics who wanted only the right to worship freely, at the same time that it gave assurance to the Anglicans.

These incidents, while encouraging alike to William and to his English followers, could have accorded just as well with a negative policy of waiting as with a positive determination to act. Because he had now chosen the latter alternative William must do more than build up golden opinions among many people. He must strengthen his connection with possible allies, feel out their desires, discard those whose rashness might make them dangerous, and learn to recognize those whose fundamental loyalty to the King, for all their criticisms, might make them unreliable in a crisis. He did not have to go outside his own country to find British subjects who wanted him to be their friend. A good number of the malcontents were already in the United Provinces, but even while William knew he could not disregard them and should not antagonize them, they were not of the group with which he most wished to join forces. Many of them were refugees, both Scottish and English, from the Monmouth-Argyle affair who had been in the country before the uprising and had fled back after its disastrous close. There was also a handful of Non-Conformist preachers who had come, especially to Utrecht, to escape punishment under the Conventicle and the Five Mile Acts. Somewhat more to William's liking were the officers of the British regiments who were becoming alarmed over the number of Roman Catholics being introduced into the army at home. Finally, discontented individuals were beginning to make their way to the country, such as the impetuous Lord Mordaunt who, after expressing vigorous opposition to James in the brief November session of Parliament, had come to The Hague the next autumn and had, at that early date, urged the Prince to make an immediate assault upon England.[22]

But William knew that the groundwork was not yet sufficiently laid, and that before further steps were taken he must have more definite backing, not only from these fiery and often irresponsible refugees, but also from the more sober and influential men in England. A few letters show that he had had correspondents there for some time, although whether this was more than the ordinary intelligence service of the day is hard to discover from the veiled phraseology. There are indications, however, that more precise reports of matters of interest to William were being brought verbally.[23] The impression that a correspondence already existed is strengthened by Burnet who not only mentions that he had been recommended to William before he reached Utrecht, but also states a little later that both the Prince and Princess had been urged by the English to denounce the Ecclesiastical Commission, and to "begin a breach upon that." [24] Unfortunately, the phrase "by those *from* England" leaves room for doubt as to whether he is referring to persons then in the Netherlands or to those who were in England.

What William needed to do now was not so much to make new contacts as to reëstablish old ones. Up to this time his closest relations in England had been with the fairly moderate Tories. The one exception to this was Henry Sidney who had not, as it happened, been definitely partisan in politics although the fact that he was a brother of Algernon Sidney had brought him under the suspicion of both Charles and James. Among the other friends of the Prince, now that the Earl of Ossory was dead and Sir William Temple had retired from active politics, the foremost were the Earl of Danby, the Marquis of Halifax, and Mary's two maternal uncles, the Earl of Clarendon and the Earl of Rochester.

All four of them were Tories who had given staunch support to Charles II in his fight against the Whigs. Of them, Danby had not yet recovered from the disgrace into which he had been thrust by Shaftesbury; Halifax had been able to keep office under James for less than a year; and by the autumn of 1686 the two Hydes could easily read the signs of their imminent fall. But this group was small, and, again excepting Sidney, correspondence with them had been allowed to lapse. As for Sidney, he appeared in The Hague briefly in the late summer of 1686 and, after giving William his views on the situation in England, retired to the discreet neutrality of travel in Italy and other parts of the Continent. References to him in letters of other conspirators, for so they may now be called, indicate that his travel was not as innocent as it seemed.

The step to renew contacts and to enlarge the circle must now be taken. Late in the year the visit of his younger son to The Hague gave Halifax the opportunity to take the initiative in reopening his correspondence with William, but his noncommittal letters, characteristic of the Great Trimmer,[25] were unsatisfactory. William wanted to get in touch not only with other Tories but also with the Whigs and the Dissenters. For this purpose he began to make plans, late in December, to send over a special envoy who could combine official business with the more important work of establishing contacts and finding out just how far the English were prepared to go, what they expected of William, and what he could expect from them. It was easy to find a pretext for sending such an envoy as the English and the Dutch were usually at loggerheads somewhere in the East Indies, and the States General were worried over James's improvement of his fleet. The States General, therefore, after a very little urging from William, resolved to send Everard van Weede, lord of Dijkveld, to inform himself for them on the state of affairs in England and to assure His Britannic Majesty of their inclination to live in friendship with him.[26]

At this point it may be well to pause and face the problem that must have confronted several Englishmen during the next few months. What did William have to offer them that they should be willing to go outside their own country for a leader, and in doing so commit acts which, if they were not treasonous, were certainly, by any criterion, disloyal? It seems to boil down to this: that, in the struggle between James II and the Tories, victory for either side could be won only by a coalition with the Dissenters. We have already seen why coöperation with James would have been not merely impolitic but actually dangerous to the Tory Anglicans. As the months went by it became increasingly apparent that, no matter what happened to the cause of religious toleration under James, those who opposed him in his attempts to achieve it were out. If he was able to win the Dissenters to his side they were out for good, not only for the duration of his reign but very probably also for that of his successors. For the Tories the greatest hope of salvaging any of their former position lay in convincing the Dissenters that they could bring about a more desirable form of toleration than James could. But it was these very same individuals who, in the first flush of the Restoration, had imposed the Penal Laws, not only against the radical sectaries, but even against the moderate Presbyterians who had helped to put an end to the Commonwealth. The Anglicans had been more bitter, during the whole reign of Charles II, against their Protestant than against their Catholic rivals, for the simple reason, pointed out earlier, that the former were more numerous and much more formidable. How were they now to adjust themselves to coöperation with their former enemies and, more to the point, how were they to convince those enemies that they wanted to be friends?

In this contest for the support of the Dissenters, James had many advantages. He could offer release from the nagging humiliations and worse of the Clarendon Code. He could perhaps even give that release the sanction of enacted law, provided, of course, that he could assemble a parliament willing to take such a step. But offsetting that lay his supreme disadvantage. He was a Papist. Whatever dispensation he granted to the non-Anglican Protestants would go also to the Catholics whom most of them hated so bitterly. Whatever he might say or do about liberty of conscience for all, he would always be open to the charge of insincerity and of acting primarily in the interests of his co-religionaries.

The weakness of James's position was the strength of William's and the basis for much of his attractiveness. He could speak with safety of religious toleration, for no one could suspect him of crypto-Romanism. He drew additional support from the fact that his home country had managed to maintain religious toleration for all Protestants, and even, to a degree, for Roman Catholics, at the same time that political authority rested safely in the hands of the Calvinists. His own devotion to Calvinism was another great drawing card, especially for the leaders among the English Presbyterians who, like their Anglican erstwhile rivals and would-be friends, disliked Anabaptists and Quakers only a little less than they disliked Papists. Finally, the Tory leaders had good reason to believe that William's views on the English constitution corresponded with their own and that, as heir to the crown whether by virtue of his own claims or those of his wife, he was the natural defender of that constitution, be it against Parliament or against Republican. In what other man could there be found such a happy combination of attributes?

The first half of 1687 saw the issues fairly well clarified. The last month of the previous year had seen the fall of Rochester and Clarendon, an event in which backstairs intrigue played at least as great a part as religion, but the fact that they were replaced by Catholics obscured the former and emphasized the latter motive which had the added virtue of high publicity value. On February 12 came the Edict of Toleration in Scotland, granting full freedom in the practice of their religion to Catholics, Quakers, and moderate Presbyterians, but not to the Conventiclers who combined republican ideas with their dissenting doctrines. The Edict had a mixed reception. The Episcopal clergy were furious and some of the Presbyterians were alarmed by the freedom given to Quakers and Catholics. But most of the non-Anglicans were pleased. On March 18 James announced in the Privy Council his intention of issuing a similar declaration in England. He did so on April 4 by the Declaration of Indulgence which suspended the Test Act and the Penal Acts. A gesture of reassurance was made to the established church in confirming to it and to its clergy "the free exercise of their religion as by law established and the quiet enjoyment of their possessions without any molestation or disturbance whatsoever." The document might be considered an admirable statement of tolerant convictions had not James, with incredible stupidity or high-minded devoutness, or both, included therein the fatal statement that "he could not but wish that all his subjects were members of the Catholic Church" — words which must have attracted much more attention than those which followed immediately: "yet he had always declared, That conscience ought not be constrained nor people forced in matters of mere* religion, that force was contrary to the interests of government, and never obtained the end for which it was employed."

Meanwhile James, who had not given up his project of parliamentary confirmation of his acts, had started, around the turn of the year, what are known as the closetings, whereby he called in individually several of the leaders of the House of Commons and many other office holders to try to get them to consent in advance to the repeal of the laws so odious to him. These days also saw the trouble with Magdelen College, Oxford, and the preparations for the formal reception of the Papal nuncio, D'Adda, who had now been in England for some months. D'Adda was given the official recognition of a state function on July 3. The day before, despairing of doing anything with the existing House of Commons, James had dissolved Parliament.

Dijkveld's mission, therefore, corresponded with a period of tension to which it undoubtedly contributed. Everard van Weede, lord of Dijkveld,[27] was admirably equipped for the task which had been given him. A mature diplomat who enjoyed the confidence of both the Prince Stadholder and Their High Mightinesses of the States General, he had already been employed on two missions to England, the more recent occasion having been as a member of the delegation which had been sent to reaffirm the treaties between Great Britain and the United Provinces at the time of the accession of James II. His sojourn in London at that time had extended from the spring to the early autumn of 1685, those tense months which had seen the Monmouth Rebellion and the first faint indications that the over-

---

*Lest James be accused of lack of respect toward religion it might be well to point out that, according to seventeenth-century usage, "mere" meant unmixed or pure. Elizabeth I, for example, had boasted that she was "merely English."

confident King might go too far. Dijkveld, of course, had not lived in a vacuum during those days. He had met and talked to the more important political leaders of the realm. The mission had been successful, eminently so, for the United Provinces were the only nation that managed to get from James II a clear-cut affirmation of the treaties existing at the time of his brother's death. But Dijkveld's task in 1685 was easy indeed compared to the one which he was commanded to undertake now. As a first step toward understanding the highly delicate nature of what he must do, let us examine the relations between James II and William at the opening of 1687, a year that was to be even more crucial in the lives of both men than the one that followed it.

James had failed in his attempts, channeled through Penn, to get the Prince and Princess of Orange to declare themselves in favor of his project to repeal the Test and Penal laws, but he was far from willing to give up the project. As a man and as a father he wanted the approval of his heirs not only because he wished to insure the lasting quality of his work, but also because he believed that he was right and that his children, in opposing him, would be wrong not only in terms of filial obedience but also of the very issue itself. Let us not look too lightly on that side of the case. Had James been less concerned about his immortal soul he might just possibly have kept his temporal crown. If, however, we consider him not *qua* father and individual but *qua* king and political leader, it is easy enough to see why the support and approval of William was just as important to him as it was to the Tories. But William, for his part, neither needed nor wanted James's support. He did need and want the support of all those in England who objected to the methods by which James was trying to establish toleration.

James's second attempt to win over William followed almost immediately after Penn's failure. It was carried out through the Marquis of Albeville who was sent to The Hague in January to replace the objectionable Skelton. He was not an improvement on his predecessor. In fact, James could scarce have done worse. An Irish Catholic, D'Albeville had a reputation in his own time for incompetence and unreliability, and both his nationality and his religion made it easy for his contemporaries to cast doubt upon his integrity. Perhaps they were justified. On the other hand,

D'Albeville was at least as anxious as his master that Great Britain and the United Provinces should be friends. He had indicated his desire by unsolicited and disinterested efforts the summer before to calm the suspicions of van Citters, Dutch ambassador to England, when unfounded rumors were flying about that James was planning war.[28] Once in The Hague he immediately showed such preference for the anti-French faction that the French ambassador, D'Avaux, who had expected him to be more malleable than Skelton, was first baffled and then infuriated.[29] It was not until D'Albeville, like James, realized that he was being rebuffed not only by the Prince but also by the States General that he became truly responsive to D'Avaux's demands.

D'Albeville had orders to protest to William over his open favors to Burnet and to try to get him to announce his approval of the repeal of the Test and Penal laws. The protest could not be ignored, for Burnet was becoming more and more outspoken in his antagonism toward James. Probably, too, William was growing a little tired of the self-important divine. At any rate he complied to the extent of sending him from the Court. He did not, of course, break off correspondence with this valuable, if somewhat irksome, ally.[30] As for the rest of D'Albeville's message, William's reply was very similar to that made a few months earlier to Penn, with one important difference. In both instances he was outspoken in his refusal to condone the repeal of the Test Act, but on the earlier occasion he had implied that he would be willing to advocate toleration for Roman Catholics as well as for Protestants, provided that it came about as the result of an act of Parliament. Now no mention was made of Parliament, and by taking this fact in connection with the letters of Halifax and others it becomes apparent that for the moment, at least, those in opposition to James feared rather than desired a meeting of that body.

William could be reasonably sure that when Dijkveld reached England James would exert every effort to succeed through the States' envoy where he had failed through his own ambassador. William also knew that the Anglicans in England, from whom he had received direct word on the subject, looked to this mission to bring reassurance to the Dissenters that they would gain more from him than from James if they but stood firm in the common cause of opposition to Popery.[31] Weeks of long conferences prepared the envoy for his task. Present at them, besides the Prince, were Bentinck, Fagel, and Halwyn. That Halwyn was included in these discussions is highly significant for he was experienced in intrigue and was an intimate friend of one Frimans, a mysterious individual who had been used before to establish contacts with malcontents in the British Isles. Nor was D'Albeville ignored, strangely enough, although he was not, of course, admitted into any of the highly secret talks at which the Prince was present. Yet Dijkveld had seen a good deal of him during the embassy of 1685 and perhaps knew that his naïveté and lack of diplomatic experience might lead to unconscious but highly important revelations.[32] The frequent interviews between the two aroused D'Avaux's exasperated curiosity and cannot but excite our own. Like him, we remain unsatisfied.

Armed, then, with complete information and full instructions, Dijkveld arrived in England on February 11, the day before the Edict in Scotland was issued.[33] Ten days passed before he had an audience with the King, who would not see him until D'Albeville had been received by the States General. The delay was not particularly long, nor should it be attributed to any animosity on the part of James. While Their High Mightinesses were being ultrapunctilious about formalities over his representative there was no reason why he should hasten to receive one from them. The first interview, when it came, was confined entirely to the ostensible matter of the mission, the relations between the United Provinces and England.[34] Apparently Dijkveld was reluctant to approach the problem of religion too abruptly.[35] The most probable reason for this reluctance is that in the interval since his arrival he had become aware of the extent to which the Imperial and the Spanish ambassadors were disturbed over the prospect that a too-intransigent stand of the Dutch on matters of religion might throw James definitely into the French camp. Dijkveld knew as well as William that among the European diplomats the religious issue had to be glossed over. Nevertheless, when the problem of the repeal of the Test and Penal laws was broached in later conversations, apparently on the initiative of the King, Dijkveld's replies, both to James and to his ministers, was always the same. Acting upon instructions he answered that William and Mary looked upon the Test Act as the safeguard of England's government. Nothing could induce them to assent to its repeal or to approve the Declaration which suspended it.*[36]

If Dijkveld's audiences with James were repetitious to the point of monotony he was certainly saved from any danger of boredom by his other contacts, which were as exciting as his interviews with the King were dull. Private credentials from the Prince established him with Halifax,[37] and paved the way for a series of conferences which began several days before his official reception took place. Mordaunt, back in England for the moment, was an important go-between for his interviews,[38] held at the home of the Earl of Shrewsbury, with Halifax, Shrewsbury, Devonshire, Danby, Nottingham, Lumley, and Mordaunt, the admirals Russell and Herbert, and the Bishop of London. These men are cited by Burnet as the "persons chiefly trusted."[39] In addition, the envoy sounded out many others, the most important being Churchill, already prominent as the close friend of the Princess Anne; and Mary's two uncles, the earls of Clarendon and of Rochester.

His object, in which he succeeded admirably, was to convince each of the varied and often jarring groups that William was their friend. Men like Danby, the Hydes, Halifax, and Nottingham, were allowed to hope for an end to their political retirement. The Church party was assured that William had their interests at heart. The Dissenters, whose support was so important to both sides at this time, were promised comprehension within the Church of England, if they belonged to the group who wanted that, or else toleration by act of Parliament rather than by Declaration of Indulgence. Even the Roman Catholics were not overlooked.

*Two accounts are superficially at variance here. Burnet emphasizes Dijkveld's consistent refusal to consider any proposals that William and Mary approve James's method of establishing toleration. Don Ronquillo, the Spanish ambassador, writing to his king on May 26 (O.S.?) about the time Dijkveld left for home, reported that the latter was temporarily enthusiastic about the Declaration of Indulgence when he first heard about it. The apparent discrepancy, which has troubled a good many writers including Muilenburg and the Editor of Mackintosh, is not too disturbing. As a consummate diplomat Dijkveld was, of course, careful about the impression he gave to the other ambassadors in London.

Those whom Dijkveld approached were naturally not the Jesuit Court circle, but the moderates. Recently disturbed over the fall of Rochester, they were apprehensive that James's ill-advised though well-meant efforts on their behalf should worsen rather than improve their condition by heightening the already strong animosity against them. Here again the whole tangled political situation on the Continent had its repercussions. The Roman Catholic opponents of Louis XIV, who indeed had more to fear from him than did the Protestants since it was upon their territories that he was encroaching, suspected that the Prince of Orange might be trying to raise a Protestant League. Therefore, William constantly had to be on guard lest his actions in England should give substance to that suspicion, even while he banked so heavily upon his reputation as the great protector of Protestantism. It is not surprising, then, that Dijkveld should have suggested to the Catholics, as he had to the Dissenters, that William, although unwilling to permit them to have political equality, was ready to see them receive the right of freedom of worship. Nor is it strange that the Catholics listened to him. They had no desire for martyrdom, and if James went on as he was going that might well be their fate. Acting upon instructions from William, Dijkveld also used the occasion to gain information about James's military strength and about the condition of his treasury, which was, by the way, excellent. In addition he probed into the resources and sentiments of the different groups in order that the Prince might know the comparative value of their support and what he would have to do to win it.

His work accomplished and his information gathered, Dijkveld returned to the Netherlands early in June, carrying with him letters which he must have guarded jealously. According to Burnet the men meeting at Shrewsbury House "concerted matters and drew the declaration on which they advised the Prince to engage."[40] That is a tantalizing statement for, if they did indeed draw up a declaration in writing which is certainly suggested by the remark, it has apparently been destroyed or lost and its content is unknown. The letters entrusted to Dijkveld, however, give us some indication of the results of his mission. Several of these are still in King William's Chest and have been published in the

Appendix to Dalrymple's *Memoirs*.[41] Dalrymple finds it "singular that most of them are men of the Tory party" but the analysis made earlier in this study should remove any surprise on that score.

Three of the writers, Nottingham, Shrewsbury, and Devonshire, speak of William's "commands" in terms that give the impression that they are references to orders instead of merely the conventional respects of seventeenth-century letter writing. Nottingham, for example, wrote "The great ambition I have ever had of serving Your Highness made me most readily obey the commands I received from you by the Heer van Dyckvelt."[42] Like all the others who had been at the conferences, Nottingham indicates that Dijkveld can give a much fuller and more exact account of the affairs than it would be wise to commit to paper. From Shrewsbury's references to himself as "one so much a stranger to Your Highness," it is apparent that he was not among those already in communication with the Prince, at least for any great length of time. Danby's letter is the longest and is a little verbose. Always a conceited person, ever since he had played such an important part in bringing about William's marriage he had been quite certain that the latter trusted him more than he trusted anyone else in England. His letter hints more strongly than the others of well-laid plans, deplores the fact that so little can be done at that time, and expresses a wish that he and other men might come to the Netherlands to talk directly to the Prince.

Halifax's letter, that of a self-assured man confident in himself and conscious of no need to kowtow to a possible rising sun, leads us to wonder just how far he was informed of the real purpose of Dijkveld's mission, or, if he was informed, how thoroughly he approved; an impression strengthened by references toward the end of Danby's letter. Halifax seems certain that James's plans are so surely doomed to failure that no drastic action need be taken. His most interesting comments are on the possibility of a session of Parliament, as they strengthen the impression that the opposition group feared rather than hoped for such an eventuality in view of the fact that it would occur only if James were sure of support, and, by giving legal status to the Declaration of Indulgence, would deprive them of one of their best weapons of attack. These men knew all too well the tricks of winning votes for they had used them themselves to gain their own ends. Halifax, however, mentions their apprehensions only to discredit them, for he did not think that the King could possibly get assurance of a majority, and he was certain that no meeting would be called without it.

Of the letters which come from men not mentioned as having been at Shrewsbury House, perhaps the most interesting is from Churchill who asserts not only his own loyalty to Protestantism—if need be he will "shew the resolution of a martyr"—but also that of the Princess Anne. Clarendon and Rochester are included and both are noncommittal. After all, even though they had been deprived of office, they had both been provided for, Rochester generously and Clarendon adequately,[43] and while they were uncles of the Princess Mary they were also the King's brothers-in-law. Whichever way the wind blew they were fairly secure, or at least they should be if they did not commit themselves too far. Sunderland writes a brief note which may or may not be significant of closer connections. More will be said of that later. The remaining letters are unimportant.

Although Tories predominate among these letter writers, both here and in the group who were present at the Shrewsbury House conferences may be seen a strange mixture of Whigs, Tories, Churchmen, and former Roman Catholics, united in a common cause. Shrewsbury himself was later counted among the Whigs but at this time he ought not to be labeled, and indeed his freedom from association with any set group was one of the qualifications for which his fellows recommended him to William.[44] A member of an old Catholic family, he had left the Church seven years before, but as he was only twenty at the time too much significance should not be attached to his conversion. Still under twenty-seven, he was extremely popular at the Court and had been singled out by James for one of the most honorable positions at the recent coronation, probably because of the valuable services he had rendered during the elections for Parliament. Soon afterwards he became a captain in the army, and before Dijkveld's arrival he had been made a colonel. His motives for joining the opposition are obscure, and his later career suggests that he may not have thought his actions through very carefully. It is possible that he was under the influence of Lord Mordaunt. The same holds true for Lumley who, like Shrewsbury, was young and an even more recent convert from Catholicism which he did not actually renounce until this very year. An army officer and one of the leaders of the troops that captured Monmouth, he had resigned his commission in January 1687, after it was fairly well known in England that Dijkveld was coming.

Of the outright Tories, Danby is too well-known to need explanation. His motives are clear: to recapture the political prominence of which he had been deprived by Shaftesbury, to which he could never hope to return so long as James held power. Ascribing to him any deep concern either for the constitution or for liberty of the subject would be nonsense. His political career had been built on bribery of members of the House of Commons and on active support of the royal prerogative. To a degree the same can be said of Nottingham, who, although he had not been guilty of bribery, was certainly no champion of popular rights. His hostility to the Crown at this time can be ascribed in part to the fact that his brother, Heneage Finch, had been dismissed as Solicitor General the year before for refusing to uphold the royal dispensing power.

Halifax and the Bishop of London complete the roster of Tories in the group. It would be wrong, however, to permit the inference that the others were Whigs. Herbert, like Shrewsbury and Lumley, had not taken a definite stand with either party. A rear admiral for some time, he had been appointed by James to the fairly lucrative office of master of the robes. His first outright opposition occurred when the King tried to secure his promise to vote for the repeal of the Test Act when Parliament, in which he sat as a member for Dover, should reconvene. The dismissal from office which resulted from his refusal might lead us to admire his incorruptibility were it not that by the time the King called him in he was already in close association with the Shrewsbury House group.[45] As with Shrewsbury himself, Herbert's later career does not bring conviction that his actions were carefully considered.

The remaining three, Mordaunt, Devonshire, and Edward Russell, were Whigs. Mordaunt, too young to have taken part in the Exclusion struggle, had not attracted political attention until the November session of James's only Parliament. Devonshire had a long record of opposition to the crown. At the moment he was embroiled in a curious and somewhat scandalous affair which led, before Dijkveld left, to his being fined £30,000 for striking his enemy, Colpepper, when the two men were in the royal palace. As the fine was imposed by King's Bench, Devonshire claimed—unsuccessfully—the privilege of peerage. The order was given that he should be imprisoned until the fine was paid but intervention by the Duchess of Mazarin brought the King to concede that payment would not be pressed if the culprit would behave himself. Although Devonshire had joined the conspirators before all this came to a head, he now had an additional grievance against the King which gave him further reason for wishing for a change. The list closes with Vice Admiral Edward Russell, cousin of Lord William Russell, in whom a family grievance united with Whig convictions. Never particularly active in politics, he was to be of great value to William at the time of the expedition of 1688 and somewhat of a burden to him later.

These men have been described at some length in order to show the kind of person with whom William was making contact. Others, who were not at the conferences, could be added, but the general characteristics would remain the same. Whigs and Tories are both included but the latter are in a decided majority, and of the Whigs known to have been involved, only Devonshire had a record of political activity. With the exception of Mordaunt and of Lumley, whose conversion was too recent for him to be typed in this respect, all were staunch, but not necessarily devout Anglicans. All of them were either peers or closely related to peers. They were men of wealth whose extensive landed property and family connections gave them prestige and influence throughout the shires.

Nor was the pattern changed materially as the conspiracy widened. Several erstwhile Exclusionists were of course attracted as wind of something afoot blew across the country, but their state of mind may be illustrated, although in a somewhat extreme fashion, by the Marquis of Winchester who was so uncertain of how to act that, Hamlet-like, he feigned insanity and spent the summer of 1687 rampaging about England with a retinue of one hundred horsemen, giving lavish entertainments at each night's stopping place. Like his prototype he may have had method in his madness. Aside from the Exclusionists, the most notable additions in the next few months were the Scots and the army and navy officers. Among neither group do we find particularly strong convictions on English constitutional problems. Those in the second category were worried over the possibility that they might be cashiered to make a place for Roman Catholics; their fears were given substance by James's permission to Tyrconnel to include several of that faith in the regiments in Ireland, and shadow by careful intrigue and propaganda emanating from the Orangists. As for the Scots, they were prompted by motives so nationalistic as to cause trouble once the Revolution was accomplished and send some of their leaders ultimately into the ranks of the Jacobites.

One group is conspicuous by its absence, especially because of the emphasis placed upon them in some of the later interpretations of the Revolution. These are the merchants of whom only a few, notably William Harbord and Samuel Barnardiston, were at all important. Actually a scrutiny of the economic policies of James II proves his interest in the cause of trade; and the firm stand he was taking against the Dutch, who were the great and often successful rivals of the English, was popular among the City companies. The chief significance of the merchants in relation to the whole movement appears to be not that they contributed much to it, but that it could not have been successful if they had actively opposed it; and the great value of Nottingham and Danby lay in the fact that, through family relationships and other ties, they were able to influence this powerful group.[46]

But it has already been noted that the leaders were peers. At first this might be thought unworthy of comment since most men who achieved political leadership were likely to be raised to that rank, and some of those already mentioned had been ennobled only since the Restoration. As the months passed by, however, more and more of the members of the old peerage were added, so that, from the English side at least, the Revolution was manipulated by the landed gentry and aristocracy with emphasis on the latter. The sophisticated historian ought not to be surprised to find the peerage in opposition to the royal power. One is reminded of the barons at Runnymede, the Lords Ordainers, the Lords Appellant, and, finally, of that strong segment of the House of Lords which remained loyal to the cause of Parliament long after the opening of the Civil Wars and might almost be said to have been dislodged from that loyalty by the attacks of the extremists rather than to have deserted. Their sons and grandsons were no less jealous of the privileges of rank than they had been, nor less determined to preserve their rights from attack by either king or commoner. Control of the principal offices of the realm was the device which they had used for centuries to protect their position, and they would fight to defend that control. For the moment their adversary was the king. The history of the next century was to prove that in winning their battle against him they tightened their control over the Commons. Just how far they represented the sentiment of the people at large is open to doubt. Certainly they were able, through local prestige, to create and manipulate opinion which they could be said to reflect. If one must make ethical judgments, these men can be called valiant upholders of constitutional principal or base and materialistic traitors with almost equal ease. Either judgment is unwarranted. In thinking in terms of self-interest and in identifying that interest with the good of the country, they conformed to the pattern of rationalization which is invariably present in any political group. Be Bentham right or wrong, we human beings *believe* that what is good for ourselves is good for others.

Father Orleans, in his *Histoire des Revolutions d'Angleterre*, first published in 1693, emphasized the point that any plans for an attack upon the throne itself were carefully concealed from most of the men who were being drawn into the plot.[47] It is safe to go even further than that and to make the assumption, based on what actually happened, that only a very small number of Englishmen, most of whom were not in the country at the time, were aware of any such project. What the others had in mind was a show of force to compel James to withdraw the Declaration of Indulgence and to dismiss his ministers, whose places they would then take. If that failed, they would go beyond the show of force to force itself, possibly with the aim of setting William up as regent.[48] Anything beyond that would have been too dangerous, and not only because of the consequences of failure. Whatever happened, two things must be kept intact: the monarchy and Anglican supremacy. More liberal Tory theory permitted the idea that the king must conform to the fundamental law of the realm, but it clung tenaciously to the doctrine of indefeasible hereditary right, and condemned republicanism much more violently than it condemned arbitrary power.

William's great task then, was so to lay his plans that he could keep the indispensable support of the Tories at the same time that he won over a group who would be willing to see the monarchy change hands. Two factors in the developing situation helped him. For one thing, James played into his hands. It will be made plain that, partly because he could not help himself, and partly because he was so intent upon achieving one set purpose, James was unaware until it was too late of the magnitude of the risk he was taking. The second factor leads us back to the struggle for the support of the Dissenters. In it we shall see how William and the Tories both could hold out hopes of toleration based on law at the same time that they cast doubts on the possibility that James could or would do so.

CHAPTER 2

The Issues Defined

In the winter of 1686–1687 the big fear of the Tory opposition had been that James might win, not only the Dissenters, but also William, over to support of the Declaration of Indulgence and of parliamentary repeal of the Test Act and the Penal laws, especially the former. Dijkveld brought assurance to the few with whom he established contact, but a curious and much-discussed letter reveals the current uneasiness in the minds of the others. This letter, dated March 7, 1687, was sent, with elaborate precautions for secrecy, to William from Anne, the wife of the Earl of Sunderland and the mistress of William's close friend, Henry Sidney. The writer informs William that there is much discussion in her circle of the possibility that he might yield to the pressure which she knows is being put on him, and tells him that any indication of his doing so would be of great damage to him in England. It was this last piece of information that was so valuable to the recipient of the letter for, taken in connection with another that will be mentioned soon, it strengthened his conviction that he not only need not, but could not, remain neutral in English politics, and that support of the Test Act was the one sure and indispensable plank in his platform.

Further comment on this letter is necessary, although not in direct relation to William. Dalrymple and others have suggested that the body of it was actually written by Sunderland himself,*

---

*Even granting the lax marital standards of the Restoration, the reference to Henry Sidney in the opening sentences of the letter argues against this.

with the postscript, which is unimportant, alone added by his wife. On that basis the letter is offered as evidence that Sunderland was in the conspiracy from the very beginning, using his position as one of James's chief ministers to direct his master along a path which he knew would lead to destruction. Examination of the original letter reveals it to be all in one hand, that of Lady Sunderland,[1] but that is unimportant as she could easily have copied something given to her by her husband so that he would be protected if it were intercepted. But much more important is the fact that the warning conveyed indicates ignorance rather than knowledge, as none of the men in contact with Dijkveld could possibly have had such doubts. If Sunderland was indeed the author of the body of the letter, he was not at that time in William's confidence. There is further evidence against the suggestion and it seems to be conclusive. Included in the published correspondence of William III and Hans Willem Bentinck, there is a memorandum, the original of which is in Bentinck's handwriting, headed *Points to be extracted from a letter of Lady Sunderland*.[2] From its content the memorandum indubitably refers to the document under consideration here. Its heading certainly tells us that Bentinck did not think the letter had been written by Lord rather than by Lady Sunderland. He had no reason to resort to a misleading heading in a casual memorandum intended for his personal use. Nor is it at all likely that he, like others, was hoaxed, and that William alone knew the truth, for Bentinck was completely in William's confidence. All in all, while Sunderland cannot be absolved from suspicion of later implication in the conspiracy, the use of the letter as evidence against him does not seem justified.*

*One curious detail may be worthy of mention. The letter was enclosed in one from Lady Sunderland to the Princess of Orange which, in its turn, was enclosed in one the Countess wrote to Bentinck about her garden. Sections of other letters suggest that references to gardening were a device to indicate secret and highly important communications. For example, when Mordaunt returned to England in the fall of 1686 he wrote to Bentinck "Meantime you know we are to correspond as brother gardiners." On March 11, 1687, probably before Lady Sunderland's letter went off (since we know that it was delayed for a few days), Mordaunt again wrote to Bentinck suggesting that letters might be intercepted and "good gardiners that we are, if we speak of plants and flowers, the spies would find mysteries in that." Other instances could be cited. One is torn between a reluctance to fall for "cloak and dagger" suggestions and the realization that, in the circumstances, similar devices must have been used and that this may well have been one of them.

Shortly after getting this letter, over which so much controversy has arisen, the Prince received another communication that is much more significant although it has attracted almost no attention. Adding a great deal to his information on the state of mind of the English and Scottish refugees in the Netherlands, it also opened the way for direct contact with the discontented element in Scotland. The writer was Patrick Hume, later Lord Polworth, a refugee from the Argyle expedition, who had been outlawed for implication in the Rye House Plot. Now living in Utrecht under the name of Wallace, he had been for some time in contact with Bentinck. He informed William that many of the British in the Netherlands, "not of the ranting, talking sort of men" met to discuss what to do and that "at present all of them look upon your Highness as the great wheel which, under God, must give life and motion to any good project." But they wanted to know what William thought of the Edict in Scotland and of the Declaration of Indulgence. As two of the Scots were about to return home it was hoped that William would see them first so that they could carry with them first hand knowledge of his sentiments. With this letter, Hume sent a document called *Memorial upon the Edict in Scotland* written, he said, by "Church of England men," which goes so much further that the sender was a little disturbed by it. Its authors urged the Prince to write James a strong letter in support of the Test Act. This should be "published to the world" for the encouragement of the people in case Parliament met. Suggestions concerning the British regiments in the Netherlands indicate that military action was contemplated, although "time and season are to be discreetly chosen." All this must have interested William exceedingly, but the lines which undoubtedly caught and held his eyes were those which declared:

One thing the Prince will do well to be persuaded of and lay to heart and it is of note for himself and himself alone: if the nations (i.e. England and Scotland) come once into an extreme of suffering, that their case require it, the Prince must either hazard himself for them and become their deliverer or else he will risk and hazard his interest in those kingdoms forever.[3]

William was sure now of the support of the Tory-Anglican group in England, and he could be reasonably certain that many of the Whigs would be glad to act against the King whom they had hated even for years before he came to the throne. Information received about the refugees in the Netherlands, of which the above letters were only a small part, for Bentinck was in constant contact with them, and Burnet, although banished from William's presence, sent in frequent reports, established the fact that he not only could, but must count on them or run the risk of having them become his antagonists and perhaps work for a republic. The only important step left was to win over the Dissenters in England, the only important step, that is, so far as England was concerned. Careful and complicated diplomatic negotiations still had to be made to set the stage on the Continent, and the political leaders of the United Provinces had to be put in the right frame of mind. But that is another story which will receive due attention in time.

The Declaration of Indulgence, although not unexpected, was greeted with consternation by James's opponents. Macaulay describes the situation a little naïvely — if it be not lese majesty to speak so of the great Whig historian. "The Anglican party" he writes, "was in amazement and terror. This new turn of affairs was indeed alarming. The house of Stuart leagued with the republican and regicide sects against the old Cavaliers of England!"[4] The naïveté lies in the fact that Macaulay does not seem to see that what put the Tory party in "amazement and terror" was the possible combination of the Dissenters with the King rather than the use of the dispensing power, although attack upon that came in very handy during the next few months. The consternation was well-founded. From this distance in time it is almost impossible to prove exactly how the Dissenters as a whole felt about the Declaration, for one comfort of those days was that public opinion polls had not yet been invented. Whatever their inner convictions, however, their immediate response, except for a few stubborn souls like John Bunyan, was either passive acceptance or outright joy. A considerable number of declarations of gratitude were sent to the Court,[5] especially from the more radical sects such as the Quakers and the Anabaptists, so that James had very good reason to believe that what he had done was meeting with approval.[6] Let us not fall into the trap of labeling these expressions of approval insincere cant. There was no reason why they should have been written beyond that of honest conviction on the part of their authors. Not for two or three months did adverse opinion, stemming from the Dissenters themselves rather than from the Anglicans, become noticeable. It is important to understand that this changed sentiment, when it came, was not spontaneous, but resulted from the work of the Anglicans. Especially noteworthy is the fact that William, acting upon advice sent to him from England, gathered together some of the leading dissenting divines then taking refuge in the United Provinces, and, after providing them with money to pay their debts and buy their passage, sent them home to take advantage of the freedom of speech and assembly granted to them by the Declaration of Indulgence, to preach against it, and to win back those straying brethren who were willing to accept religious liberty from a Catholic king.[7]

Their influence was soon felt. The expressions of gratitude diminished in number. In place of them the summer saw a regular pamphlet war with Dissenter fighting Dissenter, and the Anglican Church, suddenly become Latitudinarian, joining the fray. Hot words and exaggerated accusations flew wildly from both sides, but the most cogent arguments lay inevitably with the opponents of the Crown. James would establish liberty of conscience not by law but by a questionable use of the prerogative which, if allowed to remain unchallenged, could just as well be used later to deprive the Dissenters of their newly acquired privileges once the established religion was beaten and the Papists were in control. Even should the King be true to his promises to call a parliament to give his deeds the sanction of enacted law, the fact remained that he had issued the Declaration before, not after, taking such a step. Even should toleration be by law established, there was the awful example of the revocation of the Edict of Nantes to prove that a Roman Catholic king could treat a solemn agreement as a scrap of paper. The Dissenters could be sure of religious freedom only if it came to them by agreement with the Anglicans. The Roman Catholics, avowed enemies of all heretics, were not to be trusted. Thus ran the arguments of the Tories. They had weight, to be sure, but that should not blind us to the fact that several of the leading Dissenters were never won over by them and that James had acceptably good reason to believe, until he knew that William was actually on the way to England, that with their help he could win.*

From the furious verbal warfare of the summer of 1687 emerge the two major issues on which the Revolution was to be fought and won. The first of these was the repeal of the Test Act and the second was the terms on which religious toleration should be effected. They were narrow issues, to be sure, but on them hung a host of others, political and constitutional, and even social and economic. They were singled out and emphasized partly because agreement upon them by James's opponents made possible the avoidance of those still deeper issues on which difference of opinion was great and dangerous. As between King and Opposition, the first issue was clear cut. James wanted repeal of the Test Act, and the Tory-Whig-Anglican coalition said "No," although the subsequent practice of "occasional conformity" indicates that the latter may have had some mental reservations. The second was much more involved. Both sides had come to the conclusion, the Anglicans rather reluctantly, that some sort of concession must be made, and in both camps honest conviction was no doubt as responsible for this as realization of political expediency. But each wanted to *give* rather than to *assent to* toleration, and to do so on its own terms and by its own methods. James wished to do so through use of the royal prerogative with the additional support of law passed by Parliament. The others attacked the use of the prerogative in this instance and maintained that the desired end could and should be achieved only by a parliament elected without royal pressure and with due regard for observance of the Tests. Such a parliament would, of course, be predominately Anglican, thereby winning for that group the advantage of being the one that had granted religious liberty.

*The most noteworthy of these pamphlets is, of course, Halifax's famous LETTER TO A DISSENTER, which appeared early in August and was soon scattered throughout the kingdom. It was, however, only one of a great many, and its continued importance is probably due less to the relative merits of its arguments, sound as they were, than to the fame of its writer and to his ability to write a lucid English which is more readable today than that to be found in most of the pamphlets written by his contemporaries.

In the last days before the Revolution, but not until then, Parliament itself became an issue. James was charged, at that point, with wishing to rule without it, but that was a later, almost last minute, bone of contention. On the basis of what has already been said it is easy to see why the Tests originally received the greater emphasis, while the stand of the Opposition on Parliament was filled with contradictions up to the flight of James II. Some of these contradictions were the inevitable result of the forced marriage between Tories and Whigs, uniting the views of the former on the prerogative with the latter's convictions that Parliament should be supreme. Others grew out of the problem of how to oppose a parliament called to formalize the Declaration of Indulgence at the same time that it was maintained that James was acting illegally.

In the uneven struggle which followed James was hampered by the almost psychopathic fear of Catholicism to which reference has already been made. That might have been overcome if he had been willing to act slowly, but, conscious of his age, he was over-anxious to do his work so thoroughly that it could not be undone by the Protestant successor who would follow him, he was convinced, fairly soon, and Dijkveld had as good as told him that William and Mary would revoke the steps he had intended to take. But fear of Catholicism on the part of his people and his own felt need for speed were not his only disadvantages. More important is the fact that by the time he really got started the opposition to him had already been formed and was in effective operation. One result of this was that when he tried to build an organized support for his policy he ran up against a number of men who had already committed themselves to William. This point cannot be overstressed. Much has been made of the unfavorable response, first to the closetings, and, a few months later, to James's progresses in the west and to the questions the Lords Lieutenant were asked to put to the freeholders of their counties. Yet in each of these instances many of the men who responded unfavorably are known to have been involved with the Prince of Orange before they so acted, and there is a very strong probability that most of the others were similarly involved although we have no record of it to offer as proof. Whether or not these men would have been more malleable had they not been conscious of a well-organized backing is, of course, not known. Yet the fact remains that organization preceded active opposition. James was to a certain extent aware of the situation he faced, and his very awareness contributed to his downfall. Orangist influence among its members had been the principal reason he advanced for the dissolution of Parliament that summer. He still hoped to overcome that influence, in part at least, by winning his nephew over to his side, but instead he gave the Opposition the excellent chance to say that he did not dare face a freely elected House of Commons. Then, as the next year passed, obsessed by a fear of treachery for which there was much foundation, he turned more and more to the exclusive company and advice of the little group of Catholic and Protestant sycophants in whom he thought there was no danger. He did not even really trust the army, of which he had had such high hopes; and although the number of Catholics whom he made officers was relatively small, even in proportion to the total of that faith in the country, his attempt to insure loyalty by that device also reacted against him.

From the summer of 1687 events were beyond any control by James. Even a complete about-face such as he actually tried to make later was by then almost out of the question. And in all this the "great wheel which gave life to any good project" was indeed the Prince of Orange. Without him to use as a continuing threat the more moderate members of the Opposition, once they were victors in a struggle which they contemplated in terms that were primarily political, could not be sure of keeping the advantage thus won. With his aid the more radical group could look forward to victory by use of arms. None of them could be sure of winning without him. With him they could be reasonably sure of success, at least in the all-important step of compelling James to yield. Because his leadership was one of the two points — no repeal of the Tests was the other — on which all could agree, they were either willing to overlook or unable to see the points on which there was difference.

William's problem was thereby simplified for him. After the spring of 1687 all he had to do was to collect an army, a story in itself and a project on which he was already engaged, and to stand firm on the question of the Tests, letting his stand be known throughout Britain and Europe. His greatest, almost his only, danger was that the King might win a favorable parliament, but there were workers in England busy at the job of forestalling that eventuality. Nevertheless, as the summer drew on, he became uneasy. The full impact of the counterattack on the Declaration of Indulgence had not yet been felt, and the news which reached the United Provinces told more of the favorable than of the unfavorable reactions to the King's policy. Under such circumstances a parliament might meet which would knock the ground out from under his feet. It should be remembered that many of those who had made contact with him had emphasized to him their opposition not so much to toleration as to the exercise of the prerogative to bring it about. They had done this for a number of reasons, one of which may have been that when the prerogative was used contrary to their interests they had come to be uneasy about that which in theory they upheld. Of more weight, however, is the fact that under the circumstances, when winning the Dissenters was the all-important objective, the Tories were forced into the position of taking issue not with toleration itself but with the method of achieving it.

William was far from being sure of those men who had sent him such fervent avowals of their devotion. Their objectives were not the same as his and they were unaware of the basic reasons why he sought their support and offered his own. Less than ten years before he had narrowly escaped disaster when certain people in England, some of whom were included in this very group, had wanted to use him in the Exclusion Controversy, and he had seen then how willing they were to drop him when their ends could be achieved through other means. Perhaps overly sensitive to the selfish elements in their motives, he thought it entirely possible that many of them might be won over to James, at least to the extent of being willing to bargain parliamentary support for freedom of worship in return for reappointment to the offices which they had held. A successful parliament might turn the trick, and the old coalition of Crown and Tory-Anglican be reestablished. William was fairly certain that such a parliament might meet.[8] He was well aware that if it did his own plans would have to be abandoned or else radically revised to coördinate more fully with the Whigs. To seek information and to reassure himself, William once again sent a special envoy to England, using this time the pretext of a message of condolence to the Queen, whose mother had recently died.

The man chosen on this occasion was not Dijkveld, for he had identified himself too thoroughly with the Opposition to be useful. Instead, William called upon his cousin, Count Zuylestein, one of those gay men-about-Court who give the lie to the notion that all Dutchmen are ponderous, stolid, and serious. His reputation for frivolity lent him the disguise necessary for effective and secret contact with men whose opinion was sought, and he did not need Dijkveld's acumen for, the groundwork having been laid, all that was desired was information. From him, and from the letters he carried on his return, William learned that his fears were to a certain extent justified. His observers, it is true, did not think there was much possibility of a parliament, but that was only because they were convinced that James would not be able to gather one that was to his liking.[9] A variation of this general opinion was expressed by Nottingham who, although certain that a session would not be called immediately, was equally sure that when elections were held, as they were bound to be held eventually, no amount of maneuvering could prevent an Anglican majority, and he showed plainly that he preferred a parliamentary to any other solution. This was the last thing William wanted to hear, for it indicated that his help might not be needed. The only dissenting voice was Mordaunt. He was almost as sure that Parliament would meet as Nottingham and Halifax were that it would not and unlike the former he was certain that a session would be a calamity, for "blows given by parliament are deadly ones."[10] In those words he unconsciously voiced William's deepest apprehension.

Zuylestein, like Dijkveld, has left no written record of the report he brought to William. Had he done so and had he been granted the power of omnipotent and impartial observance, his words might have been roughly as follows. The King was eager to call a new parliament but would do so only if he was certain of winning a majority that would be willing to repeal the Test and Penal laws. Nottingham to the contrary, there was a real, if slight, possibility that he might be successful. Some of the towns in the west were doing more than assuring James of their support — they were volunteering it. Elsewhere James would be able to use the techniques of controlling the corporations, already developed during the period of Tory ascendency, to win members sympathetic to his cause. The counties presented a greater difficulty, but their representatives were a minority of the lower house, and even so, it might be possible, through a change in the personnel of the Lord Lieutenancies, to gain a measure of support. Had he given in to wishful thinking, Zuylestein might have told William that the progresses which James was making through the western shires at the time he left were being met with coolness by the gentry and aristocracy, but, if he was being truly judicious and impartial he would have had to admit that the lesser folk were showing an enthusiasm for their King that could not be attributed to the mere occasion of a royal visit, that Penn and his associates were meeting some success in their efforts to win the Dissenters in the towns the King was to visit, and that the King himself professed to be pleased with the results of his journey. Zuylestein might have added, with a scornful smile at such popish superstition, that James proposed to visit the shrine of St. Winifred in Wales to pray that he and the Queen might be blessed with a son.

Still retaining his impartiality, Zuylestein could have pointed out that the above situation was not unfavorable to his master, for it indicated the possibility of a turn of events which the pro-Orange aristocracy and gentry would resist by force. What was more disturbing were the doubts of that group that the King could be successful. Careful analysis of probable votes in the House of Lords showed that there was a safe majority against repeal of the Test and Penal laws.[11] As far as Commons were concerned, while it seemed possible that a majority might be willing to repeal the Penal laws, most observers believed that they would balk at doing the same for the Tests. Since even this moiety of James's policies would in all probability be rejected by the Lords, wherein lay reason for fearing a type of religious toleration that would favor Catholicism? Wherein lay a need for intervention by the Prince of Orange?

But all the above presupposes calm, judicious analysis. What Zuylestein actually had to say more probably reflected the confused thinking that is so evident in the letters written to William about this time by the very men with whom the envoy must have discussed the situation. In those letters certainty that James will be unsuccessful plainly struggles with the fear that he will be able to gain his objective. The Tory nucleus of the pro-Orange faction were worried about three possibilities. One was that the King might pack the upper house by using his unquestioned right to create new peers. That, however, disturbed them less than the prospect that some of their own number might desert to the King, a fear that was ever present in their minds as well as in that of the Prince. When such names as those of Rochester and Churchill and of four of the bishops could appear on the list of Lords favoring repeal of the controversial laws,[12] on whom could one depend? Finally, much as they tried to assure themselves that the Dissenters were too anti-Papist to yield toleration to the Catholics even if by doing so they themselves would benefit, the Anglican party could not be sure. Penn was undoubtedly having some influence. The bait of relief from onerous restrictions would be strong.

Uneasy as he was and continued to be over the possibility that some of the aristocracy might prove turncoat, William was less disturbed about them than about the Dissenters. He was gathering a neat little collection of letters which could prove very embarrassing to those of the former who might be thinking of changing their minds, but he had no such sword to dangle over the Dissenters. Yet religious toleration, under existing conditions, could be achieved only with their coöperation, in which case they would have to bear forever the onus of being responsible for letting Papists into the government. This was their vulnerable point, and the one which the Anglicans were attacking again and again. William for his part realized that enough of the Dissenters were attracted by the idea of toleration to make it necessary to show them how it could be achieved without danger of dishonor or the violation of their Protestant principles. This he could do only by coming out in the open and announcing himself the advocate of toleration, the implacable adversary of the repeal of the Tests, and the champion of the Protestant religion. His stand had of course been known before. One of the chief purposes of Dijkveld's mission, as has been pointed out, had been to make it clear. But then it had been conveyed verbally and to a selected few, with emphasis on his support of Anglicanism in particular rather than of Protestantism in general. The dissenting divines who returned from the Netherlands after April 4 consulted him before they left, and brought to England an impression which emphasized his Calvinism rather than his Anglicanism, and the same was true of the Scots who had taken advantage of the Edict to return to their homeland. But here again the impression was conveyed by word of mouth, and especially in England it was confined almost entirely to London where the returned divines were active. Only the printed page, the fly sheet, unparalleled at the time in its effectiveness as a weapon of propaganda, could really put William before the eyes of the whole nation.

This device had been suggested earlier, notably in the *Memorial upon the Edict in Scotland,* and even before that by "those in England" who had urged the Prince and Princess of Orange to take a public stand at the time of the creation of the Court of Ecclesiastical Commission. In the spring of 1687, just after the Declaration of Indulgence had been issued, rumors that some sort of printed statement from the Prince might appear had gone about England.[18] There were, however, certain objections. The printed page is terribly and irrevocably public, so that it is virtually impossible to retreat with dignity and honor from a stand once taken thereon. Also to be considered was the diplomatic situation in Europe where Catholic princes and the Papacy itself, none of whom William could afford to antagonize, might well view with alarm a pronouncement against steps that were designed to favor their co-religionaries. However, by the autumn of 1687 it was almost necessary to do something to quiet the rumors that were spreading rapidly both in England and on the Continent. Europe buzzed with stories that William planned a drastic crusade against all Papists everywhere. Fostered by the Jesuit cabal in Whitehall for the express purpose of creating suspicion in the minds of the Emperor and other Catholic rulers, these tales were the more easily believed because of the ill-advised activities of the Huguenot exiles, toward whom William was known to be sympathetic, and because of the policy of religious repression which was being put into effect in some of the United Provinces.[14] In England the rumors had to take a somewhat different form. There word ran about that William had announced himself in favor of repeal of the Tests or even that he was considering conversion to Rome![15] In a situation where he was accused on the one hand of intransigent opposition to all Catholics, and on the other of favoring them unduly, William had more to gain than to lose by offering himself to draw the fire of James while the Dissenters and Anglicans made their way out of the dilemma posed by a possible session of Parliament.

Ironically enough the means for action were put into his hands by James who, refusing to take as final the Prince's repeated answers that he would not approve the repeal of the Tests, made one more attempt to win him over to the family standard. The go-between this time was one James Stewart, a Scottish covenanter who had been a refugee for some years in the United Provinces. One of the many who had gone to England after the Declaration of Indulgence, he had, like the others, talked to William before his departure and had given assurances that he would act in the latter's interest. Unlike the others, however, shortly after his arrival in London he seems to have become sincerely convinced that the best interest not only of William but also of all the Dissenters themselves, lay in accepting the offer of toleration that came from James. He volunteered his services to the King and after they had been accepted, opened a correspondence with Fagel, who had been his close friend while he was in the Netherlands, urging him to use his great influence to get William to change his mind. His two principal arguments were that the Roman Catholics were too few in number to be dangerous, and that the Dissenters were faced with a return of the persecution which they had suffered under the Penal laws if the Tests were not repealed, for James was determined not to give up the one without the other.

The letters were, of course, brought to William, who decided that Fagel should write a reply to be translated into English by

Burnet.[16] The reply emphasized the devotion of the Prince and Princess of Orange to the cause of religious toleration. They were willing that it should be extended not only to Dissenters, but even to Catholics, although the latter ought not to be given the privilege of public worship. On the question of the Tests, however, they were unyielding, for they looked upon them as the great safeguard of the Protestant religion, and since they laid no punishment upon anyone, but simply disqualified certain persons from office, they could not be looked upon as unduly severe.[17]

Dated November 4, 1687, within a few weeks after it had been sent the letter had been translated into four languages, printed, and scattered in broadsheet form throughout England and western Europe. On the mainland it assuaged the fears of the Catholic enemies of France by its tolerant attitude toward their religion. In England, those who ran could read that the heiress presumptive and her husband had the interests of the Dissenters at heart, so that they had only to bide their time to receive a religious toleration which would not give equal or greater advantage to the Papists. The letter was received with joy and relief. People, it was said, were "in rapture to find the sentiments of Your Highness and the Princess in matters of religion not only so equitable, but so agreeable to the interest and to the taste of all this nation."[18] To counteract its effects the Court sanctioned publication of a pamphlet called *Parliamentum Pacificum* which suggested that Fagel's letter did not have the approval of the Prince and the Princess, and even intimated that the whole thing was a forgery. Fagel countered by a sharp retort to D'Albeville which affirmed the authenticity of the document and stated in no uncertain terms that the views represented therein were indeed those of William and Mary. This, like his letter to Stewart, was printed and circulated in England.

While all this was going on another set of letters was passing back and forth between London and The Hague, unknown to all but those who sent or received them and to a few of their friends, but even more important than the Fagel-Stewart interchange in establishing and determining personal relationships and through them, public acts. The principal writers were James II and Mary and the subject was the comparative merits of the Roman and the Anglican Churches. Initiated verbally by Mary, who, through D'Albeville, had asked her father for the reasons for his conversion, the correspondence began in November 1687, and continued into March when it was concluded by James with the abrupt statement that he no longer cared to go on with it. The opening letter, written by James, was dated November 4, before he knew of the Fagel letter, but after he must have been aware that he could at least hope for a son. He did not abandon his efforts until somewhere around the first of March. By then the Fagel letter, with its reply and rejoinder, were well known. The time scheme, therefore, suggests that it was Fagel's letter combined with Mary's own forthright statements to him that caused James to give up his efforts to win her approval of toleration rather than, as is sometimes suggested, his knowledge of the Queen's pregnancy. After this failure James made no further attempts to win over his children, but blundered on in his haste to establish toleration so securely that it could not be withdrawn.[19]

Knowledge of this correspondence was not confined to the two writers. Mary, of course, showed the letters to William, who sent the first one to Burnet together with Mary's reply to it, telling him that he might read, but must not copy them. Burnet obeyed the word but not the spirit. He must have memorized the contents as he later set them down in his *History* almost verbatim.[20] D'Albeville took such assurance from Mary's willingness to discuss the problem with her father that he believed she might be converted not only to toleration but even to Catholicism. At this point Mary realized her danger, and wrote to her sister and to the Bishop of London to reassure them, and also, through her chaplain, Dr. Stanley, to the Archbishop of Canterbury.[21] These letters went only to a few, but like the public pronouncement, they served to strengthen the conviction of those who received them that not only William, but also Mary, would never coöperate with James.

There could now be no doubt about William's stand on the religious issue. In a way the Fagel letter forms the climax of William's connections with political affairs in England before he became king. Whigs and Tories, Anglicans and Dissenters, had been brought into a successful coalition through emphasis upon the two or three points on which all could agree, and the doubtful were publicly assured of a champion. William's supreme advantage over James, that he could make an acceptable offer of toleration, whereas the other could not, was brought into sharper focus. From that time on there remained only to perfect the actual plans for action, and the correspondence of the time reveals those already to have been well under way. Further devices for secret letter writing were invented by the men who were working with Bentinck, and directions were given for the use of disappearing ink. A cipher was drawn up which substituted numbers for the names of the principal leaders.[22] The pamphlet war increased in fury, a great number of the pamphlets being printed in the United Provinces and smuggled across the North Sea for distribution in England. The subversion of the army and the navy began. Some of the leaders withdrew from London, the better to superintend operations in their home counties. Sometime during that year a very significant paper found its way into William's hands, giving an analysis of the English treasury, of the state of mind of the important personages in the country, and of the condition of the army and the navy.[23] At about the same time he began negotiations with Spain for the liquidation of personal claims he had against that government in the Spanish Netherlands, and within the next few months those were settled so favorably as to bring a sizable sum of ready cash into his private treasury.[24] In view of the fact that those claims had been hanging fire for years, it is significant that William suddenly became interested in pressing them at this time.

Before going any further into discussion of how these "plans for action" were put into effect, it might be well to define that phrase, and, still more important, to determine the objective. Henceforth, the plans for action will be taken to mean an armed invasion of England by a substantial military force with William in command; its purpose, the dethroning of James and the setting up of William in his place. In order to give this assertion the analysis it needs, it will be necessary to drop temporarily any adherence to a consecutive time scheme and to move freely back and forth through those months from the spring of 1687 to the day in February of 1689 when the plans for action were realized in success. That an invasion was being projected can scarcely be denied. The very fact that it actually occurred is evidence enough and the only question is how early that planning commenced. There is less agreement on its purpose: to dethrone James and make William king. It might be well to examine first what is frequently offered as evidence to the contrary.

This is to be found in what ought to be the most excellent of sources, statements by William himself. A few days before he sailed for England he wrote to the Emperor:

> I assure your Imperial Majesty by this letter, that whatever reports may have been spread, and notwithstanding those which may be spread in the future, I have not the least intention to do any hurt to his Britannic Majesty, or to those who have a right to pretend to the succession of his kingdoms, and still less to make an attempt upon the crown or to desire to appropriate it to myself. Neither have I any desire to extirpate the Roman Catholics, but only to employ my cares to endeavor to redress the disorders and irregularities which have been committed against the laws of those kingdoms by the bad counsels of the ill-intentioned.[25]

At approximately the same time he wrote to an unnamed official in the Spanish Netherlands:

> Although my enemies would have the world believe it, be assured that my intention is not to dethrone the King of England nor to extirpate the Roman Catholics in his Kingdoms. But I find myself obliged in honor and in conscience to go there to maintain the subjects in their laws and religion and to procure a liberty of conscience according to the laws.[26]

Moreover in William's letters to the Prince of Waldeck written after his arrival in London there are scattered references to his unwillingness to take the crown.[27] This would all look like positive proof if we left out of consideration the recipients of the letters and the background against which they were written. Neither the Emperor nor the Spanish government — one can hardly refer in the latter instance to the opinions of the imbecile King — were enthusiastic about the prospect of the expedition. The Spanish envoy in London, Don Pedro Ronquillo, indeed made a last minute effort to forestall it when he discovered that there was a very good possibility that James would enter into an alliance with Spain against France, but the letter in which he charged the Marquis de Gastanaga, governor of the Spanish Netherlands, to work toward that end unfortunately — or otherwise — was intercepted by the Prince of Orange.[28] Both the Emperor and Spain were uneasy over the threat to the principles of legitimacy and Divine Right and over the safety of their Catholic co-religionaries in the British Isles.[29] William had to give them assurance on those points whether he meant it or not. It is significant that, in both of the letters quoted, his promises to do nothing harmful to the Papists are coupled with assertions that he had no designs on the crown. The protestations to Waldeck can be explained on much the same basis. Waldeck had been one of William's most important negotiators with the princes of the Empire, including the Catholic members of the League of Augsburg, but unlike others who were carrying on similar work, he does not seem to have been completely in William's confidence. His letters to the latter after the expedition sailed are filled with warnings that the English Catholics must not be harmed.[30] Their safety was not his only concern. During that period he was in constant touch with enemies of France who needed to be assured that William had not departed from the strategic points of the Netherlands with some of the best troops in Europe for ends of his own, but rather to protect the interests of all by bringing England into the fold.[31]

In those parts of this study which deal specifically with the diplomatic background of the Revolution of 1688 it will be seen more clearly that William was far from being honest with his continental friends. His words to them constitute the principal concrete evidence that he did not plan to dethrone James and the truthfulness of those statements is open to question. Let us turn then, from contentions that are *contra* to those that are *pro*. Of course we look in vain for an outright statement by William of the nature of his plans and of their objectives. Guarded and obscure references are all we have to go on, for men who have such ends in view seldom accommodate posterity by drawing up in advance a full account of their intentions. We are left, therefore, to depend upon their actions, upon the words and actions of those closely associated with them, and upon the impressions the sum of all those words and actions made on others. For this last one of our principal witnesses is Comte d'Avaux, Louis XIV's ambassador at The Hague. He is known to have had an intelligence service so competent that practically nothing happened in the United Provinces of any importance to him without his having complete and accurate knowledge therof. If his information is correct on other matters — and it is — it is not reasonable to assume that it was at fault here. Moreover, what he said was going to happen actually did occur. To ascribe that to mere chance is to stretch the probability of coincidence very far indeed. He was, incidentally, one of the very few French diplomats who was willing to report unpleasant and unpalatable truths to his master. August of 1687 saw him explaining William's negotiations with Spain and his efforts to increase the Dutch navy by his plans for an attack on the throne of England "which is the principal thing he has in view." [32] Two months later he notified Louis that he had seen a letter of the Netherland's government to Vienna which mentioned that the Protestants "planned something of dangerous consequence to England." [33] His warnings grew shriller as the months went by, but Louis, for reasons that have never been satisfactorily explained, chose to ignore them. Mary of Modena's secretary made similar observances at about the same time.[34]

It has already been stated that there is very little evidence that the conspirators *who remained in England* were thinking of an invasion which would culminate in a change in dynasty. An armed *uprising*, assisted rather than led by William was under consideration, but that is quite different both in method and in intention. Approach from the side of the United Provinces reveals a decidedly different picture. That the refugees there were not merely considering but were preparing for an attack from outside the British Isles is evident from the *Memorial upon the Edict in Scotland* which stresses the importance of the British regiments in Dutch service in just such an event, and continued plotting on their part came to the attention of D'Avaux. That William knew what was going on among them and more than that, connived at it, is indisputable. Otherwise he would not have established contact with those men through his most intimate friend, Bentinck, whom he could truly have termed his other self, a self which had the advantage of being able to go where he, in his own person, could not. Bentinck's services in channeling the activities of the refugees in the best interests of his master were invaluable.

Among most of those in the immediate circle of the Prince it was certainly assumed that the crown was the ultimate objective. As early as September 1688, Simon Pettecum, who was one of those most thoroughly acquainted with William's plans, burst out impatiently to the imperial ambassador "Of what importance is it to the Emperor whether the King of England is named James or William?" [35] Shortly before the expedition sailed, Huygens, William's personal secretary, and brother to the famous scientist, wrote in his diary "Rooseboom discussed what would happen in England *when his Highness should be master there.*" [36] (Italics mine.) The very casual way in which this man, certainly in a position to know, alluded to the future, is highly suggestive. There is nothing surprising to him in the possibility that William might be master of England. The assumption is to be found even beyond the immediate circle. D'Albeville wrote from The Hague on November 23, 1688, that the English in the Prince's army "took an oath amongst themselves before their departure that they would never lay down arms till they made the Prince of Orange king, and laughed at a free parliament." [37] If he was not stating proven fact he was at least repeating current gossip. That the idea was not entirely absent even from the minds of those who remained in England is indicated by a letter dated December 2 from Sir Robert Howard to William stating that "they only fix upon hopes of remedy by a total change of persons." [38] We shall have occasion to deal with this letter more thoroughly later.

But it is William's own acts which are of greatest interest. In those tense days that followed the flight of James and preceded the meeting of the Convention, he expressed himself to Halifax:

Said, hee did not come over to establish a Commonwealth
Said hee was sure of one thing; hee would not stay in England if King James came again.
Hee said, with the strongest asseverations, that hee would go if they went about to make him regent.[39]

The implication is clear. William would have the crown or nothing.

This, of course, was in 1688. There are plenty of indications that the resolution was not formed after he reached England. His response to Burnet's advice to "put the fleet of Holland in good condition" has already been related, and it has been pointed out that the story is utterly devoid of meaning unless it refers to armed attack upon England. Simultaneously began the intensification of William's negotiations with Brandenburg which von Ranke and others believe were directed toward the seizure of the English throne. If von Ranke's interpretation is correct, the Great Elector not only was aware of William's plans, but had made the initial suggestion in 1686. Although this is doubtful, and it is improbable that William needed such a suggestion, it is true that the Elector's successor wrote to William early in 1689 to congratulate him on the "completion of those wishes *which some years ago I had formed* of your elevation to the English throne which is due to you . . . by blood." [40] (Italics mine.) Regardless, however, of their significance in relation to the inception of the idea, these negotiations are of the utmost importance, for they made it possible for William not only to gather an army, but to direct Louis's attention to the Rhineland rather than to the Netherlands. By the winter of 1687 he had begun to branch out to include the other German princes, and in those negotiations the invasion of England was certainly contemplated.*

This much at least is certain: before the winter of 1687–88 was over, William's preparations had reached a stage where all he needed to put his plans into action was word from England on the actual time and place. The extent of these preparations, and the smoothness with which they went into effect, argues against their having been the improvisation of the moment. Action could not have been taken earlier. William had to be sure that the varied groups of opposition in England had formed a coalition strong enough so that he could be reasonably sure that James would be without reliable support at home. The Fagel letter put the capstone on those preparations by winning the majority of the all-important Dissenters. Not until he was fairly sure of his ground in England was it feasible or even sage to extend the negotiations for military assistance to Brandenburg and the other German states.

*See *infra*, pp. 109 ff.

In this crucial winter James himself once more contributed direct assistance by requesting the return of the six British regiments in the United Provinces. He had been subtly led to do this through the insinuations of D'Albeville who was, by that time, acting in coöperation with D'Avaux and the French court. Their purpose was to build up Anglo-Dutch antagonism [41] but this, of course, was unknown to James. Even so, outside of his desire to strengthen his own military position in order that his word might have more weight in European affairs, James could not but be uneasy about these regiments. He knew that English malcontents were welcomed into them, while, for the last year or so, no new Catholics had been admitted, contrary to the general policy of the Dutch of showing no religious discrimination in their army. Moreover, colonial disputes between the Dutch and the English were grave enough, at the moment, to threaten war. Nevertheless, James hesitated for several months after the first suggestion was made to him, partly because he did not want to provoke the States General. It was not until January 17 that he yielded at last to the smooth teamwork of the French and Sunderland and requested the return of the regiments. William was not displeased. He saw that James had made a false step. Moreover, in spite of the fact that the majority of the officers in these regiments were firm in the Orangist cause, many of the others were outspoken in their loyalty to James.[42] William now saw a threefold opportunity: to clear the ranks of doubtful persons, to stir the States General against James, and to heighten tension in England. He was successful in all three. The States General at first refused the King's request, but eventually yielded to the point of saying that *individuals* who wished to return to England might do so. James thereupon ordered the members of the regiments to come home. Records of just how many left are so varied as to be completely unreliable, but it seems that several officers and men did leave the Dutch service. It is usually implied, but there is no proof of this, that all who did so were Roman Catholics. Should that be true the number who left could not have been large as there were not many of that faith in the regiments, especially among the officers. Skelton's son, however, was one of those who returned to England and he was a Protestant.[43] Obedience to the commands of their King could well have impelled several others of that faith to do as young Skelton did. All in all, however, James succeeded only in adding to the discontent at home and in entrenching that major part of the regiments that remained in the United Provinces more firmly than ever in William's cause, for, having resisted their King's express command, they could not expect to be able to return to England in safety until his reign was over. The places left vacant by the loyal officers were easily filled by new arrivals from the British Isles.

As the winter drew on, not only did the correspondence with the English widen, but several Englishmen, most of them young and sons of peers, were suddenly seized with a great desire to travel on the Continent, especially in the United Provinces. It is interesting to note that the widening of the circle of letter writers extended to men of known Whig principles who had been conspicuously absent from the earlier groups. This came about as the result of overtures from the Prince himself.[44] That this closer union of Whigs and Tories was bringing difficulties is clear from a letter of Danby who expressed a fear that mutual distrust might render their efforts ineffectual.[45] William, however, was astute enough to see that a movement dominated exclusively by Tories might stir up antagonism among the Whigs which would be more difficult to cope with than the problems created by their coöperation, and he was confident that he could deal successfully with both groups once the purpose of their uneasy coöperation was achieved.

Among the travelers the one of greatest consequence was Admiral Russell who arrived in The Hague sometime in April. The purpose of his journey was to find out for himself and for the principal members of the conspiracy in England, when the Prince would act, and what he could be expected to do. The time had come when some cards had to be laid on the table, for there was rising apprehension that a few who were still undecided might yield to the King, thus starting a stampede over to the royal cause, unless they had specific word of action, rather than of moral support, from the Prince. The situation reveals some of the complications that had been created by the necessity of drawing together several factions essentially different from one another and hence, in a crisis, likely to be more responsive to mutual jealousies than to common grievances, and, also, by William's hesitancy to take his English backers completely into his confidence. He had been wise in not doing so, for until these men were so deeply involved that only he could save them, he could not be sure of their unqualified support. Now, however, the possibility that some of those who had been approached but had not yet declared themselves might become reconciled to the King and turn informer to curry favor evoked gruesome memories of punishments following the exposure of the Rye House Plot. The Opposition had to be sure of success and only William could assure them. Russell was therefore instructed by his friends to urge William to place himself at the head of a strong body of troops, to invade England, and to call upon the people of the country to rise against their King.

William's answer to Russell was cautious. He could not but have been aware that the admiral was one of the more radical wing of the Orangists. He knew, too, that there was still danger of desertion from the Opposition and that he could not afford to commit himself unless others did so too. He was, however, in a position to exact conditions, for not only was he indispensable to the success of the movement, he was also in possession of enough incriminating letters to send many men in England into exile — if they were lucky. He agreed, therefore, that if several of the most important men involved in the conspiracy "in their own name and in the name of others who trusted them, invited him to come and rescue the nation and the religion, he believed he could be ready by the end of September to come over." [46] His self-controlled response in Russell's presence may have given the admiral reason to believe that he was not too anxious to act, but a little later, surrounded only by his Dutch friends, he exclaimed "Now or never" with a vehemence that showed plainly how relieved he was that the moment to act had come.

Russell returned to London to find that the King had issued another Declaration of Indulgence and that enough of the Dissenters were greeting it with enthusiasm to arouse such intransigent divines as Baxter and Howe to new heights of fury against the dangers of Popery. Once more James helped more than he soothed unfavorable reaction, this time by his order that the Declaration should be read in all churches, and by his subsequent arrest of the seven bishops who petitioned against this order. Before their trial the Prince of Wales was born and a sullen people refused customary celebration of the event.

Yet in spite of the widespread expression of discontent, Russell was unable to get any immediate response to William's demand for a commitment. The steps the Englishmen were being asked to take were the kind that wise and moderate men usually take only in desperation, and the situation was not desperate. Herbert, Lumley, and Shrewsbury wrote to William at once, but their letters were merely individual expressions of loyalty and guardedly phrased at that, while of the three writers only Shrewsbury had a following worthy of attention. His note is particularly revealing in that he complains of being restrained by "wiser people" from going over to The Hague that summer, for fear of arousing the anger of the King.[47] These wiser people were probably of that group who knew the direction the conspiracy was taking but hesitated to join it, hoping for some other solution to their problem. Russell had been in England more than a month before he was able to send William any assurance that his conditions were being met, and that merely took the form of a promise that the expected message would soon be forthcoming.[48] At that time Nottingham, who later withdrew, was in on the secret. Halifax had been sounded out, but was reported as being backward.[49]

Meanwhile Zuylestein was dispatched again to London, the occasion this time being to bring the King and Queen the personal congratulations of the Prince and Princess of Orange on the birth of a son. His arrival brought consternation to several of those most deeply involved in the conspiracy, for it suggested that William might be planning to desert their cause. But, as had been the case a year earlier, the ostensible reason for Zuylestein's errand was a disguise for his real purpose. Even as the Englishmen did not quite trust William, so was he unsure of them, and, more than that, disturbed over their unwillingness to commit themselves. Zuylestein's duty was to put pressure on the laggards. He accomplished his purpose. On June 30 the period of hesitation ended with the drawing up of the so-called invitation. Almost immediately thereafter Admiral Herbert, disguised as a common sailor, conveyed it personally to the Prince. He took with him also a note from Henry Sidney in which this man who had been so long in the confidence of the Prince expressed doubt as to the outcome of the venture and, by the very irresolute character of what he wrote, counseled William to think carefully before taking irrevocable action.[50]

Few documents have been so overrated as this letter of the "immortal seven." It is nothing more than a very cautiously worded statement of the assistance the Prince may expect to receive in England if he should come over. The first sentence: "We have great satisfaction to find by (Russell) and since by Mons. Zuylestein that your Highness is so ready to give us such assistance as they related to us" could lead an uninformed reader, then and in the present time, to believe that the initiative had come from William. Nowhere is William *asked* to come. The writers simply assume that he is going to do so. Although they assure him that "nineteen parts of twenty" of the people were ready for a change, they express doubt that many would be willing to risk their fortunes or their lives to bring it about. If, however, the Prince could guarantee adequate safeguards against the possibility of reprisal many would join his forces. No solution to the existing problems is suggested beyond a seizure of power by force of arms. There is complete silence on how and in whose interests that power should be used or through what channels it would operate. Nothing is said of the kingship itself. The only reference to Parliament is found in an expression of apprehension that the King may be able to summon one that will do his bidding.

The letter was not signed, but bore instead the ciphers for the names of Shrewsbury, Devonshire, Danby, Lumley, London, Russell, and Sidney. Of these only two, Devonshire and Danby, had had political careers of any importance. The names of Halifax and Nottingham, which would have added both weight and dignity, were lacking. Halifax had not even been definitely approached, not only because of his attitude when some hints were made to him, but also because his letters to the Prince during the spring had shown, beyond any doubt, that he did not consider such drastic action necessary. Nottingham had at first consented to sign, but when the showdown came he refused. He, like Halifax, believed that the English people could settle the problem themselves without resorting either to foreign assistance or to force. His comrades accused him of lack of courage and discussed among themselves the advisability of assassinating him to prevent him from betraying their secret. They finally decided not to do so on the grounds that since he could not find the courage to commit himself with them, he probably would not have the spirit to report them. It apparently did not occur to them that he was a man of honor.

The "Invitation" lies now, along with the letter from Sidney which accompanied it, in that collection in the Public Record Office in London which is designated as coming from King William's Chest. To unfold it, to read the very words that William himself once read, is to grasp something of that strange continuity of life which only the raw material of history gives. What were the emotions of this sickly, ambitious little man as his eyes moved over and his mind comprehended the essence of this message? Undoubtedly it fell short of what he wanted: it was unsigned; two of the most important names were missing. But he had gone too far to retreat if he had wanted to, and he did not want to. The dream of years was within reach of realization, and the backing of the great Tory statesmen was not indispensable to him. If he could keep together those who had already declared for him he could be reasonably sure of success, for he was counting very little on military or any other kind of support from the English and a great deal on the strength of the army he was gathering to take with him.

From what has been said it is evident that the birth of the Prince of Wales and the affair of the seven bishops had nothing to do with the Revolution in its all-important formative stages, for by the time they occurred matters had progressed so far that those events contributed propaganda value alone. Yet in that connection they cannot be too strongly emphasized. Russell's conference with William took place before the second Declaration of Indulgence was issued.[51] The arrest of the seven bishops for petitioning the King concerning his order that the Declaration must be read from all pulpits, did not take place until June 8. Their trial went on concurrently with the discussions at Henley-on-Thames which ultimately produced the "Invitation" and the course of the trial, together with the verdict of "Not Guilty" given the day before that invitation was completed, showed that Englishmen could still trust to the courts even under a king who could make or dismiss judges at will. In the weeks that followed immediately James was to discover that not even that creature which was most completely his own, the Court of Ecclesiastical Commission, could be trusted to do his bidding.

Nevertheless the very fact that James had dared to proceed against the bishops stirred still further an already excited people and made them the more willing to listen to the doubts which were cast upon the birth of the Prince of Wales. That latter event, which James had looked upon as a signal blessing from God, turned out in the end to be the chief occasion of his fall. Long before the child was born he had begun to make his contribution to his father's fate. Although examination of the time relationships proves that organization for resistance was well under way in England before rumors of the Queen's pregnancy were officially confirmed, the possibility of a male heir to the throne intensified activity on both sides. James was almost delirious with joy. Absurdly and, in the light of future events, fatally certain that the child would be a boy, he no longer felt any need of winning the support of William and Mary, but was sure that it was with himself alone that the Dissenters would have to come to terms if they wanted freedom of conscience. So he threw caution to the well-known winds, and for about six months acted, in his own opinion, like a true king: in the opinion of his people, like a tyrant.

The Opposition, as soon as they had recovered from the first effect of the blow, realized that the birth of a prince could be an advantage to them rather than otherwise. The cautious Dissenters and the high Tories who preferred to wait for natural causes to bring them a Protestant ruler would now be faced with the necessity of accepting a Catholic dynasty or taking steps to end it. To win over this group, especially the Tories, rumors that the pregnancy was spurious were noised about almost as soon as the rumors of the pregnancy itself. These were followed, after the actual birth, by stories of a supposititious child. The comment of G. N. Clark is noteworthy: "The catholics thought it was a miracle and the protestants said it was an imposture. It was neither." [52] He is right; no one today questions the Stuart blood of the Old Pretender. But that was not so in his babyhood. Nevertheless, the stories, which ripened into outright accusations after his birth, were the result of planned activity rather than of spontaneous suspicion. Similar insinuations had been spread some years earlier preceding the birth of Mary of Modena's third child. Now they appeared again. The whole story is revolting and one would prefer to pass over it in the silence it would deserve were it not for the part the whole affair played in assuring the success of the Revolution.

For the accusation that the child was supposititious* was one of the biggest talking points used to win the masses of the people over to William at the time of his landing, and the extent to which it took root among them is testified by its growth into folk legend through the famous folk song:

> Rock-a-bye baby, in the tree top.
> When the wind blows the cradle will rock.
> When the bough breaks the cradle will fall
> And down will come baby, cradle, and all.

When the Protestant wind blew the cradle would rock, and if it blew strongly enough to break the parent bough, the cradle and the baby would go down with it. Few mothers today, humming the lullaby through to its catastrophic last line are aware of its significance, but those who heard it first were not so ignorant. To them it meant that their king was trying to subvert the true laws of succession, which were in the hands of God, by palming off on them a spurious prince. Here was reason enough, if others were lacking, to rise up against him. The argument was telling even among the better educated and wealthy. Some, perhaps, accepted the tale with fingers crossed and tongues in cheek. Others may have been dominated subconsciously by wishful thinking. All

*This somewhat awkward term is employed because it has, over the years, become standard with reference to this child.

who accepted the story as true, whatever their reason for accepting it, or whatever the process by which they convinced themselves or were convinced by others, found in it a justification for rebellion. Its effect was especially important among those Tories (and they formed the backbone of the population), who abhorred the King's attempts to bring about toleration even for Dissenters, let alone for Roman Catholics, but yet had been, up to this time, reluctant to join in any plans for an uprising because they were deterred by the sanctions imposed upon them by their belief in the doctrine of indefeasible hereditary right. The inviolability of the monarchy and of the Anglican Church were the twin pillars of their social structure. The King's attacks upon the one could not, in their eyes, justify their own attack upon the other. But if he attacked the one and sought by a trick to make a mockery of the other, the strictures of obedience were no longer binding upon them. The event was to prove that the birth of an heir, which James looked upon as an answer to his prayers, was indeed a God-send instead to his opponents.

Anyone who questions the importance of the story need only turn to the pamphlet literature of the last half of 1688 to have his doubts removed. Just how much William had to do at first with instigating the rumors is not so clear. Certainly some of the most scurrilous leaflets on the subject originated in the Netherlands, including the first printed questioning of the Queen's pregnancy. This appeared in a pamphlet by Burnet called *Reflections on the Letter of Mr. Fagel* written at the surprisingly early date of January 22, 1688. That it could have been published without the foreknowledge of Bentinck or even of William is unlikely. It is, of course, well known that although prayers were offered for the Prince of Wales by Mary's chaplain, and although Zuylestein was sent with official congratulations, very soon after the child's birth William professed to accept the rumors as truth and gave public notice thereof by ordering the prayers to be discontinued. Soon after, he and Bentinck discussed the advisability of distributing a broadsheet in English that had been recommended to them by Mr. Johnstone, a nephew of Burnet, in the following note:

The following paper about the Prince of Wales would doe much good in England, where even those who believe that there is a trick put upon the nation, will be glad to know why they think so, and those that only suspect the thing will be glad to find reasons to determine them. . . [53]

This may or may not refer to one of the many broadsheets that actually were circulated. If it does not, it was not because skepticism or scruples kept William from using the story as is amply proven in his Declaration of reasons for invading England which he climaxed with the statement that he came to protect his wife's inheritance from a false claimant.

Mary's part in the whole affair is somewhat different and of the utmost importance. She received the first intimation that the Queen might be pregnant from the latter herself. Always on friendly, even affectionate terms with her stepmother, Mary rejoiced with her. Not for several days did it dawn upon her what this might mean. Let her own words tell her reaction, for they do so with a poignancy that no paraphrase can convey: "Outside of the interest of the Church, the love which I had for the Prince brought me to wish him all that he merited. . . I regret that I have only three crowns to bring him." [54] Comprehension and apprehension from then on worked together to make it easy for this usually naïve and credulous woman to see cause for doubt in minor incidents that she probably would have overlooked completely had it not been for the threat to the man whom she loved so much more than he deserved. Only on that basis can one explain the coarseness, so foreign to her, of the questions she put to her sister Anne about the circumstances of her stepmother's pregnancy and the birth of the child.[55] The answers convinced her that her father had committed a horrible crime and that "there was no other way to save the Church and the State other than that my husband should dethrone him by force." [56*] Her conviction was of the

*The quotation is taken from a memoir Mary drew up at the close of 1688 in which she summarizes the events of that year and her own reaction to them. The particular passage relates the story of the confirmation of her suspicions when Zuylestein returned from England. Taken in context it suggests that her conclusion that her husband must dethrone her father was reached then, i.e. in the summer of 1688. Possibly she was projecting an attitude she held at the time she was writing into her account of what happened earlier. It is, however, improbable that that was the case. For one thing the time lapse is not long enough to give very strong support to any contention that we have here an example of misleading after-

utmost importance to William; without it he would have had to seek some other and probably less effective pretext for his venture.

The summer after the birth of the Prince and the trial of the bishops saw a new rush of Whigs and a handful of Tories to join William's cause. Most of them came over to the Netherlands in person, and some of them, Shrewsbury for one, brought welcome contributions of money. An excellent courier service kept William in touch with those who remained at home. Most of the news he got through such channels was encouraging, some of it unjustifiably so, as, for example, a letter from Henry Compton, bishop of London, in which he promised much stronger support from his brother bishops than they were subsequently willing to give.[57] Others would have been discouraging had William been willing to heed them. Halifax continued to insist that all would be well, pointing to the trial of the bishops as proof. Once more he denied that it would be possible to gather a popish parliament, and he scoffed at the charge that James, confronted by an unruly Commons, would resort to immediate prorogation.[58] Halifax did not actually know how far the conspiracy had gone, but he was too shrewd not to be strongly suspicious. Nottingham, who did know, refused to be moved by Zuylestein's urgings. Nothing had occurred, he said, "that a little time will not effectively remedy." [59]

The words of Halifax could be shrugged off. Others could not be so easily disregarded. In August, Danby wrote that the expedition ought to be deferred until spring, but William, knowing that to delay the project was to abandon it, merely redoubled the zeal with which he was making preparations.[60] New arrivals brought word that the invading army should be kept as small as possible to avoid antagonizing the English people. This advice, too, was

---

thought. Moreover, subsequent passages in the memoir indicate that Mary did form at that time a conclusion which determined her attitudes and her actions from then on until the end of the year.

Even if we assume that the impression the memoir conveys is misleading, the passage is still interesting. Mary must have written it on or about January 1, 1689 (N.S.). The last word she has had from England was that her father had been taken into custody ("le Roy avoit été arrêté"). At that point, then, she takes for granted that her husband's aim was to dethrone James. The significance of all this is obvious. Is it at all likely that she would have expressed herself as she did if William's intention had been merely to establish a regency?

ignored. Tory fears of an overwhelming armed victory and of Whig dominance were beginning to make themselves felt. Because he had to, William moved closer to the Whigs in spite of his dislike of their policies. But they formed the majority of those who had come to pledge their wealth and join his army, and they were not so likely as the Tories to be squeamish about revolution. Even so he came into conflict with the more radical wing of the party and nearly lost the support of Mordaunt in so doing.

It is in his Declaration of reasons for undertaking the expedition to England that one can see most clearly how William made certain concessions to the Whigs at the same time that he bid for the continued support of the Tory-Anglicans with whom he had first entered into negotiation. This document was drawn up by Fagel but modeled upon one which had been brought from England by Sidney. Burnet did the translation into English. In it the royal dignity is protected from direct attack by the use of the old device of throwing the blame for arbitrary acts on evil counselors. This could serve to soothe the Tory conscience. Much is made of the sufferings of the Church of England, very little of freedom of religious worship. Other grievances are the use of the power to suspend the operation of laws, the dismissal of judges, the efforts to pack Parliament and to admit into it members who should be disqualified by the Tests, and the attack upon Mary's heritage by the setting up of an impostor as a Prince of Wales. On all these points both Whig and Tory could agree, although the Whigs were not particularly disturbed about the rights of the Anglican church and emphasis upon royal electioneering must have been a little embarrassing to the Whigs and even more so to the Tories who had so recently benefited from that device themselves. The big concession to the Whigs came toward the end, in the promise to submit all problems to a freely elected parliament. This was a point insisted upon by Sidney, who knew the temper of the Whigs. William disliked it and feared it, but he realized that he had to give in.[61]

One little group remained unsatisfied. Led by the aging John Wildman, who forty years before had authored *An Agreement of the People*, they called for a denunciation of the whole structure of the existing British government. From their point of view

James had not broken the laws. The laws themselves were at fault and should be changed. More specifically they protested against the continued dominance of the Church of England which would derive renewed strength from decisions made by a parliament composed exclusively of its members or close sympathizers. In spite of the fact that Mordaunt and one or two of the leading Scotsmen were with them, the members of this group were quickly silenced. No one else wanted to lay bare the real skeletons in the closet of England's government.

CHAPTER **3**

The Diplomatic Background

A few months after William received the famous *Invitation* he responded to it by setting sail from the Netherlands with a crack Dutch army of some twelve to fifteen thousand troops loaded on a formidable fleet. He left behind him a continent just entering upon the third of what the textbooks refer to as "The Wars of Louis the Fourteenth," and a native land mortally certain to be drawn into that war. It is no wonder that among his countrymen and his allies there were many who thought such a powerful military force could be put to as good, or even better use at home. Their tentative objections were stilled by the assertion that William acted as he did in order to prevent England from joining with France and to bring her instead into that great European coalition being formed to stop the threat of French aggression. Historians in general have accepted that assertion.

"Il y a des choses que tout le monde dit, parce qu'elles ont été dites une fois" quotes Rousset concerning one of the crucial events in the continental background of the Revolution of 1688, the attack upon Philipsburg by Louis in the autumn of that year.[1] If the historians' assertion, made so often because it was made once, is correct, then the timing of the Revolution was a fortunate act of fate. Without the synchronization of events England presumably would not have brought her supposedly indispensable aid to the anti-French coalition. And how lucky for England that the continental crisis corresponded in time so nicely with her own! For, if we go on the basis of this motive, that crisis alone was responsible for William's interest in England, an interest that took tangible form in military action without which the uprising of 1688 might well have ended in an ignominious and disastrous failure rather than in a "Glorious Revolution."

Are we not giving just a little too much credit to fate? The roots of the English revolution go back many years, as do those of the continental crisis with which it coincided. The nexus between the two was William of Orange. A definite affirmation or denial that his purpose was the one so often stated could be made only by unlocking the mind of this man who, so much more than his great-grandfather, merits the description "William the Silent," whose actions speak so much more loudly than his words because he said so little and committed so few of his thoughts to paper concerning this climax of his life, the expedition to England. It is, therefore, not his words, but his actions, that must be examined, in the threefold context of English, Dutch, and European affairs. Any such examination will, of course, show that much of what happened on the Continent as well as in England lay outside the scope of his direct control or even of his interests. Nevertheless, when the timetables of insular and European events are placed side by side and studied in relation to William's participation in both it becomes clear that the over-all diplomatic situation was of primary importance in assuring the success of the English venture, whether or not it provided the occasion for it. In the final months this side of the problem occupied more of William's attention than any other, and no wonder. Even a minor slip-up might have made it necessary to call off the whole project. The two crises *had* to synchronize. That they did so was not entirely accidental.

To understand this diplomatic background, so intimately bound in with what was to happen in England at the same time that it was in many ways so unrelated to insular events, it is necessary to make a brief survey of the European situation as it was when James II came to the throne. Any such survey must of necessity start with France for she bestrode the European world like a Colossus. These years were the zenith of Louis XIV's career. Already victorious in two wars, he had been able to extend his boundaries still further in peacetime by the operations of the Chambers of Reunion, and indignant as his neighbors might be over the encroachments onto their lands, the best they could do was to bring about in 1684 the Twenty Year Truce of Ratisbon whereby it was agreed that for two decades at least the French king was to retain possession of Strasbourg and the other territories acquired by these questionable procedures.

To state that a zenith has been reached implies that the next step is one of decline, and in spite of the fact that the height now reached by Louis XIV was more a plateau than a sharp peak, the forces that eventually would lead downward were already beginning to appear. For all its favorable aspects Ratisbon was still but a truce, inconclusive, indefinite, and temporary. Meanwhile the French hold over the minor German princes was slackening. Agreements and unions had been formed among several of them for mutual assistance and for maintenance of the treaties of Münster and of Nimwegen. As for others, Spain, Sweden, the United Provinces, and the Hapsburgs, each of which had at one time or another responded favorably to French blandishments, had now been brought into a circle of more or less consistent opposition. True enough, such formal alliances as had been made were defensive and did not mention France by name, but their intent was obvious. Crowning blows came with the defection of Brandenburg in 1685 and with the decision of Bavaria, at almost the same time, to side with the Emperor rather than with France. England was undependable: the Pope bitterly hostile. The day had come when even the mighty incentive of subsidies was not enough to procure reliable allies for Louis.

Moreover his opponents were becoming more and more able to cope with him. They were developing a corps of skilled diplomats familiar with French techniques and competent to pit their brains against the men Louis was sending to the European courts at the very time that those men were feeling the effect of a servile atmosphere which made many of them more anxious to please and flatter their king than to tell him unpleasant truths. A similar situation existed in military affairs. Although Vauban, the great engineer, was still living, Louis's outstanding general, Turenne, had died some years before. His successors preferred Versailles to the battlefield. His opponents had had time to study his methods, to learn how to deal with them, and to model their own armies on those which the great French strategist had trained. In short, two points only were in Louis's favor. The Emperor and several other German rulers were pinned down by the Turks in the East; the situation in Germany was not stabilized for so subject were all of the princedoms, from the largest to the smallest, to bitter rivalry among themselves, that it was by no means impossible that Louis might be able to bribe some of them back into his camp or at least into hostile neutrality toward one another.

Yet for all this Louis's reputation was still formidable. His domestic power and resources were tremendous. He was served by a staff of highly trained and experienced officials beginning, it is true, to feel the effects of overcentralization and of royal craving for flattery, but still one of the most efficient in Europe. The king himself had had a quarter of a century in which to learn the complexities of European diplomacy and the best methods by which they could be handled. He headed a united country in which effective opposition had been stifled either by force or by a growing nationalistic pride in the dominant position of France. The Colossus might be deteriorating, but the signs thereof were not visible to Louis's contemporaries.

When we shift our scrutiny from France to England and to the United Provinces, those two states inseparably linked by and through William, we should keep in mind that for almost half a century they had been on bad terms with each other. Three wars had been fought between them in the quarter century that stretched from 1650 to 1675, to be followed by an uneasy peace now seriously threatened, at the time of the accession of James II, by clashes in the East Indies, in Africa, and in the Caribbean. The tension was heightened, during the next three years, by James's strong colonial policy. One point, although it was of doubtful value to either of them, these two countries had in common: neither was very attractive to other European states as an ally. Briefly stated, the reason for this was that the presence of some degree of popular direction and control made the government of each undependable in international affairs in that foreign policies could and did reflect changes in the relative power of rival groups within each state. Louis had discovered this when he had trusted John de Witt in 1667 and later when he had relied on Charles II in the opening stages of the Dutch War. The Great Elector, so unreliable himself, learned it to his dismay at Nimwegen. Even William had had to cope with the problem thus created not only when he tried to get his own countrymen to act, but also when he discovered that his hopes of bringing England in on his side in the last stages of the Dutch War were frustrated by a parsimonious, recalcitrant, and thoroughly bribed parliament. Yet undesirable as both countries were, England appeared to be more so, and for this reason, if for no other, one can surely hesitate to accept without question the assumption that William, who knew the situation so well, embarked on his dangerous expedition for no other reason than to win her to his side, and that the central European governments backed him for that purpose.

For what *did* England have to offer that one should believe her presence in or absence from a coalition could spell success or failure? We are not speaking now of the England of the mid-eighteenth century, made wealthy by imperial exploits and by a head start in modern industrial and agricultural development. We are speaking of a country that had been pushed out of the lucrative trade of the easily-conquered Spice Islands to rest content with a few posts on the mainland of India, from which she would ultimately gain a great deal, but only after long years of hard struggle that were still ahead of her. We are speaking of a country whose imperial possessions in Africa, in the Caribbean, in North America, were everywhere the leavings, the least desirable portions, which she had picked up or had been allowed to retain after Spain, Portugal, the United Provinces, and even, to a lesser extent, France, had taken or kept what they wanted.* At home and in the nascent empire there was wealth, to be sure, and more would

*It is almost as hard for an American to swallow his pride enough to accept this point of view as it is for an Englishman, especially with respect to North America. Yet the French and Spanish possessions on this continent, in terms of that time, were far wealthier than the English colonies on the Atlantic seaboard. As for the New Netherlands, the United Provinces had not deemed it worth their while to try to retain it, preferring to concentrate their efforts on driving England from the Spice Islands of the East Indies.

be gained by conquest in the years to come, but it would have taken a sharp eye to detect these facts in the 1680's.

Nor had England's military record been anything to boast about in the century since the defeat of the Armada. An exception can be found in the brief period of ascendency under Cromwell in which he had, it might be pointed out, been fortunate enough to have France as an ally, and for opponents, decadent Spain and the United Provinces even less united than usual just then because of factional internal strife. One after another of England's efforts to wield an influence on the Continent had ended in ridiculous or disastrous failure: Mansfield, Rhè, and the brief and humiliating participation in Louis XIV's war against the United Provinces; while on the seas were to be recalled such shameful episodes as the Dutch destruction of part of the English fleet and their capture of the rest of it in 1667. We cannot say with even that slight degree of assurance always attendant upon an historical "if" that England would have been more successful had her kings been willing to give Parliament a greater share in the direction of foreign affairs. Especially during the Restoration the disapproval so often and so loudly voiced in Commons all too often sprang at best from unenlightened and insular self-interest, or at worst from bribery by Louis XIV or even William III. Parsimony and opposition for its own sake frequently condemned royal policies to failure before either their wisdom or their compatibility with national interest could be tested. All in all the most generous interpretation that can be found of the sorry showing and the causes from whence it sprang is that England, in the throes of trying to become a democracy* was faced even this early with one of the still-unsolved problems of that form of government: inconsistency and apparent vacillation in foreign policy. In the next century, indeed before that, in 1689, she would slough off this nonsense, for such it seemed to contemporaries, to become an oligarchy,

---

*Or a republic, if you will. Both terms are unsatisfactory in that they suggest the absence of a monarchy which, of course, was contemplated at this time only by a few extremists. It was the presence in the government of an active and vocal representative element that created the problem, and in spite of the fact that the basis of representation was far from meeting the criterion for either a democratic or republican state, it was a start in that direction.

but for the time being she had, and had had for years, an unstable government and that instability could not but affect her relations with the rest of the world. Ever since the death of Elizabeth I, English foreign policy had been a source of annoyance and at times of something worse to the continental powers.* By the time James II came to the throne the heads of these states had begun to understand that the reason for the characteristic unreliability was somehow connected with the nature of the country's government, but they were still baffled when methods they were accustomed to use among themselves proved inadequate to bring England to consistent action.

Prominent among these methods was the giving and receiving of subsidies. This practice was as much a part of the diplomacy of the seventeenth century as its counterpart of international loans has been to the nineteenth and twentieth, and it played a similar rôle. Although powerful and effective, it was never sure, for a state that believed it had thus secured the support of another might find that a third had intervened with a larger offer, or that purely national or personal considerations, temporarily outweighing gold, had entered into the picture. Of the subsidizing powers France, of course, was usually in a position to outbid all others, with the United Provinces a close rival although they were beginning to get the reputation of not fulfilling their promises. The whole subsidy farce was played according to certain mutually accepted and understood, if never openly expressed rules. A money transaction† meant that the giver could count upon the recipient until more was offered to the latter by someone else, or until those national considerations referred to above came into play. So effective were the intelligence systems of most of the important powers that each knew fairly exactly when one of its allies was receiving tempting offers from a member of the opposing camp. When that

*The words *state* and *power* are used in this chapter although they are perhaps a little modern for the time. *Princes* might be better, were it not that that term cannot cover the United Provinces. The compromise terms are adopted because they include all types of government then in existence.

†Usually the payment went from one sovereign to another, but there was also a procedure whereby funds went to political advisors in order to get them to throw the weight of their influence in favor of one particular policy or another.

happened it was necessary to choose between outbidding the rival or cutting losses and looking for new friends. Meanwhile, if Country X promised Country Y to act in a certain way, or even to supply a stipulated amount of military assistance, the head of Country Y knew where he stood because he was dealing with a sovereign individual who had the power to act within his own state.

In England, as European rulers were beginning to realize, such was not the case. Later generations have been shocked to learn that Stuart foreign policy was, to some extent, determined by French gold during the Restoration period. The men of that time, many of whom were themselves accepting bribes from the same source, had little reason to be either shocked or surprised, however much they may have blustered at Westminster. What did amaze Louis's enemies and pain and even infuriate Louis himself, was the ineffectiveness of the subsidies once they had been given.* Diplomatic negotiations were carried on with a king who was constitutionally free to make treaties without consulting his parliament. Nor was there anything in English law, although an appeal to English honor might have rendered a different decision, to prevent that king from accepting French money as his brother sovereigns on the Continent were doing. Nevertheless, if living up to the terms of a treaty made in consequence of the subsidies called for increased taxation, as it did whenever any direct participation in war was involved, Parliament could and did act. It has already been suggested that the reasons why its members blocked the king's policies, as they so often did, were by no means consistently high-minded. This, however, is not the place for value judgments on any phase of what was at best a highly questionable, albeit frequently effective, system. What is important historically, what stood out in the minds of the diplomats of the seventeenth century, was the fact that nowhere in England could these diplomats find a single source of power strong enough so that they could rely upon it to play the game according to continental rules.

Louis XIV and William III were the two men most deeply concerned with trying to win England to a consistent role. Neither, before 1688, had expected her to play one that was important.

*Especially after 1677.

Each had tried the same devices to achieve his aims. One was to support the King so strongly that he could derive from the assistance thus given that edge of power necessary to swing the balance in his favor. The other was to support Parliament to the same end. Both men erred, Louis to a greater extent and for a longer time, in assuming that the struggle was as simple as that: King vs. Parliament. What was going on was an internal contest between rival political groups for the control of the state, with all the complex mixture of highmindedness and sordidness that such a contest always presents. To throw the weight of support on institutions that were merely media for the conflict could do no good unless the real conflict itself were resolved.

The policy toward England which William pursued in his capacity of Stadholder was always determined to some extent by his personal interest in English institutions, and as the crisis of 1688 drew nearer this latter factor very naturally became more and more dominant, so much so, in fact, that further study of it must be reserved for fuller treatment within its chronological context. As for Louis, his letters during the five years prior to the Revolution[2] give clear indication that he preferred to do his best to establish royal absolutism in England, for in his thinking absolutism was synonomous with consistency.* At the same time he continued to make use of the alternative of immobilizing or neutralizing the country by fomenting domestic discontent. He had undoubtedly done this during the Exclusion Controversy, and suggestions that he was somehow connected with the Monmouth affair are too strong to be ignored. If in 1688 he did indeed, as some writers have believed, deliberately attack Philipsburg rather than Maestricht in order to facilitate William's departure from the United Provinces, the only logical reason for his doing so was

*This should not lead us into the common error of assuming that Louis's subsidies enabled either Charles or James to "rule without Parliament." The subject is too long to go into here beyond pointing out (1) that French subsidies were not so large as they were formerly supposed to have been and (2) that the sums promised were by no means always delivered, and (3) that even if we assume, although we should be far from justified in so doing, that the above mentioned monarchs wished to dispense with Parliament, they were relieved from the primary necessity of calling this body together — i.e., the need for additional funds — more by increase in the normal revenue than by any help from Louis.

that he expected England to be thrown into a turmoil which would compel her to concentrate on domestic rather than foreign affairs for some months or perhaps years to come. There are two possible reasons why Louis should have resorted to this procedure instead of relying completely upon the first, and to him preferable alternative. One is that subsidies were never completely successful with the later Stuarts, not only because of the parliamentary interference already referred to, but also because both Charles and James, who probably rather disliked Louis, were inclined to put national and personal considerations above their French cousin's to a greater degree than did many of the continental rulers. Louis, who was aware of this and frequently exasperated by it, knew perfectly well that he was getting a more accurate version of James's sentiments from the shrewd D'Avaux in the Netherlands than from Barillon in London. The second reason is closely connected with the first. While English power was not great enough to be of paramount importance in any of the continental struggles, it could have been, on some occasions, enough to turn the scale if it had been applied with constancy. But constancy as we know, was lacking, which created difficulty not only for Louis but also for others, for no one could be certain when England might step into some quarrel, or when, having stepped in, she might withdraw. Having learned from the experiences of the 1670's and early eighties that subsidies were not a certain guarantee against the effects of popular pressure, Louis may have determined to keep England so occupied at home that neutrality would be a necessity for pro- and anti-French factions alike.

Other continental powers faced with the problem of trying to get the British to follow a steady course sought a different answer. To them it seemed important that King and Parliament should settle their differences and that consistency should come through agreement and coöperation rather than through the preponderance of one institution over the other. This is brought out clearly on more than one occasion, two of which are worthy of special attention. The first occurred early in 1685 when the Emperor Leopold sent a special embassy to London, having been prompted in his decision not only by the friendly advances James was making toward the United Provinces and by the unexpectedly peaceful succession, but also by the news that James had assembled what appeared to be a favorable and coöperative House of Commons. That it was the last of these circumstances which was decisive in persuading Leopold to believe the time had come when it might be worthwhile to give England a little attention is borne out by the fact that the ambassador was instructed to impress on King and leaders of Parliament alike how important it was for the peace of Europe that they should get on together.[3]

The friendly atmosphere prevalent in the first session of James's only Parliament, encouraging alike to the ambassador and to the Emperor who sent him, disappeared before the year was over, and with its disappearance once more we find a European statesman urging peace between the two factions which seemed to outsiders to be perennially warring against each other. This time the spokesman of what appears to have been a fairly general sentiment was Gaspar Fagel of the United Provinces. Convinced that the unstable condition of England contributed materially to unrest on the Continent, he wrote to his fellow-countryman, Heinsius, then on a special mission in London, ordering him to put it strongly to the King that the peace of Europe depended on good relations between him and his Parliament, for without those good relations respect would be lacking for his high office and the foreign policies he was formulating could not be taken seriously by continental diplomats. This part of Fagel's letter has been referred to frequently. What follows is even more significant for its shows Fagel's awareness that decision in this matter did not rest entirely with James. Heinsius was further charged to make the same argument to the leaders of Parliament, to urge them to subordinate their differences with the King to the need for a government capable of pursuing a strong foreign policy.[4] Even as the hopes of the Imperial ambassador had been disappointed, so were the pleas of Fagel ignored. If consistency depended on peace between King and Parliament, that consistency was not to be achieved under James II.

To have such an urgent exhortation come from Fagel was ironical, for the United Provinces also presented the disadvantage of unreliability in that decisions adopted by either the States General or the Stadholder could be blocked by the other. This country, however, possessed certain merits which England did not have. Its fleet, although somewhat neglected during the earlier half of William's stadholderate, was still powerful; its seamen ably trained. A corps of skilled diplomats, including William himself, knew the European scene much more thoroughly than did any of the English. The wealth of the country was great enough to rank them with France as one of the few able to give, rather than compelled to ask for, subsidies. Although not rich in natural resources as far as their continental possessions were concerned, the Dutch had behind them the opulence of an enviable empire, and they had in their population at home artisans skilled in making the best use of such resources as were available to supply their armies with the needed matériel for warfare, and their merchant fleet and navy with the necessities of both war and peace. The great drawback of the Netherlands was that the burghers of the Dutch cities simply did not like war. It disrupted their trade and drained their profits through taxation. Unless a situation arose which threatened their pocketbooks they usually remained unmoved by the pressures of power politics.

In the general European diplomatic situation, and in Anglo-Dutch relations in particular there were, as is almost always true, a host of contradictory elements. English and Dutch leaders were seeking alliances that were disliked by large sections of the populations of each country, and, because of the elements of popular control mentioned earlier, the domestic conflicts engendered by these differences of opinion were very important. The most obvious instance of this is the English disapproval of James's reputed friendly relations with Louis XIV, but the very obviousness has obscured certain facts which need consideration. For one thing, James's complete reliance upon Louis *after* 1688 should not lead us to assume that he was equally subservient before. Actually he was aware of the lack of community of interest between his own country and France, especially in colonial areas, and he took definite steps to protect the rights of his subjects when they were encroached upon by French traders. Unfortunately that aspect of his foreign policy seems to have received as little publicity in his own time as in later years. On the other hand, if and when James worked to strengthen ties with the United Provinces, that policy, although satisfactory to the anti-French element, aroused the opposition of those who were financially interested in the conflict with the Dutch. The old antagonism that had kept itself alive for many years by hugging the memory of the "massacre" of Amboyna and had been revitalized by quarrels in the East Indies and embittered by the loss of choice trading posts to Dutch rivals, was by no means dead.

In the United Provinces one can discern a similar picture of conflicting inclinations. Up to within a few months of the Revolution of 1688 the leaders of the great and powerful merchant group were almost solidly pro-French and had been so for years. If we turn our eyes away from the framework of continental politics to that furnished by colonial affairs we can see why this should be so. The intrigues of Europe held little interest for the burghers of Amsterdam and the smaller cities except insofar as they involved control of the Baltic, for the economic pulse of the States General was quickened or retarded by what happened in the world of nascent empires. In that world England and the Netherlands were rivals for the support of France. In the first two of their trilogy of wars since 1650 victory had gone to the side which had French assistance. The third did indeed end in defeat for England, in spite of the fact that she entered it with a French alliance, but this war alone of the three was not fought primarily on colonial issues. Generally speaking, above any other possible diplomatic situation the Dutch dreaded a strong alliance which could unite English and French naval forces to cripple the commerce of the United Provinces by blocking the exits to the Atlantic. Whenever this contingency threatened it was France, not England, that the mercantile group wished to detach and if possible, to win over to their side; for it was England who was trying to intrude upon the claims which the Dutch had staked out in the East Indies and in the Caribbean, as it was England whose fishermen were challenging the Dutch in the North Sea.

When James came to the throne there was a shift in this general pattern which did not, however, become apparent until the year of the Revolution. France, first under Colbert and then under his son and successor Seignelay, had been trying to break into the carrying trade and cloth industry where supremacy lay with the

Dutch and the English. In the brief period under consideration Seignelay's policies had the temporary approval of the powerful Louvois, usually unmoved by the commercial interests of his compatriots, and his coöperation made the French course of action more dangerous than it might otherwise have been.[5] Efforts to keep out English and Dutch cloth, to restrict the freedom of Dutch merchants, and to counteract the English navigation laws, furnished grievances to England and the United Provinces that were at least as strong as those they felt toward one another. Among the accidents in the timing of the Revolution, by no means the least important is the fact that when William committed himself to his venture circumstances over which he had had no control furnished him with a talking point that could be used effectively with those very sections of the Dutch and English population between which there was normally the greatest degree of antagonism.

The complexities and contradictions in the international situation remain in evidence as one extends his scrutiny from England and the Netherlands to the general European picture. Religion still played a part as a motivating force and although it was by no means as important as it had been at the opening of the century it was used as a propaganda weapon at the time of the Revolution of 1688 to a degree that makes it necessary to give the issue a little more than passing attention here. The truth of the matter is that no Roman Catholic or Protestant statesman, whatever his country might be, could have found a foreign policy that would have been entirely compatible with his personal religious beliefs. Louis's revocation of the Edict of Nantes and James's policy of toleration did indeed constitute threats, the one to freedom of conscience in France; the other to the established position of Anglicanism in England. Yet the Hapsburg policy toward the Protestants of Hungary was every bit as hostile as that of Louis toward the Huguenots. The United Provinces and Brandenburg sent protests to Vienna — and accepted Leopold as an ally. In the bitter quarrel between Louis XIV and the Pope the latter had Protestant supporters. Many Protestants were willing to speak high sounding phrases about the defense of their religion, especially when and if that defense also involved common action against France. When the time came to act they were just as willing to accept help from any source.

Actually several of the abler statesmen of all faiths would have preferred to see the religious issue soft-pedaled in the domestic and foreign policies of their own and other countries. Perhaps the best instance that can be cited in support of this assertion is to be found in the letter from Fagel to Heinsius to which reference has already been made.* After expressing his hope that parliamentary leaders would try to work with the King, Fagel becomes more specific. The zeal and opinionatedness of the English Protestants, he says, have been a constant source of trouble to all Europe. He even goes so far as to blame them, unfairly it may be but none the less explicitly, for the repression of the Huguenots and for all of Louis's encroachments since the treaty of Nimwegen, and he brings the letter to a close by urging Heinsius to do all in his power to open the eyes of the English to the need for more judicious action. A month later, having heard from London that feeling there was growing more rather than less bitter, he wrote "If the members of Parliament will reflect on what is happening, I believe it will be clear to them . . . that the religion for which they now appear to act can have no greater danger than that they and His Majesty should fall into disunity and dissension." [6] It should be pointed out that the above attitude was not peculiar to Protestants; that Roman Catholic leaders also wished that the religious issue could be kept in the background, and that neither the Pope nor the Emperor was happy over the steps James was taking to make life easier for those of his subjects who were not Anglicans.[7]

Religion, then, was an ostensible but not necessarily a basic motivation in determining diplomatic alignments. There is also the question of the power struggle and personal ambition. These are truly hard to evaluate. The task is all the more difficult because we have had for so long the pat, but not necessarily correct, formula to apply: Louis XIV, greedy for power and glory, was trying to dominate Europe to such an extent that, to combat his ambitions, a coalition was formed against him in the mid 1680's which was at last successful when England was prevailed upon to fulfill her historic function of maintaining the balance of power. But

*See above, p. 85.

examine the formula for a moment, and see its dangerous resemblance to the thinking of Monday morning quarterbacks who call the plays after the game is over. That Louis was a bundle of vanity there can be no dispute. How far his ambitions were personal and how far they were national, it is impossible to say, for the fortunes of Louis were the fortunes of France. Whatever the wisdom or folly of his policies two points should be noted. The sixteenth-century domination of the Hapsburgs had left France with a real and justifiable fear of that once-powerful dynasty whose family domains encircled her so tightly, and if, by the reign of Louis XIV what had once been self-protection had become aggression, the transition had not been easy to perceive nor the process easy to stop. Secondly, at the time when nation states were emerging out of the old dynastic conflicts, it was the fortune of France to have that combination of internal resources and skilled administrators, including the king himself, which enabled her to reach the goal of strong government earlier than her rivals. Under a lazy and incompetent ruler France might have lagged — had not his place been taken by a Richelieu or a Mazarin.

It is to the smaller princes of the Empire that we should turn if we desire to see the element of individual ambition operating most forcibly. These men possessed small territories over which their personal control was great. Their chief concerns, one might say amusements, were their armies and their castles, which they were fashioning on French models and, to some extent, supporting with French money. An additional source of revenue which, like the one just mentioned, involved international affairs, came from the tolls they exacted from merchants who must traverse their lands. Here, then, we have the two determining factors in their foreign policies. The second is highly complicated and not particularly germane to our subject. As for the first, it was in these minor states that French subsidies were most effective, for without them the princelings might not enjoy their playthings. Not until their resentment at the hauteur of some of Louis's demands co-incided with very good offers from his rivals were they effectively welded into opposition against him.

In summary, the accession of James II occurred at a time when Louis XIV was quiescent and sure of only a small number of weak allies. If there was not very strong opposition to him, neither was he particularly threatening. Complex motives determined the relations of the leading countries toward one another and most of them had almost equal reason to like or to fear and distrust their neighbors. It was from this background that William III drew his diplomatic support for the Revolution of 1688.

Of William's personal enmity toward Louis XIV there can be no question, but it would be well to examine the reasons for his attitude. Why was it that he, almost alone of the European leaders, stood in such intransigent opposition to Louis that he never, at least after Nimwegen, was to be numbered among those who indicated a willingness to be friendly or even neutral? Part of the answer is undoubtedly that an outstanding reason for his popularity in England was his reputation for being anti-French. He had built up a strong following there on the basis of a certain attitude, and he had the intelligence to perceive that he must continue to maintain it or risk losing the support it had gained for him. But it is also important to understand that his position was somewhat defensive and not entirely of his own choosing, for Louis, on his side, showed no disposition to win over the Prince but treated him instead with a consistent hostility in sharp contrast to the flattery he could, when he chose, bestow on those he wanted to charm. This was especially marked after Louis learned of William's double dealing in the early stages of the Nimwegen negotiations.[8] From then on Louis confined whatever pacific gestures he wished to make in the United Provinces to their High Mightinesses of the States General, for he had learned years before that the Stadholder was practically powerless without their backing. To the incentive of policy, therefore, William added those of dislike and even hatred that grew out of the humiliating realization that he was not only being slighted but also that his position at home was being threatened by the King of France. William hated Louis, and his emotion, deepened when decisions of the Chambers of Reunion resulted in the loss of some of his personal estates in the Spanish Netherlands, grew bitter indeed when his own patronymic principality of Orange, an enclave in southern France, was seized by Louis the very year that James became king.

William's relations with England were necessarily dual in character. There existed what might be called a personal status that grew out of family ties and the political position he held as her probable future king,* a position which made it impossible for him to avoid entanglement in the seething rivalries that were primarily domestic. But also his official status in the United Provinces made him one channel through which the diplomatic affairs of that state and England were conducted. Naturally these two capacities, personal and official, were inseparable, existing as they did within a single individual, so that the actions of the Prince in either aspect were motivated and influenced by his interests in the other. In the course of the thirteen years that followed his rise to power in the Netherlands in 1672, both he and his country had been now on bad terms with England, now on good. The personal variations were, however, much greater and more complex than the national, for they were closely connected with the highly volatile English political situation.

At the beginning of 1685 the only obvious obstacles to friendship between William and the English court was the presence of Monmouth in The Hague, where he had been for some months, apparently in William's good graces, and certainly in those of the still-homesick Mary into whose austere life he brought a refreshing bit of gaiety. A question no historian has solved is whether or not William was giving asylum to his cousin with the secret approval of Charles, perhaps even at his request. On the surface Charles expressed a displeasure which the Duke of York not only took at face value but also attempted to assuage by acting as mediator between his brother and his son-in-law.[9] To this evidence of good will he added, when the time came, the prompt and personal notification of Charles's death and of his own succession. Many subtle motivations could be read into this action, such as that James wished to impress William with the promptness with which the ceremonies of proclamation had been performed, but the simplest and most human interpretation is probably the most nearly correct. James, the man, wrote to another man who was

*Either as Mary's husband or by virtue of his own rights as nephew of James II which made him the first male heir to the throne. Although it was possible that through the first claim he might receive only the title of Consort, he assumed, as did everyone else at the time, that the real government would be in his hands.

not only his nephew but also the husband of his daughter to tell him of a death in the immediate family. Seen in that light the letter is more significant than it could ever be if judged by hypothetical hidden meanings. William, in James's eyes, was of the blood, and the family interests were his.

William replied by sending messengers to carry his good wishes. Possibly he also included proof of a private agreement between himself and Charles concerning Monmouth if, indeed, such an agreement existed.[10] The important thing is that he gave evidence of wanting to be on good terms with his uncle, who responded by setting up concrete terms for continued friendship: Monmouth should be sent out of the United Provinces, his followers should be dismissed from the English and Scottish regiments in Dutch service, and William himself should adopt a more conciliatory attitude toward France.[11] When William agreed to the first two but not to the third James appeared so unconcerned that one can legitimately wonder whether or not he attached much importance to the condition. Letters he wrote to the Prince in the first weeks of his reign were very friendly,* and the same impression of His Majesty's attitude was conveyed in the letters of his principal ministers.[12]

Although these friendly gestures were probably more important to the personal than to the diplomatic aspect of the relations between the men involved, they had an important bearing not only upon the latter but also upon William's political position in his own country and throughout Europe as well. It was highly essential to his prestige at home and abroad that he should appear

---

*As Dalrymple has pointed out (*Memoirs*, II, App. pt. I, p. 290), James has left behind him an almost infallible criterion on this point. When he was feeling friendly toward William his letters close with "You shall find me as kind *as you can desire*." (Italics mine.) When he was suspicious, annoyed, or uncertain the concluding words are "as you can expect." Although it is impossible to state with finality that the variation was intentional, it corresponds neatly with James's known frame of mind over the ten year period covered by the letters. The letter written at the time of Charles's death (see *supra*, p. 1) ends "as you can expect" which is not strange, for after all Monmouth, a known threat to James, was in William's court. Soon after the other ending appears and continues to be used with only one or two exceptions down to April of 1688. The exceptions occur in the spring of 1687 when William was refusing to endorse the Declaration of Indulgence.

to be on good terms with James. For the simple fact was that he was badly in need of friends. His unpopularity at home had never been greater than it had been during the preceding year; the apparent failure of his foreign policies, culminating in the Twenty Year Truce of Ratisbon which he had opposed, had lowered his influence in the States General at the same time that it had increased that of his opponents there. This, of course, had its effect upon his status on the international scene, for the man who cannot command a following at home has little influence abroad. The enmity between himself and Louis was so deep and so bitter, had in it so much of personal as well as political antagonism, that any definitive settlement of continental tensions favorable or even acceptable to France would leave William facing a future in which he would be a nonentity. Many of the Dutch leaders would have welcomed such a settlement, not merely because it would bring the peaceful conditions in which their commercial society could flourish, but also because it would cut the ground out from under their restless, ambitious Stadholder. James, therefore, became a key figure. He could not be friends with both Louis and William. If he came out strongly and openly in favor of the former he could do little to affect the balance of power in Europe, for everyone knew that his country was not strong and that his people were divided between pro- and anti-French sentiments with the latter so dominant that it would be almost impossible for the King to take any decisive action to the contrary even if he wanted to. But he could strike a blow that might well be mortal at his nephew's already diminishing prestige.

The French were as concerned as William. Behind the scenes in the Netherlands the Comte d'Avaux, Louis's envoy, exerted every effort during the first months of 1685 to convince the burgomasters of Holland that France, not William, was the chosen friend of James, and that their best course of action was to throw their lot in with Louis, or at the very least to place the United Provinces out of the current turmoil by cutting down their military expenditure and dismissing part of their army. That accomplished, William's efforts to stir up action in Europe would pass unheeded. But D'Avaux was unsuccessful: the evidence against his arguments was too strong. Regardless of the fact that James may have been playing the double game that the dispatches of Barillon suggest but do not prove* he gave the impression of being anti-French, or at least not pro-French. Skelton, the English ambassador at The Hague, so obviously had orders to exhibit a warm feeling toward William that even D'Avaux was finally forced to recognize it. Throughout James was showing his support of William as over against the Amsterdam faction but at the same time he did what he could to win over the latter, showing much forbearance toward them, and formally renewing the treaties with the United Provinces which had been in force under Charles II. This was a direct blow at France for, as Louis pointedly observed to Barillon, those treaties, having been made when England was considering reëntrance into the Dutch War on the side of Louis's enemies, contained provisions which were unfavorable to him.[13] Those conditions no longer obtained, yet James was renewing

*These dispatches, usually taken at face value, need careful study. Many of the reports are based on secondhand rather than on direct statements of James. It is ironical that D'Avaux's accuracy should have been questioned so much and Barillon's so little, for the former was much the more acute observer and he seems to have been willing to tell Louis unpleasant truths whereas Barillon either wrote with an eye to pleasing his master rather than informing him, or else he was genuinely mistaken. At the time in question Barillon was receiving strict orders to prevent the establishment of good relations between James and either William or the States General. Simultaneously D'Avaux was sending both Louis and Barillon copies, obtained by those highly devious methods of which he was a master, of reports sent by the members of the special Dutch mission in London to Fagel and the States General which clearly indicated James's friendly disposition. Faced with this evidence that he was unsuccessful in carrying out his orders, Barillon took refuge first in the assertion that the Dutch envoys were sending home false reports and later in the suggestion that James was deceiving them. The fact seems to be that if James was playing a double game it was Barillon who was the victim. See C. J. Fox, *History of the Early Part of the Reign of James II*, Appendix pp. lxxxi *et. seq.* for Barillon's dispatches at this time. Dalrymple, *Memoirs*, Appendix, Pt. I, 154, suggests that James reaffirmed the treaties with the Netherlands because Louis was holding back on his promised subsidies. In view of the fact that the establishment of good relations between James and the Dutch, *including William*, took place before the subsidy issue became really important it is more probable that the reverse is true, and that Louis withheld subsidies, among other reasons, because James had acted contrary to his wishes *in re* the Dutch. A careful reading of the dispatches in full and in their proper sequence, rather than in the chronologically out-of-order extracts that appear in Dalrymple does much to substantiate the above point of view.

the treaties despite the fact that he had been urged not to do so.

Outside of France other statesmen noticed what was happening with some surprise — they had expected James to be pro-French — and with moderate pleasure, for, while they would welcome England they did not expect much of a country so conspicuous throughout the century for inconsistency in foreign policy. Spain, always grasping at straws, began to lay hopeful plans for drawing England into what she hoped might be an offensive alliance against Louis XIV.[14] Brandenburg, more skeptical, was concerned not so much with England itself as with the effect of James's attitude upon the Dutch merchant oligarchy who could at best only with difficulty be persuaded to interest themselves in continental affairs and not at all if they were too involved in colonial conflicts with England.[15] Fuchs, one of the Great Elector's ablest diplomats, was sent to The Hague to discover, if he could, the truth about Anglo-Dutch relations. He found the leaders of the Netherlands in general inclined to believe that James was sincere in his gestures of good will.[16]

That James should have entered into more favorable relations with the United Provinces than with any of the other continental powers of the anti-French bloc is not necessarily due to a more friendly attitude toward them than toward the others. Part of the explanation is that the conditions surrounding and to some extent determining his relations with them, even in spite of colonial differences, were less complicated than those which existed elsewhere. Spain and the Emperor were, as usual, in difficulties not only between themselves but also with France over the future allotment of the territories of the still-living but seemingly perpetually moribund Carlos II, and any arrangement made with either of them depended to a large extent on the policy of the one toward the other. The Emperor, moreover, continued to be engaged with the Turks on his eastern frontier and what he did in western Europe depended not only on his successes in the Danubian area but also on his decision as to the relative importance of western versus eastern affairs. Noteworthy, too, is the fact that most of the continental powers showed but mild enthusiasm for winning England's friendship. The Imperial ambassador, for example, his springtime optimism considerably diminished by the November session of Parliament, reported that with all the good will in the world England was not worth courting. Her military forces were weak and she was in no condition to play any effective part in foreign affairs so long as she continued to be torn by internal dissension.[17] It is worth noting that it was England's weakness rather than her good intentions which engendered the skepticism. Even Louis seems to have been more concerned over the effect that James might have upon policies adopted by the States General than by English friendship for its own sake.

As for James himself, his ambition seems to have been to play the arbitrator in European affairs. It was a pathetic ambition that led him to make frequent and grandiose pronouncements about his desire to establish the peace of Europe. It could not be fulfilled, partly because neither he nor any other Englishman in or out of James's councils fully grasped the complicated state of continental affairs, but more because England at that time simply did not have the might which the arbitrator must have. She could cause trouble but she could not cure it.

Nevertheless, up to the spring of 1686 England's advances were being fairly well received on the Continent and she herself was the object of a certain amount of gratifying attention. After all, she was a member of the family of nations and her sister states were still hopeful that the new king might be able to carry out a policy that was stronger than his brother's had been. Then the sense of England's weakness combined with rumors of an Anglo-French alliance to place her in the position of being suspect. There was good ground for the former; little if any for the latter, but as it is the latter which contributes most directly to the Revolution of 1688 it is the one which must be studied. Examination of it leads us once more to the Prince of Orange.

In spite of his subservient attitude toward James up to the end of the Monmouth rebellion — the only time in his life that he was ever subservient toward anyone — William, as we know, had by no means discontinued his connections with men in England who were either actually or potentially in opposition to the King, and his policy toward James was always conditioned by the effect it might have upon those whom he wished to make or keep as his followers in any possible conflict with his uncle. D'Avaux tells

us that his personal instructions to the members of his first mission
to James were submitted to an Englishman for approval.[18] This
assertion is supported by further evidence in a letter to William
from Rochester who, having seen some of these instructions and
realizing that they ran counter to the best interests of James, not
only warned William of what might have been the consequences
had they fallen into the wrong hands but also charged him in stern
but respectful terms not to let anything similar happen in the
future.[19]

The inclusion of the veteran Dijkveld in the commission that
went to London later in the year to negotiate renewal of the
treaties was another indication that William was keeping close
watch over his own interests at the same time that he was striving
to give James the impression of friendliness. In addition to being
a highly trained diplomat, Dijkveld was as much in William's
confidence as any of his countrymen with the exception of Bentinck. To assume that this man spent more than three months in
London without consulting with those of Orangist sympathies is
to assume that he lived in a mental and social vacuum. We do not
need to go with D'Avaux to the extent of accusing him of laying
at this time the groundwork of the Revolution, but we can be
reasonably sure that he explained William's policy toward James
to the former's English friends and found them to acquiesce if
they did not quite approve.

Of even greater moment was Bentinck's journey to London at
the height of the Monmouth rebellion. Whatever the outcome of
that affair might be, and it was still in doubt when Bentinck left
The Hague, its importance to William was so great as to make it
essential for him to have someone on the ground to protect his
interests. Who better to send than this closest of his friends who
had so many contacts in England through earlier missions there
and through his marriage to a member of the prominent Villiers
family? One can but regret that the association between the Prince
and Bentinck was so close and the latter's understanding of the
former so complete that there was little need for written reports
or memoranda. Yet even more than in the case of Dijkveld we
can be sure that Bentinck did not spend several weeks in England

without discussing the affairs of his master with those to whom they were of especial interest.

With the end of the Monmouth rebellion or, if you will, with the return of Bentinck, there was a notable change in the relationship between William and James. No longer did the attitude of the Prince exude a most unfamiliar and unpleasant subservience toward his uncle. James's proposal to fill the vacant command of the British regiments in the United Provinces by the young Lord Pembroke was first agreed to and then disapproved of on somewhat specious grounds. Refugees from the rebellion flocked back to the Netherlands, and even granting William's lack of power to prosecute them he certainly did not use those powers he had to the extent he had led James to believe he would. By midwinter we find him contributing to the rumors of a forthcoming French attack somewhere and sometime in the spring;[20] and by the first of the next August he indubitably placed himself at the head of those who claimed that an Anglo-French alliance existed and that the two allies would inaugurate a general war by an attack upon the Netherlands.

As there was no change in James's foreign policy which could account for William's attitude or substantiate the rumors of any leaning toward France, the explanation must be sought elsewhere. William's own domestic situation may have had some bearing. During the time under consideration his relations with the Amsterdam faction had improved noticeably owing not only to the latter's consternation over the treatment of the French Huguenots, which was drawing them out of the pro-French camp, but also to William's own wise and patient actions. He no longer, therefore, needed the prestige of James's favor to bolster his position at home. Simultaneously, friendly advances, to which James's attitude had contributed, from Sweden and Brandenburg were improving his standing in western Europe. Yet these circumstances can be but of minor significance. The real key to the change in William's attitude is to be found in his relation to the domestic politics of England.

Although it is impossible to state with any degree of exactness the extent and composition of the Orangist party in England before Dijkveld's mission of 1687, such a party undoubtedly existed and was known to contemporaries by that name. Not necessarily an opposition group to begin with, it became so for reasons that have already been discussed. Shortly after the Monmouth rebellion this party began to turn against James. It has been shown that a long term view prompted them to refuse to endorse policies which they assumed would not be carried on by William, whom they expected to succeed James in the fairly near future. William, for his part, could not, if he expected to keep their support, continue to work hand in glove with James. This meant that James's leaning toward an anti-French, pro-Dutch policy must be rebuffed, and that he had to be forced into a position of appearing to cater to Louis.

The relation between these inter- and intra-national affairs can be established by a short review of their correlation in time. William began to turn cool toward James almost immediately after the Monmouth rebellion had been quelled. This coolness became more marked after Parliament was dismissed in November. By the beginning of 1686 William was indubitably lending approval to the rumors of Anglo-French alliance and a possible outbreak of war,[21] in spite of the fact that these rumors were denied from London by both Heinsius and van Citters.[22] As his relations with the English opposition grew closer, so did his insistence on the probability of war increase. The climax came on August 1, 1686 (N.S.), when he sent Fagel to the States General with an almost hysterical message that he had received reliable news of an Anglo-French plan to start war. Basing on this a plea for an increase in the military budget, William went so far as to insist that his demand be placed on record so that, if the States General refused to comply, they could not later accuse him of not having given ample warning.[23] It was about this time that the famous interview with Burnet took place and that Henry Sidney made his brief visit to The Hague.

Beyond doubt in that spring and summer of 1686 someone was trying desperately to create the impression that James and Louis had concluded or were in the process of concluding an aggressive alliance aimed particularly at the United Provinces. Only two grains of truth can be found in the bushel of chaff and when discovered they are scarcely worth the search. One of them was especially negligible. In spite of his friendly attitude toward the Dutch, James was already showing clearly that he was going to defend the colonial interests of his subjects more stoutly than his brother had done. It was, however, defense, not offense, that he had in mind, and with their own consciences by no means clear, for they knew they had been and still were encroaching on English preserves, the Dutch merchants might be disturbed but they could not justifiably be aggrieved. The other bit of truth was that Louis and James had indeed concluded an agreement, but this, too, was concerned exclusively with colonial differences chiefly in North America, and far from showing servility, it upheld the rights of the English trading companies in a way that was somewhat disconcerting to Louis. Yet on these meager foundations grew a host of rumors.

Van Citters reported the tales he heard in London directly to the States General but his letters usually contained also the evidence he had for believing they were unfounded. It is interesting that just about this time certain Englishmen observed that he seemed to be very angry with William about something.[24] Shortly after William sent his urgent message to the States General, van Citters wrote directly to him telling him that he had been warned by d'Albeville that there were those who sought to provoke England and the United Provinces to war but that William must be assured that James had no such desire.[25] On the same day van Citters reported to the States General that James's financial position and the internal unrest in the country rendered him in no condition to make war on anyone unless he was furnished with money by France.[26] Given the nature of James's policy at that time the money was not likely to be forthcoming.

A few days later van Citters sent another report which was indeed explosive, the dynamite coming in an enclosure. This was supposedly a copy of a statement read by James to his Council advocating immediate attack upon the United Provinces who, it was asserted, would be practically defenseless at the moment because their potential allies in the Empire were engaged with the Turks. If Parliament would not grant money for such a war the King would use his prerogative to find other means of taxation. This war would not only put down a hated rival and give the King a chance to increase his standing army, but it would also strengthen his power to impose Roman Catholicism on his subjects. Last and most important, or so the statement implied, it would gain for them the favor of the French king:

> To establish the Catholic religion and to confirm it here, it is necessary to become in some way dependent on France and to place the decision concerning the succession to the Crown in the hands of their king, because it would be better that his (James's) subjects should become vassals of the King of France, being Catholic, than that they should remain as slaves of the devil in enjoying this great liberty which they so abuse at present.[27]

Every fear of the average seventeenth-century Englishman was carefully played upon in this document: a large army, taxation by prerogative, Popery, French domination. Dutch apprehensions of their own destruction and the destruction of Protestantism everywhere were similarly stimulated. Whoever drew it up knew what he was doing. That the document was spurious there can be no doubt, but when he sent his report van Citters believed it to be authentic. Within a day or so James got wind of the story and sent for van Citters. Denying the whole thing vigorously he showed especial fury over the suggestions of making England a vassal of France and of letting Louis decide the succession. van Citters then wrote:

> Thereto I can say nothing more . . . except that since I have had the honor of having this interview everyone seems to hear an entirely different kind of talk.[28]

He was quite convinced that James was sincere and that the entire incident had its origin in a hoax.

Although very little is known about this document it must have been drawn up and allowed to fall into van Citters' hands by someone who wanted to deepen the antagonism between James and the States General and to frighten the latter. There is no evidence that William knew anything about it. Nevertheless it worked toward his benefit, for in spite of van Citters' report the suspicion that had been insinuated into the minds of their High Mightinesses remained.[29]

Although there is good reason to believe that William's change of attitude toward James was related to his interest in English domestic politics he was not yet ready to take any definite steps toward the formation of a system of continental alliances which could be integrated with that interest. But he was not the only one who was making plans. Others beside himself were concerned with forming alliances and from such projects he could not stand entirely aloof for all he might not wish to be involved directly. Of primary importance was the conclusion of the League of Augsburg that July. Its members were the Emperor, the kings of Spain and of Sweden for such estates as they had in the Empire, the Elector of Bavaria, and several of the other German princes, but not, it is important to notice, the Elector of Brandenburg. The purpose of the League was to guarantee the treaties of Westphalia and Nimwegen and the Twenty Year Truce of Ratisbon; to make that guarantee effective the members agreed to contribute to an army of sixty thousand men to be placed under Prince Waldeck.

William has often and erroneously been called the leading spirit of this League apparently because it was eventually merged into the Grand Alliance of 1689 in which he did play a major role. As it happened, however, not only did the United Provinces refrain from joining but William himself when urged by the Imperial ambassador Cramprich to press them to become members refused to use his influence, giving as a reason his belief that the League would be ineffective until Brandenburg and Brunswick-Lüneburg were in it.[30] Fresh as he was from a conference with the Great Elector he must have known that that condition, for he practically put it as such, would not be met. It is fairly easy to see why he was reluctant to give his support. He had lost so much ground by the Twenty Year Truce and his position at home and abroad was still so uncertain that he had to feel his way very carefully. Accused of being a warmonger by the opposition in his own country he could not risk losing the ground he had gained in the past months by any indication that he was lending his approval to a scheme that could well provoke Louis to action. Moreover he was wavering between an all-out Protestant alliance, which would exclude the Hapsburgs, and an anti-French alliance which could include them. Terming the League of Augsburg "innocuous," he intimated that he preferred an offensive to a defensive alliance.[31] Probably the real truth was that he had not yet determined exactly upon a course of action which would reconcile his varying and sometimes conflicting needs at home, in England, and in connection with his relations with the anti-French bloc on the Continent.

Another event of that same summer was William's meeting with the Great Elector during the latter's visit to Cleves in August, an event which, like the formulation of the League of Augsburg, has been given undue significance and must, like the other, be treated mainly in order to reduce it to its proper importance. On a mistaken assertion by Pufendorf that Marshal Schomberg was present at the conference [32] has been reared the story that plans for the subsequent invasion of England were made at this time. Schomberg, as we now know, was not there but the establishment of that fact seems to have made little difference. In the first place even his presence would not prove the assertion; in the second, proof of his absence has not been able to shake the traditional belief that here at Cleves, William and his uncle worked out in more or less detail the former's policy toward England.[33]

Admittedly the evidence is almost entirely circumstantial either way. Brandenburg did give William strong support in 1688 but we should be going ahead of our story if we pointed out here just why that need not be taken as proof of the assumption. On the other hand lack of positive proof coming from the time of the conference itself cannot be given too much weight because if the project of an expedition was discussed the subject was, of course, too dangerous to be committed to paper unnecessarily. What is more significant is that there is no retrospective reference to any such discussion at any later time when mention of it would not have been dangerous. But the whole conjecture depends for its validity mainly on the assumption that William and the Great Elector, planning as we know they did at this time, some sort of concerted action against France, believed that nothing effective could be done without England. It so happens that there is very good indication that the Great Elector did not think anything of the kind. This is contained in a fascinating memorandum he himself drew up in answer to the wavering Leopold's plaintive inquiry as to what could be done about France.[34] In this memorandum Frederick William sketched plans for a full scale *attack* upon France. Once peace with Turkey had been made an army of 199,000 could, he asserted, easily be raised from various parts of the Empire, from the United Provinces, and from Spain. This army, he claimed, and he was no fool in assessing military strength, could defeat France. Although some mention is made of the possible actions of the Northern powers in this event, England is ignored. The omission certainly indicates that Frederick William did not believe her coöperation indispensable to victory. As for the possibility that she might come to Louis's assistance, he does not seem to have given that a thought.

This meeting was nonetheless important in laying the general diplomatic groundwork for the next few years. We know that the two men did discuss the problem of France, the need to detach the smaller German states from her following, and the necessity of getting Spain to pull herself together and contribute something to the subsidies that were almost the only way of combating Louis in the contest for allies. We have reason to believe that they discussed the possibility that Frederick William's oldest son by his second marriage might be accepted as William's heir, a belief that is given substance by the fact that the young man shortly afterwards took up residence at The Hague where he became somewhat of a pet of Mary's. The Elector may also have unburdened himself about some of the many troubles he was having within his own family, especially those created by the antagonistic attitude of the sons of his first marriage, William's cousins, toward their stepmother. Those troubles weighed so heavily on him just then that he had almost called off the visit to Cleves. In the time left, and there could not have been much of it even if the domestic grievances had not been aired, William and his uncle may well have talked over the former's position vis-à-vis England. To the Elector, unaccustomed to any concept of inheritance which did not transfer the life interest in a woman's rights to her husband, William was of course the future sovereign of England and his standing in

Europe was to some extent based on that expectation. The two men were on good terms, with an easy familiarity between them that was lacking in the Prince's relations with his maternal uncles. But William did not need the Great Elector to plan his policies.

For the next year William took almost no part in the diplomatic intrigues of Europe. The Imperial envoys, Cramprich and Kaunitz, found him so uninterested in any of their proposals that they urged the Emperor to cease dealing with him and turn directly to the States General.[35] Early winter saw the annual threat that Louis, come spring and in conjunction with James would attack the Rhineland or the Netherlands or both. But the threat was feeble. Louis was known to be so gravely ill that European chancelleries were beginning to consider how to adjust their policies to his demise. James was so absorbed in domestic problems that he could not be aroused to what the envoys sent to him considered a proper interest in foreign affairs, nor could he be convinced that the Emperor, Spain, and the Pope were less interested in his efforts to establish religious toleration than they were in the possible effect of his actions on their own ambitions. Moreover the stand James had taken on French demonstrations at Namur in the autumn of 1686 had, justifiably or not, been credited throughout Europe with having for once stopped Louis in his tracks. The specter of Anglo-French aggression seemed laid for the time being.

European politics ran on their uneasy, inconsistent course. Imperial armies met with growing success in the Danubian area and the news of the victories met with varied and contradictory receptions in the West. It was joyfully acclaimed throughout Germany, where any uneasiness over the possible effect of those victories on relations between the Emperor and members of the Empire were overshadowed by glory and by the hope that peace with the Turk would make possible a firm stand against France. In Italy the Pope hailed success in a Holy War to which he had contributed much. In England, James II likewise considered this a Holy War but disregarded the fact that he had contributed nothing. In Spain one branch of the Hapsburg family basked in the reflected glory of the other. There was, however, little rejoicing in France where the possibility of a defeat of the Turks did more than raise the prospect of war with the Empire. It threatened French commercial interests in the Levant. In England while James rejoiced the mob glowered and went into action when the Spanish ambassador lit a bonfire to celebrate the fall of Osen; and people in higher places were heard to remark that it was as if seven churches had been lost to Protestantism. Here too, Levantine trade may have been the important factor rather than religious zeal. William for his part greeted the news with noticeable lack of enthusiasm, believing with good reason that an Emperor who saw the prospect of rich victories in the East would only with difficulty be led to action in the West. The people of the United Provinces, like those of England, feared the waxing strength of a Catholic power. In spirit, at least, William and Louis were united with the average Dutchman and Englishman in a strange, confusing sentiment.

Nor was the confusion confined to the attitude toward what was going on in east Europe. Displaced Huguenots traveled from one to another of the Protestant courts in ceaseless efforts to build a religious league. Although they found these zealots somewhat troublesome, William and the Great Elector considered the idea but bided their time. Talking largely of counteracting with a Catholic League, Louis at that very moment was at grips with the Pope in a struggle that can well be compared to the great medieval conflicts between the Papacy and Philip Augustus or Philip the Fair. There seemed little likelihood that the Holy Father would enter any league formed by the French king; it would be impossible to make one without him. James, undoubtedly a sincere Catholic whatever else might be said of him, found moral support for his domestic religious policy in France, very little, if any at all in the Empire, and even less in the Holy See itself.

William's lack of activity during these months must not be interpreted as inertia. It was for him a time of decision, and before the inescapable choice from which he could not turn back could be made he had to take a careful survey of the existing conditions. His problem was this: should he come out as the champion of Protestantism or should he take his stand as the opponent of France? The ultimate aim was the same; the means and agencies to accomplish it differed. There are signs that he wavered between the two possibilities. The decision, when he finally reached it, was a compromise based on circumstances prevailing on the Continent as well as in England. From Dijkveld's information and from other sources such as the letters of Lady Sunderland and of Patrick Hume he had learned that while he must refuse to accede to the lifting of the Test and Penal laws by James's methods, he must also avoid playing into the hands of James by supporting religious intolerance as opposed to the other's stated policy of toleration. He had to win over the English Dissenters or lose his whole game, either through an all-out victory for James or, he feared, by default to a republic. Nevertheless he could not carry toleration to the extent of openly seeking Catholic allies for by doing so he might add to the current rumors that he himself was about to be converted. Neither could he afford to antagonize the Emperor, whose prestige was momentarily high by virtue of victories over the Turks. The result was that, while William formed specific alliances with Protestants in preparation for his expedition to England, he was careful to avoid giving offense to the Catholics and above all to the Emperor.

It was while Dijkveld was in England that William once more emerged from his isolation to play an active part in European affairs. His policy was two-pronged: to prevent any over-all settlement with France and to encourage the princes of Germany to put an end to their differences with each other. Both objectives were directly related to the plans he was formulating with relation to England. For these plans to be successful Louis must be pictured as a potential aggressor. Hence the consistent support William gave to any rumors of a threatened French-instigated war. Hence, too, his equally consistent insinuations of insincerity and hidden malevolent motive whenever Louis suggested a definitive peace. Because Leopold's ambitions on the Danube led him to yearn for quiet on the Rhine, one such peaceful overture coming at this very time had had some chance of success. It failed, in part at least, because the princes of the Rhineland could not, like the Emperor, hope for compensation to the eastward. But before the threat had vanished William had spoken out more clearly and forcefully than he had done for many a month to point out to Cramprich that Louis was not to be trusted and that if the Emperor was misled into accepting the proffered peace the time might come when he would find himself jockeyed into the undesirable position of an aggressor through his inability to accept Louis's interpretation of its terms.[36]

Let others who are concerned with the over-all picture of Europe in these years determine whether or not Louis could be trusted. Probably he could not. But had he been as free from guile as that later peacemaker of Versailles, Woodrow Wilson, it was nonetheless essential to William that Louis *should* not be trusted and that James II should seem ready to join him in his schemes. Yet envoy after envoy wrote home from England to say that James was, if anything, inclined to be friendly to the anti-French bloc and at most, in agreement with Louis only to the extent of wishing to be a guarantor of any definitive peace that might be made. These estimates were usually joined to opinions that James was ineffective anyway because of his troubles at home. Under those circumstances it is almost incredible that William should have been able to conjure up the ogre of an offensive Anglo-French alliance. Fate played into his hands and must have strengthened his Calvinistic faith in predestination.

His reëntry into German affairs to achieve the second objective of his policy came at the same time that he broke his silence to denounce Louis's proposal for a settlement and to warn the Emperor of a trap. The public, but not the private, occasion of this reëntry was the sending of Jacob Hop, pensionary of Amsterdam, as a commissioner to Berlin to see if the United Provinces could use their good offices to end the tension in northern Germany in which Denmark, Brandenburg, and the Emperor himself were involved. Even the United Provinces were concerned through conflicts between their own trading companies and the Brandenburg North African Company, as well as through issues touching upon the dues which Denmark levied upon trade into the Baltic. Until the atmosphere cleared or at least showed appreciable signs of improvement, William could not expect the North German states, especially Brandenburg, from whom he hoped so much, to interest themselves in his projects, to say nothing of giving him active support. Consequently when the States General suggested that Hop should be sent William agreed heartily not only out of deference to the Great Elector who had requested mediation[37] but also because it was to his own interest that the tension be ended and, perhaps most of all, because it was important for him to have someone on the spot who could send him information.

It is, however, extremely unlikely that Hop, as is sometimes asserted, was entrusted with knowledge of William's plans concerning England. For one thing nowhere in his long, tedious reports to William[38] is there any reference to "the secret," the term generally used in other correspondence to refer to those plans. It is, moreover, improbable that William would, at this early date, have confided in Hop who was one of the leaders of the party in the States General that opposed his foreign policy. Approving the choice of such a man was wise for in addition to being a well-timed gesture of conciliation it gave one of their High Mightinesses a chance to see for himself the complex nature of existing foreign affairs. But to have entrusted him with "the secret" would have been foolhardy.

Moreover it was unnecessary. William was not depending on Hop alone to bring peace to North Germany or to lay the groundwork for an alliance of those states with the United Provinces. Hop's mission was public. Two weeks before it had been approved by the States General, William had dispatched into the same territory a personal and private agent, Simon von Pettecum, president of the Prince's council and a man whose personal attachment to him was strong. Pettecum was assigned the task of opening discussions with the German princes that led eventually to treaties, ostensibly between them and the United Provinces, but actually more personally between them and William. These treaties made the expedition to England possible. Any doubt as to the relative importance of his mission and Hop's, at least in William's estimation, is dispelled by the instructions which Pettecum received from his chief on how he should act in case his path crossed that of the accredited envoy:

You know in what manner you should govern yourself toward him, that is to say, very civilly, but without saying anything to him of the subject of your journey.[39]

Information on the first part of Pettecum's mission, to the Lüneburg dukes and to the Landgrave of Hesse-Cassel, can be gleaned only from references to his reports in letters written to him by William, for the reports themselves appear to have been lost or destroyed. That Pettecum was ordered to make definite proposals we know, but not what those proposals were.[40] It seems clear, however, that William was offering some sort of inducements to keep the Lüneburg dukes from responding favorably to French advances, but it is certain, as we shall see later, that he did not at this time broach to them the subject of an expedition to England although he himself undoubtedly had it in mind. In the latter part of September Pettecum was directed to go to Berlin, ostensibly to mediate in an unusually bitter quarrel between the Great Elector and his oldest son, but actually to hold secret conversations with Schomberg and Fuchs. With Schomberg at least the English affair must have been discussed for the Marshal was in the confidence of Henry Sidney and had already corresponded with him on the subject.[41]

Pettecum stayed in Berlin until January 2, 1688. On his way back to The Hague he stopped at Celle where he received the assurances of that Duke that he and his Wolfenbüttel relatives were "firm in the good party," and then went on to Hanover, whose ruler, Ernst August, although not in the "good party" was obviously anxious to learn what was going on. From Pettecum's amusing report on what happened we can see a little of the pressures that were being applied at this time. The chief ministers of the duchy, de Platen and von Gröte, fell over themselves in their haste to see the envoy immediately on his arrival. Pettecum blandly, and with full knowledge of the game he was playing, assumed that they wanted the latest gossip on the quarrels at the Brandenburg court and entertained them with stories thereon until the Hanoverians, unable to contain themselves any longer, interrupted to ask him his opinion on France. After saying sententiously that he knew nothing, Pettecum went on to belie his own words by stating that Louis without doubt had designs on either the United Provinces or the Rhineland, but that the Elector was pressing the Emperor to make peace with the Turks, that the Emperor would almost certainly do so, and that in any case Turkey, suffering from an internal upheaval at the moment, was so badly disrupted that she could not hold out much longer.[42] The apparently unrelated remarks had heavy significance for the listeners. Peace with Turkey meant war in western Europe, and a prince of Germany allied to France was not in a pretty position. Without actually committing himself, then, Pettecum had given as a covert threat to Hanover what he had very likely used as an inducement elsewhere, to wit: that a coalition was forming against Louis XIV which waited only for an apparently certain peace in the East to swing into action, and that it would be well to get in on the right side before it was too late. Although he himself made no specific offer at this court we learn from his report on his conference with the Duke, which took place the same day as the above conversations, that William had written to Ernst August about subsidies from Spain.[43] It is safe to assume that if subsidies were offered here they were offered elsewhere.

To sum up: Pettecum's task had been to lay the groundwork for a system of alliances in Germany. In his contacts with Schomberg and perhaps with the Great Elector these were spoken of in connection with William's English policy. Elsewhere they were not. Even in Berlin, Pettecum probably walked very softly for the Great Elector was known to oppose the opening of hostilities before the enemies of France were ready and he did not think that that time would come until the war in the East was over. In this respect the mission may have been disappointing for by now William knew that he could not wait much longer before taking action in England. Otherwise Pettecum was reasonably successful. Suggestions had been dropped which had set the North German princes and their councilors to doing some hard thinking. But there was still a great deal of work to be done.

One of the touchiest situations existed in Brandenburg. The strongest of these states, it was also the one with which William had the closest personal ties. But in addition it was also the one in the best position to act independently, and its ruler's Machiavellian policy for more than forty years had been to strengthen his own dominions with small regard either to honor or to assumed obligations. He was interested in William's project, but not so much so that he could or would be altruistic in his assistance. In these, the last few months of his life, tired and old and emotionally distraught by bitter quarrels with his sons, he was more hesitant to act than he had been before. On February 5 he wrote William that he had told two Huguenot refugees who had come to urge him to take up arms in defense of Protestantism, that the appearance of a religious war must be avoided at all cost, and that the time for action was not yet ripe.[44] Moreover he was displeased by the dilatory manner in which the States General were carrying out their treaty with him. It was probably to soothe the Elector and to prepare his mind for the pressing need for action that William sent the young Lord Leven to Berlin in the latter part of February. A Scottish refugee, son of one of the most intransigent opponents of the Stuart kings and himself in contact with malcontents both at home and in the Netherlands, Leven was a good man to point out to Frederick William, whom he already knew from previous service in Berlin, that affairs in England were coming to a head.

William knew that he could not wait much longer. He had led the English to expect his support, and in that expectation they had so ordered events that resistance against James had come to be for them, as well as for William, a case of "now or never." William could not do what everyone else on the Continent wanted to do: wait for the conclusion of the Turkish war before taking definite steps. We see then, that his actions were determined not by the need to bring England into the ring against France but by the compelling necessity to bring his German allies into action against James II. He had to manufacture reasons since he could not be frank. If what he did provoked France to take up arms before his allies were ready, the risk had nonetheless to be taken or England was lost to him. Furthermore it should be emphasized here that England would not have been lost so far as the continental enemies of France were concerned. These could still have won her if they had really tried. It was the provocative actions of the Great Elector, egged on by William, plus the coolness of the Emperor and the Pope, that were throwing James more and more and always with reluctance, into the French camp.

On May 9 the Great Elector died. It is probable that the story that his last words were "London–Amsterdam," supposedly indicative of his concern over William's plans, is no more and no less apocryphal than those of other deathbed utterances. It is also probable that William, although he may have felt some personal grief, learned of his uncle's death with a little relief, for his cousin, the new and never-great Elector, was less astute, much more open to suggestion, and on very good terms with William. Moreover the occasion gave a good excuse to send another envoy into Germany. True, if the occasion had not existed it would have been necessary to create it. About ten days before this, Russell had delivered his message and William had given an answer which amounted to a promise to be ready to lead an army into England by autumn. Negotiations in Germany could not, therefore, be put off any longer. Consequently after some delay caused by the illness of his wife, Bentinck was sent to Berlin. That he was chosen speaks volumes that fortunately do not have to be set down on paper. The closest friend of the Prince! *Fides Achates* and *alter ego* rolled into one! Only a personal visit of the Prince himself could have done greater honor to the new Elector or have been more indicative of the high importance of the mission.

Bentinck set out on his journey on or about May 17, empowered not only to give condolences and good wishes to the Elector but also to negotiate for assistance for the forthcoming expedition and to arrange for a meeting between William and Frederick.[45] Definite arrangements were made for the payment of money to Brandenburg. On the subject of an interview between William and Frederick, however, Bentinck ran into difficulties. The new Elector was either really too busy, or else he was too impressed with the relative importance of his own affairs as opposed to William's plans, to take time out to come to Cleves, the place designated by the latter. It is understandable that William should not wish to go further into Germany at this time, not only because a journey to some point nearer Berlin would cause too much comment, but also because he, like the Elector, and perhaps with better reason, felt that in those crucial days he could not spare the time. Failure to agree on this point was rather serious, for apparently the final conclusion of the treaty was to be made personally between the two men. That it was to be an agreement between them as individuals rather than as representatives of their states is indicated by the fact that William said that Hop could handle other matters. It was to be highly secret and would deal, among other things, with affairs in England.

Although Bentinck had to leave Berlin without settling the question of the interview, he apparently had received enough encouragement so that William felt able to go ahead. On his homeward journey Bentinck was supposed to go by way of Celle, Hesse-Cassel, Wolfenbüttel, and Hanover. The Landgrave of Hesse-Cassel was to be asked to enter into a treaty "such as we hope to make with Zell(sic) and Wolfenbüttel" and to be assured that if Spain could be persuaded to give subsidies to the Dukes that the Landgrave would likewise come in for a share.[46] Probably it had not been originally intended that Bentinck should go to Hanover as William knew that Ernst August had concluded a treaty with France, and in spite of the latter's insistence that there was nothing in it prejudicial to German interests, the Prince was suspicious. The death of the Archbishop of Cologne, however, which occurred while Bentinck was in Berlin, put a different face on things and not only gave William an additional problem but also provided him with another device for putting pressure on laggards.

As it happened, Bentinck's visit was cut short and he did not go to any of the courts just mentioned. His son had died during his absence, and now his wife, ill when he left, took a turn for the worse. Torn between sincere sympathy for his friend, whose happy marriage had at one time stood in such stark contrast to his own, and extreme anxiety over the need to finish the business quickly, William gave in to the more human sentiment and recalled his envoy by a letter which the latter must have received shortly after he left Berlin.[47] Madame Bentinck rallied, and three days later William tried frantically to reach his friend with orders to complete the work. It was too late. Bentinck was on the way home.

Up to the middle of June, then, so little had been accomplished that the Prince may well have been discouraged. Negotiations with Brandenburg, keystone of the structure, were dangling. The efforts of Amerongen to form an alliance with the Elector of Saxony had come to a halt, and although they were not actually terminated, it was obvious that they would be, at the very best, delayed, at a time when every day was important.[48] The other hoped-for allies had not even been approached. And, worst of all, the expected summons from England had not yet arrived. In spite of this the returning Bentinck found William in better spirits than he had left him.[49] What reason did the Prince have for being encouraged? Perhaps news from England about the disturbances raised by the trial of the seven bishops had quieted his ever-present fear that affairs would settle themselves before he could intervene, but it could also raise apprehension of a premature explosion. It is more likely that William's optimism was connected with the death of the Electoral Archbishop of Cologne.

He died on June 3 and his death at once raised the question of succession not only to the archbishopric itself, with its electoral vote, but also to the bishoprics of Liege, of Münster, and of Hildesheim which he had held and which were now vacated by his death. Cologne on the Rhine, and Liege and Münster, the one bestriding the Maas to control the path from France to the United Provinces, the other on their eastern border, were all three of extreme strategic importance not only to the Dutch but to the princes of western Germany as well. Toward the end of 1687 Louis had succeeded in getting his creature, William von Fürstenberg, Cardinal Bishop of Strasbourg, accepted as bishop coadjutor of Cologne which implied his succession. All Europe knew that Fürstenberg was so completely under Louis's influence that his becoming archbishop would virtually give France a vote in the Electoral college and further voice in the Imperial council. Worse than that, even if Fürstenberg succeeded only to Cologne, Louis would have a base in the heart of the Rhineland separated by a scant hundred miles from his outposts near Luxembourg. The princes of Germany, whom William had found so apathetic, so anxious to wait until the end of the war with Turkey would transfer the full power of the Imperial armies from the east to the west were "in clear and present danger."

The whole situation played into William's hands. Dutch gold pouring into the Rhineland helped to win the three bishoprics from Louis. When the election for the archbishopric was held Fürstenberg received a majority but not the requisite two-thirds of the votes, which placed the matter in the hands of the Pope for settlement. The last thing in the world that the Holy Father wanted was to have the candidate of his bitterest enemy installed in one of the most important sees of the Church of Rome. He gave his decision in favor of the other contestant, Prince Joseph Clement of Bavaria. Louis refused to accept the decision. The fight was on.

All this covered a period of some months from the death of the archbishop in June well into the following autumn, and coincided therefore with the period during which William was collecting and equipping his army and fleet. Much to his advantage, the incident aroused the German princes to anger. The greatest number of them, up to and including the Emperor himself, had reached the limit of their patience with Louis's arrogant intervention in what they considered to be none of his affair. He had given them orders once too often. Even the Pope was furious enough to turn his attention from the Holy War against the Turk on the Danube to the prospect of a Holy War on the Rhine. This was an additional point in William's favor. Catholic and Protestant were united. No longer need he fear that his own expedition would be characterized as a Protestant League or that he might lay himself open to criticism if he showed a friendly attitude toward Catholic princes. To make matters even better for him James, as happened so frequently, played into his hands again, this time by trying to act as mediator in the dispute. Mediator indeed! All that that unlucky man accomplished was to confirm the continental powers in their suspicion that he, like Fürstenberg, was the pawn of France.

Nevertheless affairs marched at a snail's pace. At Berlin the Elector, still preoccupied with ceremonial, either postponed the desired interview with William or suggested places such as Halberstadt so far distant from The Hague that they could not be considered. Bentinck had been ordered to request, if an interview was out of the question, that Danckelmann's brother, Thomas, to whom the secret could be safely entrusted, should be sent to The Hague with full power to conclude a treaty. But Thomas was in Vienna, and a week or so after Bentinck left Berlin his brother wrote that affairs there were so delicate that he could not be recalled for some months.[50] Months, when every day counted! Schomberg chafed under what he considered the unnecessary rituals of the electoral court and the delays in providing him with money he wanted for fortifications at Wesel.[51] Perhaps for this reason, after the death of his wife early in July he expressed a wish to join the campaign in Hungary, a wish which, if granted, would deprive William of his ablest commander. Elsewhere Waldeck reported that the Landgrave of Hesse-Cassel, who prided himself on having always been firm in the good cause, was feeling slighted because he thought the Lüneburg dukes were receiving more attention than he was. Bentinck had, of course, expected to call on him, but had been prevented by summons to return home immediately. The Landgrave accepted his excuses with some grace but showed that he wanted a letter of regret and an official substitute. Something had to be done.[52]

Accordingly on July 22 Bentinck set out to complete the work he had left unfinished in June. He went first to Hesse-Cassel where he concluded a treaty by which the injured Landgrave, soothed now and willing to coöperate, undertook, for a consideration, to provide troops for the United Provinces for one year.[53] Thence Bentinck went to Hanover for a last and unsuccessful appeal to Ernst August who, entrusted of necessity with a dangerous secret, promised to respect the confidence but refused to join the alliance.[54] A treaty was concluded with the Celle and Wolfenbüttel dukes on August 5. The day before that the Duke of Württemberg had been drawn into the circle although probably not by Bentinck. All of these treaties are similar in that the princes with whom they were made agreed to furnish a stipulated number of troops for the service of the United Provinces in return for subsidies. Celle and Wolfenbüttel specifically stated that their men were to be used *only* for defense.

The climax came on August 6 when Bentinck completed arrangements for a treaty with the all-important laggard, Brandenburg, at a conference with Fuchs. The meeting took place in cloak-and-dagger secrecy at an isolated tavern near Hamburg, in the early hours of the morning, with the participants using great precaution to conceal their identities, although it is hard to see against whom all these safeguards were taken or why they were considered necessary. The following summarizes what Bentinck had to relate.

James II and Louis XIV, he told Fuchs, had entered into a treaty and were planning to attack the United Provinces and to extirpate Protestantism. Inducements had been offered to the Emperor to persuade him to remain neutral, at least, by promising him that Alsace and all other Hapsburg possessions on the Rhine, evidently those which Louis had acquired by the Chambers of Reunion, should be returned to him. Instead of being tempted, however, the Emperor had so resolutely refused that he had threatened, in case of any repetition of such an offer, to reveal the whole project.

After those comments on continental matters Bentinck turned to England. The King, he said, planned to call a parliament. The subservience of the lower house would be assured by making certain that men known to be in agreement with the royal policies would stand for seats in all constituencies, and should any of them be opposed the proper officials were to be ordered to validate their elections regardless of whether or not they had the majority vote. From such a House of Commons, James could get not only approval of his religious policy but also the money necessary to increase and equip his fleet. He would use that fleet the next spring to join France in the proposed attack upon the United Provinces and upon Protestantism. To avert the threat to their own liberties the English leaders were constantly urging William to take action. If he refused, they and their followers would look elsewhere for help. The result would be either a republic or a victory for James. Honor and interest alike impelled the Prince to act. The prospects were good. The English nation awaited him. A fleet of forty-five warships was ready to carry him over. What was lacking was military support from Germany to protect the United Provinces should Louis fall upon them in William's absence.

At this point Fuchs, who was thoroughly acquainted with the lack of accord between William and many of the men in high positions in the United Provinces, interrupted to ask what those men thought about their Stadholder's plans to intervene in English domestic politics, inquiring specifically about the attitude of Amsterdam not only because of the importance of that city but also because it was there that the ill-feeling was strongest. Bentinck answered "joyfully," says Fuchs, that the Prince had not, of course, broached the subject to the States General openly because there was still a great need for secrecy, but that Fagel and Dijkveld had full knowledge of what was going on and so did three out of the four burgomasters of Amsterdam. He gave the distinct impression that the latter were giving enthusiastic support to William.

This interview, which we know only through Fuchs's report,[55] is amazing. It is hardly credible that Fuchs should have believed all that he was told; even less so that Bentinck himself did not realize that much of what he said was either fictitious or based on flimsy rumor or misleading. For more than two years the story of an alliance between James and Louis had been spread in various forms but had never gained much credit partly because of lack of proof but still more because of the existence of positive evidence to the contrary. The particular version used at this time, that the objective of the alliance was the overthrow of Protestantism, may be traceable to reports spread more than a year earlier by excited Huguenots that the treaty of Dover had been reënacted.[56] If so one cannot but wonder that William had waited so long before taking action. There seems to be a grain of truth behind the story of Louis's advances to the Emperor for he was, as we know, anxious to convert the Twenty Year Truce into a definitive peace and he had hoped that by making some concessions to Leopold he could induce him to put pressure on the lesser German princes. The report on the situation in England was fairly accurate, although for obvious reasons it held no suggestion that William himself had done anything to bring on the crisis. The story of the device whereby James expected to get a friendly Commons, is, however, mystifying. Interesting though it is, there is no basis for believing that James himself had ever entertained such a project. That does not necessarily indicate that Bentinck was deliberately deceiving Fuchs on this point, for the tale may well have come from some of the more violent English malcontents. So far it is possible to assume that William and Bentinck were combining rationalization with wishful thinking. That cannot be said of the assertion concerning the attitude of the Amsterdam burgomasters. Bentinck, who had himself taken part in the advances made to those men, knew that their response had been almost unfavorable and certainly by no means enthusiastic.*

The air of urgent secrecy surrounding this interview vests it with undue importance, for Brandenburg had already decided to conclude the treaty and Fuchs was interested mainly in specific stipulations for payment of the troops that were to be loaned and in pressing for a promise from William that he would take definite action to recognize the Elector as his heir.[57] The interview, therefore, culminated negotiations which had been initiated some months earlier. It is interesting mainly as the only available record of the arguments which Bentinck used, and although he may have varied his approach in other courts it is permissible to assume that the essential approach was the same in each instance. With it as a background it is possible to make a general survey of the situation as it existed during the first week in August of 1688.

By this time William had formed alliances with five of the German states: Brandenburg, Hesse-Cassel, Württemberg, Celle, and Wolfenbüttel. All treaties provided for loans of troops to the United Provinces in return for subsidies.[58] They were made in the name of the United Provinces, but through William's agents; the States General did not as yet know what was being done or the real reason why troops were required. The princes with whom the alliances were made were Protestant. None was a member of the League of Augsburg. With the exception of Brandenburg they were not particularly powerful. All but Hesse-

*See infra, pp. 140–142.

Cassel had played in with France from time to time and there was real danger up to the very last minute that the Duke of Celle might go over to the enemy. Waldeck indeed spoke very slightingly of this Duke, implying that it was money and money alone that kept him "in the good cause." [59]

How much of William's plans was revealed, and how soon, is open to question. Brandenburg clearly was in on the secret as early as the preceding winter.* The others probably knew very little until Bentinck's visit to the Rhineland in July and August. Exceptions may be found in some of the councilors rather than in the princes themselves. Goritz, for example, a member of the council of the Landgrave of Hesse-Cassel, had been taken into confidence as early as July.[60] The nearest indication of what any of them, princes or councilors, were told, is contained in Bentinck's statements to Fuchs, namely: that William was going to England to stabilize that country's government and to prevent it from joining forces with France for an attack upon the United Provinces. The part of the allies was to provide troops for protection of the United Provinces when the Dutch army should be withdrawn for the English expedition. What the German princes, other than Brandenburg, thought of these plans we do not know, but there are indications in letters from Waldeck to William after the Revolution was over that suggest that some of them considered that William might have done better to keep all his men on the Continent where they would be available against France.[61] Certainly the German princes did not want to provoke a war. In their own estimation they were taking defensive action. Yet there is more than a little reason to think that the four lesser princes were more interested in the money they would receive than in the general diplomatic considerations, at least until Louis broke the peace in September.

The new Elector of Brandenburg, although the most important of these allies, never kept up a sustained interest in Wil-

*This in spite of Japikse, *Willem de Deerde*, II. 244. References in the correspondence of Bentinck with Ham and Danckelmann in July show clearly that the matter had been discussed when Bentinck was in Berlin in May and June. Also William says in a letter to Bentinck that Hop can take on the renewal of the alliances but that the affair in England cannot be left to him.

liam's project. This is not surprising for the man was unstable, but it is also true that he had a great many irons in the fire and that this was not merely only one of many but also one in which he was concerned but indirectly. Even after the treaty was concluded he continued to be so dilatory about fulfilling his promises that Schomberg was almost frantic, to say nothing of being disgusted with the way money was being spent at the court for lavish ceremonies. In spite of all efforts to gain and hold his attention Frederick appeared to give more thought to Prussian and Polish affairs than to William's. Then, suddenly, at the end of August he sent peremptory summons for that same interview that William had begged for earlier. William naturally did not want it at all now, for the need was gone and every day was precious at home. But he did not dare refuse.[62] The meeting, which took place at Minden on September 7, seems to have been quite unimportant.

One cannot but wonder, therefore, why Frederick should have demanded it so urgently that William dared not refuse. Two reasons may be hazarded. The Elector's self-importance may suddenly have expressed itself in the notion that if this affair was going through he must make his own part in it quite clear so that there could be no doubt about the value of his contribution. Moreover, Danckelmann had all along been anxious to tie the alliance to the question of William's heir. He apparently hoped that as a *quid-pro-quo* William could be induced to make some definite assignment of his rights in the Netherlands to Brandenburg. Fuchs had been directed to bring this up at Celle, but had obtained nothing more than a vague promise. Whether or not Danckelmann pressed for the Minden interview for this purpose, he did expect to see Bentinck there and to take up the question with him, as it was one that was a little touchy for a mere minister to discuss with the Prince. Danckelmann now wanted a definite will in favor of Frederick. William was setting out on a dangerous project. If he were killed or even if, at which Danckelmann dared not hint although the thought must have been in his mind, the expedition failed and William found himself in the same position that Monmouth had been in three years earlier, on whom would his rights in the Netherlands devolve?[63] But

Bentinck, his wife worse again, did not go to Minden. Frederick himself did not discuss the matter with William — he may have been carefully forestalled — and nothing was done about it. Certainly William could never have made any such definite arrangement with Frederick for to have done so would have constituted a dangerous threat to the independence of the United Provinces. If the demand had ever been directly posed as a condition for assistance William would have been in a quandary. That it never was made was probably the result of a good deal of skillful parrying both by William himself and by Bentinck. After one last complaint from Danckelmann when the Minden interview was over no more is heard of the matter.[64]

Although the five German states composed what might be called the inner ring of the alliances, there were peripheral arrangements of several years standing with Sweden, Spain, and the Emperor. With the first of these there was a defensive alliance which William was able to evoke when France attacked Philipsburg.[65] The six thousand troops thus provided gave just that much additional strength to the defenses of the United Provinces, but the effect on the English situation was negligible. Spain and the Emperor were more important. The promise of Spanish subsidies had been used to bait the offers to the German princes at a time when William was unable to offer anything tangible from his own government because he was not yet ready to take the latter into his confidence as he would have to do to obtain additional funds. A few days before he went to Minden he had a highly secret meeting with the governor of the Spanish Netherlands of which nothing is known beyond the fact that it was related in some way to the expedition to England. Treaties between the Emperor and the United Provinces for the purpose of maintaining the Peace of Münster and the Peace of Nimwegen were reaffirmed in September [66] but no military assistance came from Vienna at this time.

The Hapsburg states are of much less significance for the assistance they gave than for the problems they created. If William, whatever his reason may have been, was trying to form an all-out coalition against France he could scarcely omit them, for it was upon their lands that the greatest encroachments had been made by Louis in the past. Had his concern been merely continental in scope there would have been little difficulty. It was the English connection that made for complications. Strongly legitimist and Catholic, with a loyalty to the Pope that stood in sharp contrast to the behavior of the Most Christian King of France in whom English fears of Catholicism were somewhat illogically concentrated, the Hapsburg rulers were alarmed at the prospect of an attack upon a brother monarch and a fellow Roman Catholic. Spain, with its weak government and imbecile king, could be dealt with fairly easily. The Emperor was a different matter. The need to keep in his good graces was a determining factor in internal policies after William was in control in England. In relation to the diplomatic aspect of the Revolution, especially just before the expedition left the Netherlands, there is more than a little suggestion that it was the need to keep the Emperor from outright opposition that led William to insist that a coalition against Louis must include England and that the only means of bringing her in was for him to get control of her government.

CHAPTER 4

Waiting for the Protestant Wind

After midsummer of 1688 William's relations with England ceased to be those of an outsider. He was now a potential usurper who stood an excellent chance of becoming a *de jure* king. The significance of his position derived from the strength of his military preparations and from his refusal to make any appreciable compromise with his own followers or any compromise whatsoever with James. He was going to invade England and not once did he offer to call off or even delay the invasion in order to give the English people and their King an opportunity to settle their dispute by themselves. Any indication that a solution might be reached without his intervention simply stiffened his determination and gave new speed to his preparations. The impending invasion, therefore, was of paramount importance. Its objective was debatable; its imminence was not. No settlement could be made until it was over. Because of that the England of this autumn became a strange dreamland in which King and people acted with the futility that comes from knowing that the most vigorous activity can be rendered nugatory by decisions as yet unmade. In this interlude, more than at any time after his coronation, William determined what was going to happen in England. The English people were not free agents. They paid the piper, but William called the tune.

Conscious though almost everyone was that something was going to happen, only a minority knew what to expect, and several who thought they knew were mistaken. Early in the summer the activities in the Dutch naval yards were noted and people talked of a possible attack somewhere along the North Sea coast.[1] But would this be an attack made by one nation upon another? If so, the mass of the population, whatever their political opinion, could be expected to close ranks to repel it, not only because of a natural impulse to self-defense, but, especially on the east coast with its centuries of rivalry with the Dutch, because of antagonism toward a traditional enemy. Even after the end of September, when semi-official reports from the United Provinces had made it fairly clear that this was to be a personal, rather than a national, venture, much confusion still lingered, and it is highly significant that when William's armies at last landed, many people who took up arms did so in response to a call to repel the foreigners, and found to their surprise that they had risen against their King.[2]

The combination of doubt and certainty, half knowledge and full knowledge, conviction and suspicion, was omnipresent, and it was disastrous to any chance for settlement not reached through trial by combat. James was affected no less than his people. By the last week of September he knew that what lay ahead of him was not a war with the United Provinces, but an invasion concerned with domestic affairs. So much he knew as proven fact. He was convinced, but he did not know, that William, if victorious, would claim the crown, but he did not know upon what pretext. Neither did he know the extent to which his own more prominent subjects were disaffected; if not actually disloyal, at least too uncertain of the outcome to be willing to commit themselves irrevocably against an invader who might be successful. Some of the people whom he distrusted might, if they had felt they had his confidence, have been more willing to stand by him firmly; some whom he trusted completely were false. Both the King and such people as were willing to try to counsel him were hampered by an almost total absence of any information about the terms that would have to be met. Charles I at least was given Nineteen Propositions to accept or reject. James was given nothing. Moreover the allusion to the earlier crisis can be misleading. The people who submitted terms to Charles were in a position to determine what they should ask of him, and whether or not his answers were satisfactory. No one in England was in a similar position in 1688.

So much has been written upon the steps that James took once he knew of a certainty that William was coming that it would be needless repetition to record them here in detail. They shall be examined only in relation to the all-important fact of threatened invasion. James has been accused of acting too late. A pertinent question might be: too late for what? It was not within his power to call off the invasion. He could only try to unite his people to meet it, and some of the most powerful among them did not want to be united. Any concession that he made was called either insufficient or insincere, and attempts to make up for insufficiency merely heightened the charge of insincerity. It is easy to assert that a man does not intend to keep his promises if he is never given a chance to prove otherwise. The time has long gone by when anyone can say whether James would or would not have stood by his word, but one does not have to be a sentimental Jacobite to point out that he had never been notorious for duplicity. On the contrary, he had been all too forthright in stating his aims.

True, he issued writs for parliamentary elections and then recalled them when he became certain of William's intentions. That might indeed be called a broken promise, but it should be noted that it was the *breaking*, not the *making*, thereof that was caused by the threat of rebellion. Even so, the rescinding of these writs was probably James's most serious mistake. Had he gone through with the plans he would have deprived his enemies of one of their greatest talking points against him, and he actually had less to fear from Parliament than they did. But it was a strategic rather than a moral error, and it is not difficult to see why it was made. Throughout the autumn James insisted that it was impossible to hold a parliament during a state of civil war such as he expected and such as did, to a certain point, come into being. There is much to be said for his contention. At the time the writs were recalled the invasion was expected within a few days, and it would have occurred much earlier than it did had not unforeseeable circumstances caused delay. No one knew where William would land. There was a prospect of local uprisings. How free would elections be in areas under the control of the Prince or his adherents? What should be done about those men among the invaders who could rightfully claim a place in the House of Lords, or, for that matter, about those who might be elected to Commons while they, too, were in arms against the King? Should they be allowed to take their places? Would either, Lord or Commoner, come? If they stayed away, not only would it be hard to call the parliament "free," but the leadership of the outstanding members of the opposition would be missing, a condition which could hardly be considered satisfactory by that group. Or should James II grant a blanket immunity to men whom he was convinced were plotting his deposition? The problem is perplexing, and it is small wonder that James was unable to solve it in the short time allotted to him for its consideration.

To hold a parliament, then, would have been difficult, however desirable and wise it might have been to do so. Placing the kingdom on the footing it had been at the time of his succession, which was, so far as James could make out, what the people wanted of him, should have been simpler, had not the prospect of invasion and the web of conspiracy raised obstacles. James acted to that end only to find a hydra monster before him. For each grievance that he removed, others appeared. Some suspicion of a man who all too quickly reverses an unpopular policy is natural, and to such a degree the people of England were justified in refusing to trust James. Moreover, it is disconcerting for any group to gird themselves for resistance and then find they have little to resist. Under such circumstances, to magnify what has not been granted, to minimize what has been done, and to look for new causes for complaint are not surprising actions. That, however, does not account for the way in which the country refused to accept what was given to it. No sooner did the King issue a proclamation saying that elections to Parliament would be free, that Catholics would be excluded from it, and that the inviolability of the Church of England would be maintained, than questions were raised concerning another statement in the proclamation to the effect that the several acts of uniformity would be confirmed in all their clauses except those *that inflicted penalties*. Did that last phrase, asked the bishops, mean that no penalties were to be inflicted upon Non-Conformists who held benefices? If so, the Act of Uniformity was void. The King answered that that was not his intention.[3] The bishops continued to question his sincerity. When some of them showed signs of coöperating, they were warned off by no less person than the Princess Anne.[4]

The same pattern was apparent elsewhere. Corporations whose old charters were returned, including London, complained about procedure and method, and men refused to accept the responsibility of office. Reinstated Lords Lieutenant quibbled over the validation of their orders. Old John Bramston's statement about gentlemen not wanting another kick in the breech has been quoted *ad nauseam*. But while the Catholic wind still blew these gentlemen had a chance to make sure that they would not get another kick. They did not take it. They waited for the wind to shift.

With a united country to back him the prospect of an invasion need not have been too worrisome to James. He could not achieve that unity. On the contrary, he faced a divided people and a strong opposition. Those who formed the opposition, however, cannot be called a party, for that would indicate cohesion and organization which did not exist. Neither can it be called Orangist, for that would imply considered adherence to William, either as a possible ruler or as a deliverer who would return, with the people's gratitude, after he had performed his task, to the place from whence he had come. Such considered adherence did exist among a number of people, especially in high places, but it was by no means widespread in spite of the propaganda carried on by broadsheet and ballad.

Roughly speaking the opposition falls into two broad groups. In the first we find the common people: in the towns, the petty tradesmen, the apprentices, and even the domestic servants; in the country, the small farmers and the agricultural laborers. Not all such persons, by any means, were opponents of the Crown, but discontent was widespread among them, some of it justified and some of it the product of deliberate agitation. Likely to be overlooked in a time when the franchise was restricted, they were nevertheless important: to James, because, in case of conflict, it was upon them he must rely for recruits for the rank and file of his army; and to William, because their determined opposition or support might well turn the scale of his enterprise. The extent to which they were politically mature and articulate, or grasped the issues of the time, is locked in the obscurity of a recordless people, but we should do well not to underestimate them, for among them were to be found the old soldiers of the Commonwealth, the followers of Lilburn and Walwyn. Some of them may even have been present at Putney and might have heard Rainborough say that "the poorest he that is in England hath a life to live as well as the greatest he." Or if these same men themselves were no longer living they had left to their sons and grandsons the tradition of that brief and glorious interval in the closing stages of the Civil Wars when the people of England raised their voices against both King and Parliament, only to be turned upon with fury by the officers of the New Model Army. It does not seem, however, that the new generation was thinking as clearly as did the old, for frustrated hopes had brought, as is so often the case, confused thinking. Where the men who had sponsored the *Agreement of the People* had cut through to the heart of their problem, the very nature of the government itself and of their position in it, their descendants focused their resentment on phantoms: the French, the Irish, and the Papists. In their religious fanaticism they had acquired that kind of interest in the Hereafter which is so often accompanied by an unrealistic appraisal of the Now. Their opinion was swayed by the sermons of the popular dissenting preachers and by broadsheets and ballads, which show a decided deterioration from the political writings which reached the people during the Civil Wars. The Prince of Orange was presented to them as a savior, so that they anxiously watched the weathercocks for a "Protestant Wind." The coming invasion was a symbol of hope. But hope for what? We cannot know simply because they did not. Yet its imminence kept them disturbed and easy prey to the rumors that assailed them from all sides. Aware that something momentous was going to happen, they found it hard to settle down to ordinary living, and by their nervous unrest they increased the widespread tension.

The second group is composed of the Protestant landed aristocracy and gentry. The reason for their opposition to James has already been stated. They saw in his disregard of the Tests a threat to their positions and to their continued monopoly of the political offices, most of which carried with them such ample opportunities for financial gain that they were looked upon as property. However, throughout the past year the unsettled conditions which had accompanied James's reorganization of offices, the mistakes or outright abuses made by inexperienced and overzealous men, had brought about enough bad government so that sincere desire for reform and for a solid legal basis for administration, especially on the local level, had been added to the more selfish interest. Many had begun to see that until the legal status of the dispensing power was settled reform according to law was meaningless. In October we begin to see subdivisions in this group, one of which we had better call pro-James. The men who formed it were willing to coöperate with the King on the basis of the reforms which he had already made and to rely upon the ultimate calling of Parliament to settle those issues which were still unsolved. Some of them, such as the Musgraves and the Duke of Newcastle, had been turned out of office only a few months before, and had never wavered in their essential loyalty to the Crown in spite of their opposition to some of its policies. Others, like Dartmouth, who had remained, and had been retained, in close contact with the King, constantly tried to persuade him to change his course. Now that they seemed to be successful, they bitterly resented the continued intrigue of the Orangist faction, especially the attempts of the latter to manipulate parliamentary elections to their own benefit. Several people in high places are to be found in this group. Among them we find Nottingham who, as we know, had gone so far in dealing with William that he had drawn back only from the last step: affixing his cipher to the letter of June 30. He did so because he preferred legal to military solution, and he had good reason now to hope that his objective was attainable. As for the Hydes, they had wavered in their opposition as they now wavered in their support. The part played by the last and greatest among them, the Marquis of Halifax is, as we shall see, open to several interpretations. But even those who, like Nottingham, hoped for the best, realized that no final decision could be made until after William had landed. Then, perhaps, actual warfare could be averted and conditions and terms discussed. Meanwhile, the efforts of many of this group were concentrated on defense measures. Others preferred to bide their time. We see them now and then at the King's councils, but they are strangely silent.

When we come to consider the remaining group, the indubitably pro-Orangists, we find that still another division is necessary, this time between those who were willing, and even anxious, to accept the assistance of the Prince, but who had either not considered the possibility of making him king, or else, realizing that that might happen, still believed that they could control events; and those who were, from the outset, thinking of dethroning James. Earlier in this study it was pointed out that it is improbable that many of the Orangist party *who remained in England* had serious thoughts of a change in rulers. Had they thought the matter through clearly perhaps they should have been able to see that their actions were almost incompatible with any other solution. That they did not do so can be attributed in part to the fact that their own immediate aims, such as recapturing office and influence, were paramount in their minds, and in part to the fact that the whole design was moving so swiftly to its climax that they had little time to think on its possible consequences. It is in this situation that we can see most clearly how the *fact* of the invasion determined conditions in England before it occurred. Men who might have been willing to come to a working agreement with James were deterred from doing so by their awareness that at any moment the Prince might land. By their unwillingness to use legal methods when the means to do so was offered to them, they made a change in rulers inevitable.

The division between those who did and did not think in terms of such change does not follow clear party lines. The Whig-Tory dichotomy was new at that time, and should not be overemphasized. Nevertheless it seems that most of the Whigs, such as Delamere, Lovelace, and Shrewsbury, belonged in the first category; while many outstanding Tories, such as Abington, Portman, and Seymour, belonged in the other. Just where Danby belongs is almost as difficult to determine as where to place Halifax. That he was deeply involved with the Prince, is of course, already established; that he wished to set him on the throne is not. Nor can we go too much by his opposition to such a step after the flight of James, because by that time he had become angered by what he considered to be slights from William. As late as October he stated the dilemma in which not only he himself, but many others were placed:

> We are in an ill-condition now in this country all ways, for if the King beat the Prince popery will return among us with more violence than ever. If the Prince beat the King, the Crown and the Nation may be in some danger.[5]

He was beginning to realize that the terms of decision had been taken out of English hands.

It is only by keeping the primary objectives of the pro-Orange group constantly in mind that we can understand their actions. The game of high politics was being played, with the principal offices of the realm as the stakes. It was obvious from the moment that the movement really got under way that the Whigs had no intention of making their peace with the King, for even if we grant them the most callous cynicism possible on the constitutional issues of the Revolution, the fact still remains that they were Whigs because of a fundamental belief in the need for controlling the royal power, and they did not believe that that control could be safely, firmly, and legally established so long as James in particular, or any Roman Catholic in general, was king, nor until the issue of the dispensing power was settled. But what of the Tories in whom a belief in the royal prerogative was as fundamental as its opposite was in the Whigs? Here we should remember that they had been the first to approach William. Most of them were so deeply engaged that they were no longer free agents, and the conspiracy for an invasion, with or without the objective of changing rulers, had gathered such a momentum that they could not stop it if they wanted to. So long as William was actually going to come whether they wanted him to do so or not, they could not afford to swing back to King

James and let the fruits of possible victory go to the Whigs by default. Neither could they afford to risk the heavy financial investments they had made by their contributions to William. Moreover they had ample reason to expect victory for they, even more than the Whigs, were aware of the thoroughness with which the plans had been made and the extent to which success had been assured long before the irrevocable step of actual invasion was taken. Their chief task then, was to do all they could to make sure that they would derive at least as much advantage from whatever happened as did the Whigs. It is for this reason that we see Danby and his friends, Sir John Lowther and Sir Henry Goodricke, working as hard in the north to protect their seats in Parliament as to pave the way for William. It explains also the strange mix-up in Lancashire between the Earl of Derby and Lord Delamere, where it seemed for a while more probable that the Revolution would turn into a fight between two supposed followers of William than into opposition to his opponents.

It is not only the distance in time that blurs our vision of the English scene in the autumn of 1688, for when we seek to sharpen our focus by bringing those days closer to ourselves through immersing our minds in the remains which they have left, the confusion is still there. At all times, whether of crisis or not, the motives of men are mixed, and even the wisest individual seldom acts with consistent intelligence. Many men in this crisis were working together, but they cannot be said to have been working toward a common goal, and even in their coöperation they were often at cross purposes with each other. Vague and varied discontents and frustrations were directed toward a particular object, the King, with all too little thought given to the question of whether or not he was personally responsible for the things which were felt to be wrong, or whether he had the power to set them right. This explains in part why a people in whom basic loyalty was still strong, could rise up for "The King and a Free Parliament" and by so doing pave the way for a usurper. It explains the pillage, the burning, the panic of the days of the Irish fear. It makes it possible to understand why the captive James could return to London amid the mild cheers of the common people.

A movement drawn from such a situation could easily have been formless and because of that, a fiasco. Even in those narrower circles where objectives were defined, though they may have differed according to the group that defined them, and grievances real, though they may have been merited, factional rivalry among the leaders could easily have led to failure. Only the presence of a strong centralizing force could give purpose and direction. That force was provided by the frail diminutive figure of the Prince, shadowy and unreal to many, but by its very dimness supplied with a glamour which closer acquaintance would dispel.

Tense as these days must have been for James and for those who waited in England, they were even more so for William. The preparations for the expedition must not be hurried, for haste could all too easily become synonymous with inadequacy. It was equally imperative that it should not be postponed until the coming spring, in spite of the danger of autumnal seas and of a winter campaign, and notwithstanding the gloomy fore-warnings of those who did not believe it could be accomplished at that season of the year. Delay might bring accommodation between James and his people, or Louis's excursions into the Rhineland might take on proportions which would compel both the German princes and the States General to insist that their troops be kept on the Continent, thereby wrecking the whole project. In the meantime there was much to be done and few whom the Prince could trust to do it. Illness deprived him of the services of the Pensionary Fagel, long one of his most trusted advisors and helpers. Madame Bentinck was dying, and only his greater loyalty to the man whom he had served since boyhood kept her husband from being constantly at her side. In this time of high excitement William's own grasp of and attention to detail was almost superhuman.

He was determined to have a strong military force with him when he arrived in England; in spite of the warnings of his English friends who, worried lest a foreign army should create an unfavorable impression, counseled him to keep his land forces to a minimum and to concentrate on his navy. Vehemently he answered them that he had no intention of exposing himself and the United Provinces to danger by invading Great Britain without an army that was strong enough to meet anything the King could muster, for he refused to rely either on the prospect of desertion among the royal troops or on a spontaneous uprising of the people.[6] The army he was collecting was, indeed, smaller in numbers than that of James, but it was composed of some of the finest regiments in Europe, seasoned soldiers who would be more than a match for the untried recruits that his opponent was gathering. He knew he could depend on this army, and he was not going to forego its support in return for mere promises.

The expeditionary force was being equipped to the last shoe button. During the late summer and early autumn the saddler, the baker, and the armament maker worked ceaselessly and under constant pressure from William or his immediate lieutenants such as Bentinck and de Wilde, to provide the necessary supplies. Transport ships gathered in the harbors and men scoured the country to bring together the means for another form of transportation, horses and wagons; for an army landed on the coast of England would be helpless if it could not move itself and its equipment. Money had to be collected, for the saddler, the baker, and the armament maker would not work for promises, nor the ship owners rent their vessels without some payment in advance and security for the future.[7] William staked his own personal fortune as did many of the English. French Huguenots also were willing to invest in the project. But that was not enough. It was the Dutch government itself, persuaded by Fagel, which supplied most of the funds when they loaned to William money which had been gathered to strengthen the border fortresses.[8] Even so he had only enough to finance his expedition to the end of December.[9] Beyond that he had to trust to luck.

Although the most important phases of the military preparations were centered in the Netherlands, others that were to be extremely useful in the long run were being looked after on the other side of the North Sea. When the King sent out orders to place the country in a state of defense such men as Danby rejoiced in the opportunity thus given them to raise the militia and put officers of their own choosing in control,[10] thereby at least neutralizing those troops if not actually winning them over to the side of the disaffected. William seems to have had very little to do with these arrangements and even less with the work being done to prepare the way for treachery within the regular army. That there was boring from within is hardly open to question in view of the desertions which took place later, but our knowledge of the operations involved rests on rather insecure evidence.[11] The assumption that those operations were exclusively confined to the higher officers is substantiated both by what we know of the treasonous activities and by the fact that when the showdown came both the lesser officers and the common soldiers remained loyal. Trelawney, a brother of the Bishop of Bristol who had been one of the famous "Seven," the infamous Kirke of the aftermath of the Monmouth rebellion, and John Churchill, later Duke of Marlborough, were undoubtedly the officers most deeply involved. William knew of their activities, at least to the extent of having information about the number and disposition of troops,[12] but he does not seem to have taken part, before his landing, in any of the plans beyond preparing a declaration calling all soldiers to his banner, and that was not to be issued until after the invasion was an accomplished fact.

This situation does not hold true with respect to the navy. Through his brother, who was a naval officer, Churchill was also working for the subversion of the fleet. Nevertheless the most important activities for winning over that branch of the service were directed from the Netherlands by William himself. The fleet was of vital importance. Intelligence reports revealed that in size it was inferior to that which would be mustered by the invader but if loyal and stouthearted in defense it could work serious damage even though it might not be able to prevent the expedition from landing. In it were veterans of the Anglo-Dutch wars who, remembering both ignominious defeats and glorious victories, might long to revenge the first and repeat the second. There were, however, indications that James had lost popularity here, as in the army, by appointing Catholic officers, and the religious issue thus raised was played on strongly by those who were working for William. Admiral Herbert was placed at the head of the Dutch fleet, outranking in actuality even such men as Evertson. To the natural complaints of his compatriots William answered that he was placing Herbert in command because he relied on him to win over the English seamen. Through the weeks immediately preceding action, Dutch boats kept constant surveillance over the British navy, even to the extent of discovering the sentiment of the seamen aboard the ships.[13] When the expedition finally sailed William was reasonably sure that it would meet with little resistance from England's fleet not only because the latter was outnumbered by his own navy, but also because he knew that the work of subversion had been thoroughly carried out, extending not only to the officers, but also to the common seamen some of whom were known to have declared that they would not fight against a Protestant and in defense of a Catholic.[14]

Liaison with the English was maintained through agents sent over by William himself; by Lord Dumblaine, Danby's son, who ran a frigate back and forth across the North Sea to carry people, messages, and money from England to the Netherlands; by the reports of the Dutch envoy in London, van Citters; and by information received from the English who came to join the Orangist army. From all of these sources William received dependable information of the temper of the English people and of the steps that James was taking to meet an invasion after he at last became convinced of its inevitability. This information received was probably important in determining that the place of the invasion should be the southwest rather than the northeast coast, for James was known to have disposed most of his strength in the latter area and in the vicinity of London and to have taken further precautions by ordering all cattle and horses along the coast of the North Sea driven twenty miles inland so that the invaders could not use them either for food or for transportation. Such measures cancelled out whatever advantages there might be in the work Danby had been doing in that region to raise forces for the Prince.

One thing that stands out clearly is that William was much better informed about what was going on in England than those who remained there were about his plans. They never knew when and where he was intending to land. He had said the previous spring that once the decision was taken he believed he would be able to sail by the end of September, yet in the middle of that

month the agent Van Leeuwen found Danby, Russell, and Lumley greatly disturbed because so little seemed to be happening in
the Netherlands, and fearful lest they be betrayed to James.[15]
Shortly before the first of October, Lovelace returned from
The Hague.[16] This seems to have been the last direct contact any
of these men or the others who were engaged in the project had
with William, and from then on they were even more dependent
upon rumor than James, who had his channel of information
not only through D'Albeville, but also via France, from the
highly observant D'Avaux. As time went on many began to
despair that the project could be undertaken so late in the
season.[17] Their worst fears seemed to be realized when a recon-
noitering expedition under Herbert was driven back to Hel-
voetsluys by a storm. Hearing of this, Lord Lorn, son of the
Earl of Argyle, left London for the Netherlands to urge the
Prince not to be discouraged by the mischance but to prepare
for a new attempt.[18] His trip was unnecessary. The damage was
not great and William had never entertained the slightest intention of changing his plans. Nevertheless the qualms of those
who sent Lorn were justified. If they knew positively that the
expedition would be postponed the wise thing for them to do
was to enter into measures leading to a compromise with James
before it was too late. But they certainly should not do so if
at any minute a hostile army might call quietus to such an
undertaking.

Military preparations were important, but just as urgent was
the need to prepare a favorable state of mind. This had to be
done in the Netherlands as well as in England, for William was
about to make a step which would not only call for the expenditure of great sums of Dutch money, but would also denude
the country's borders of troops and its seacoasts of a protective
navy. During the preceding spring and summer only a few
men outside of the Prince's official family had known of his
intentions. The story of those few is interesting not only for
what it tells us of their reactions, but also for the additional light
it throws on William's own state of mind. It has come down to
us through an account written by one of the men concerned,
Witsen, a burgomaster of Amsterdam.[19] He tells us that early

in 1688 Fagel mentioned to him and to two or three others that affairs in England were approaching a condition where it would be necessary for William to interfere whenever he received a request to do so from the important people of the country, and that in those circumstances it would behoove the States to stand by their Stadholder. A little later Dijkveld also brought up the subject. On both occasions Witsen refused to commit himself, but he was greatly disturbed. His uneasiness increased when, some time afterwards, the Prince himself sounded him out. Then came news of the birth of a son to James, and in his next talk with William, Witsen insisted that the occasion for the intervention had passed as he, William, no longer had a right to the crown. "The prince" wrote Witsen, "took this amiss and declared angrily that his right was as good as his." Almost immediately thereafter Dijkveld came once more with warnings that the Protestant religion was in danger. Witsen suggested that they trust in Providence and wait a few months. Two days later he was asked to come to The Hague. Reluctantly he went. The first person with whom he talked was Dijkveld who gave him many accounts of how well disposed the important people in England were toward William and how their plans could hardly miscarry. Bentinck, who came in while the conference was going on, backed Dijkveld emphatically. Witsen remained noncommittal. The next day he saw the Prince, who put it to him that the money already raised for defense was enough to finance an expedition to England and that any delay would merely give James time to strengthen himself. He expected to undertake the venture alone, but he strongly hoped that the States would stand by him. What was wanted of Witsen was active support in the Amsterdam council and elsewhere. Witsen, despite the pressure put on him, refused to do more than say that he would take a stand neither for nor against the project. The two of his fellow burgomasters whom he consulted agreed with him.

Witsen's obvious dislike of the whole enterprise stands out clearly in his account. Timidity was combined with a feeling that there was something not quite right about the project. His reactions were those of an individual but they probably would not have differed too much from those of the majority of his countrymen. Throughout the spring and summer, while his hopes were hardening into preparations, it was touch and go whether or not William could get the indispensable acquiescence of the Dutch. He was not popular among his own people, especially the leaders of the all-important city of Amsterdam, many of whom believed him to be a warmonger and wished heartily that he would cease his restless interference with the warlords of Europe. Wars were expensive and bad for trade. Nevertheless, through careful maneuvering and a judicious presentation of insinuation mixed with truth, William finally got what he wanted.

Throughout the summer the States General had been kept completely in the dark concerning the true reasons for the military preparations. Arrangements for the loan of troops from German princes had been made, as we have seen, without their knowledge or consent, the Prince acting on his own authority as Captain and Admiral General of the United Provinces. This authority, however, could not be used at home where the levy of troops was left to the individual provinces and cities. To them William implied that the preparations were defensive and retaliatory measures against France although, as he admitted to Bentinck, this was only a pretext.[20] The truth, or some of it, had, however, to come out, and the immediate occasion was the simultaneous presentation of memorials by D'Albeville and D'Avaux on September 8, demanding the reason for such extensive arming "in a season," as the former put it, "when ordinarily all such preparations, principally on the seas, cease." [21] As a result of these memorials a committee was appointed to consult William. According to their report the Prince outlined the reasons for danger as consisting entirely in the threatening attitude of France toward Dutch commerce and religion. England was mentioned only with reference to Louis's alleged attempt to detach her from friendship with the United Provinces. He declared that he had placed the country in a posture of defense in order to conserve those friends and allies that he had, and that he had borrowed troops because it was hard to raise an army by levy unless there were actual hostilities. He made no mention of any intention of using the army in England. That he had acted on his own accord he defended on the grounds of the need for a secrecy which would be impossible to maintain if there were open discussion in the States General.[22]

This report of the committee indicates the line that William was taking: emphasis upon danger from France. That he considered it a pretext is proven by the statements in his letters to Bentinck to which reference has already been made, although the counteractions of Louis came dangerously near to turning the pretext into truth. The same held true when it finally became necessary for him to declare to the States General, on October 7, his intention of taking the fleet and the stronger part of the army to England. Once again the danger from France was stressed. England was brought into the picture because Louis and James, said William, were banding together to destroy Dutch commerce. James's supposedly pro-French policy and his religious policies were so unpopular with his people that only two alternatives offered themselves. One was the establishment of a republic, and the States General, said William, had reason to know from experience what unhappy results could follow from that. Another was direct assistance to the people of England from the States General, given for the purpose of helping them to maintain their laws, liberties, and religion, and of saving them from a hateful alliance with France. The Dutch would, thereby, be but protecting themselves, for any success of Louis and James would place the Netherlands in peril. He did not attempt to conceal from them his own and his wife's interest in the affair. As prince and princess of the blood they had expectations to the crown which gave them reason to be concerned that there should be no dispute between the King and his people which might imperil their own rights to the succession. Immediate action was imperative. Lacking it the English people might take matters into their own hands and settle them to the great disadvantage of the United Provinces and of the Prince himself.[23]

To sum up: the United Provinces were led to believe that in permitting their army and navy to be used for an invasion of England they were engaging in a defensive war with France as the oblique enemy and their own commerce and religion as the object of attack. They seem to have given fairly wholehearted support to the project, although their reasons for doing so were

mixed. The French troop movements, the affair of the archbishop of Cologne, and the actual attack on Philipsburg, which
by this time had taken place, were indeed ominous. Fears on
the ground of religion had been intensified by the tales of
Huguenot refugees which were horrible enough to shake even
the burghers of Amsterdam out of their pro-French inclinations.
A desire to prevent a similar situation from coming about in
England sprang from real humanitarian motives and was stimulated by the sermons of their Calvinist ministers who readily
adopted the religious aims of the Prince as their own.[24] Commerce, however, was another matter, and one which could not be
so easily personalized toward France who had never been and
was not now, in spite of recent measures, a really serious com-
petitor. But England had been, throughout the whole of the
century, and was becoming more so as the result of James's
naval and colonial policies. Dutch traders who had been characterized in the Cromwellian period as having more concern
over a basket of raisins than over religion, who had been bel-
ligerently anti-English, as well as anti-Orange, could now see
a chance to gain the upper hand over their rival by insinuating
themselves into her government. Also, there may have been something in D'Albeville's suggestion that their High Mightinesses
were glad of an excuse to get their unruly and ambitious Stadholder out of the country.

The French and religious issues took the paramount position
in creating a favorable state of mind in the United Provinces.
In England the game had to be played in a somewhat different
fashion. For one thing, William could not and did not do anything overt there until he had landed, because if he did he must
state reasons and conditions which would give James something
definite to counteract. A barrage of propaganda was, of course,
laid, but it was done in part by Orangists in England and all of
it was of such a nature that William could, if necessary, dis-
claim it. The propaganda and the later official pronouncements
follow pretty much the same pattern and can be considered
together. The most important thing was that the people should
be prepared to accept the invasion, if not with eagerness, at least
without hostility, for a temporary victory gained by force alone

would avail little if the bulk of the population remained antagonistic. This became especially true after William had been induced to say that he would leave the outcome to the decision of
a freely elected parliament. In England not quite so much emphasis could be placed upon danger of an Anglo-French alliance,
for no person of any political astuteness could fail to remember
that Charles II had found it impossible to maintain just such an
alliance in the face of the stubborn opposition of his people expressed outside of Parliament even more than within it. The
French bogey, therefore, was shaped to fit the fear that James
might accept the use of French troops against his own people,
a fear that had its foundation in the negotiations to the same purpose during the Civil Wars, in the once-secret, but by now fairly
well-known clauses of the treaty of Dover, and in rumors that
leaked out from the Court of Barillon's efforts to bring about
just that very thing in this crisis. Given the English frame of
mind at the time it was easier for most of the people to accept
these rumors as true than it was for them to believe that James
was angrily refusing all of Louis's offers, as he actually did up
to a very late point when indiscretion born of desperation led
him to grasp at straws.

The chief effect of this French rumor was to produce confused
thinking, especially among the common soldiers and seamen,
including those who were being recruited to the militia and the
trained bands. When the invasion took place many of the land
forces who would very probably have fought more vigorously
against William if the French red herring had not been drawn
across the trail refused to do so either because they thought he
had come to protect them from French troops or because they
thought soldiers of Louis XIV's army were going to be bri-
gaded with their own. As for the seamen, many of them were
more interested in preventing a landing from France, which they
imagined was going to take place, than in forestalling the one
from the Netherlands, which was a reality.

Much the same situation held true with respect to Ireland.
With some cause, for the oppressor always has reason to fear those
whom he has oppressed, the English feared the Irish even more
hysterically than they feared the native Catholics and the French.

When he was at last prevailed upon to take steps to defend himself, James called over some of the Irish troops. In all not more than three thousand seem to have come, but the number was large enough to give substance to fears. Some clashes between Irish and English troops, plus others between the Irish and the townspeople where they were quartered, aggravated them. William played upon the hysteria by pointed references to the Irish in the proclamations which he prepared to issue to the army and the navy.

But playing on hysterical fears was not enough, for such fears could too easily be dispelled when nothing happened to substantiate them. In fact, we shall see that this procedure eventually backfired in a rather disconcerting manner. Moreover, while they could be counted upon to have considerable effect upon the common people, it was not likely that rumors would be very important with the politically mature leaders whose support William knew he had to keep during the tense days that were ahead. The principal line of propaganda in England, then, became that of stress upon maintaining the true laws, liberties, and religion of the country. This would appeal to everyone but the most Jacobite Catholics and most dyed-in-the-wool Tories and many of the latter were won over by the claim that James was subverting indefeasible hereditary right by a supposititious Prince of Wales. It could also smooth over factional strife, at least for the time being, as both Whigs and Tories could place their own interpretation on "true laws and liberties and religion."

Perhaps the biggest advantage, however, in insisting that his objective was to maintain the established laws was that it enabled William to claim that resistance to him was resistance to legally constituted authority. This was done by casuistry, it is true, but it worked. It formed the basis for that part of his Declaration wherein he called upon the people of England for their support. It appeared in his directions to his fleet when he ordered his admirals to inform any members of the English navy who offered resistance that they would be treated as enemies of the *kingdom* of Great Britain, thus drawing a distinction between loyalty to the King and loyalty to the nation.[25] He used it to form the concluding and the clinching point of his appeal to the soldiers and sailors to desert the ranks of James's army and navy and join his own:

. . . I hope God will put it into your hearts at this time to redeem yourselves, your religion, and your country from those miseries which in all human appearance can be done only by giving mee your present assistance who am laboring for your deliverance.[26]

In addition to appealing to the sentiments as well as to the convictions of the English it constituted a measure of safety against the danger of a charge of treason to those who were engaged with William, a protection, it is true, that was more illusory than real, for the widest interpretation of the statute of treason could scarcely provide foundation for it.

William left little to chance. Weeks before the invasion could be commenced he drew up not only the Declaration but also the appeals to the soldiers and sailors to which reference has just been made. When word from England indicated that the King might succeed in coming to a peaceful settlement with his people a second declaration was prepared, urging that no one be fooled by engagements that could be broken, by promises that could be retracted, and by concessions that could be withdrawn once the danger was over. Thousands of copies of all these proclamations were printed and sent over to various parts of England where they were placed in the hands of secret agents who were ordered to distribute them as soon as they received word of the Prince's landing. The equipment of the army included a printing press which was to be used for new broadsheets if the need arose.

The army and the navy were ready. The Dutch people had been won, some to acquiescence and many more to support. Louis XIV, acting almost as though he were conniving with William, sent his armies into the Rhineland where they no longer threatened the borders of the United Provinces. The English people waited for a Protestant wind, some with dread, others with eagerness, and more with a confused mixture of both, for in their minds they were not clear as to just what that wind would bring, and few who were unacquainted with the conspiracy could welcome the prospect of an invasion which would at the very least mean a disruption of trade and at the worst a bloody war.

To William the end of preparation meant the beginning of achievement. The man who as a ten-year-old boy had accompanied his uncles out to the ship that took them home to Restoration, was ready, now, to embark upon a voyage that would bring the Restoration period to a close. He had gone to England three times before: as an inexperienced youth of twenty, still ignored by his own countrymen and therefore both susceptible to and suspicious of the easy flattery of the English Court, and impressed by the fact that his uncle the King treated him as a man; as a bridegroom of twenty-seven, seeking to clinch his claims to the crown of England by marrying its first heiress in spite of her tearful protests that she wanted none of him; and as a mature warrior and politician, for it is never quite right to call him a statesman, of thirty-one, disturbed not only by the efforts of the most violent Exclusionists to divert the succession to his illegitimate cousin, the Duke of Monmouth, but also by the possibility that the very prerogatives of the crown itself might be so circumscribed as to make it useless to him who wore it. His concern with England was old and deep, stretching back to his childhood and to the memory of a mother who had never considered the House of Orange as anything but the servitors of her own family. The first language he spoke was English. The features of his face, the color of his hair, bespoke his Stuart heritage. The very name he bore, William Henry, had been given to him only after a violent altercation between his grandmother and his mother in which the latter lost. Her choice had been Charles. She was unimpressed by, if not unaware of, the coincidence that gave her only son the name of the last man who had successfully planned and accomplished an invasion of England.

It is no wonder that even his firm self-control was not enough to cover the emotions of those last few days. He has been characterized as cold and phlegmatic, but the descriptions of those who knew him intimately leave little room for doubt that the characterization is false, and that the calm stoicism with which he faced most of the crises of his life was the result of rigid self-discipline. Now that discipline almost broke under the combined prospect of danger and fulfillment. He was under no illusion about the danger. He knew that his friends had insisted on the presence of

Marshal Schomberg so that the army would not be left without an able commander if he himself were killed in battle. He was not blind to the possibility that the Jesuits, who were the worst advisors of King James, might think of an assassin for him as they had for those two great grandfathers whose names he bore, and with the same justification. But when he took leave of the States General he was calmer than their High Mightinesses. It was only when he parted from his wife that his command over himself relaxed, and there he was safe, for only the prying eyes of historians who read her memoirs have witnessed that scene.

Even at this late date no final decision seems to have been made about a landing place. The common interpretation is that the intention was to land in the North, and that only the continued northeast wind determined the choice. Certainly William was expected in the region about the Humber by his own henchmen as well as by the King. Even so late as November 5 (N.S.), Burnet talked glibly of the comparative advantages of Kent and Essex[27] and made no mention of the Southwest, but Burnet was seldom as intimately acquainted with William's plans as he thought he was. In spite of this apparent indecision there are several facts which indicate that William never seriously planned to land in the North or East unless he was forced to do so by the weather. For one thing, Admiral Herbert objected, insisting vehemently that those who considered that destination were landlubbers who knew nothing of currents, tides, and ports; and also that to concentrate the fleet there would leave the channel open to the French.[28] Moreover William knew, as has already been said, that the greatest preparations to repel him had been taken in that area, whereas the Southwest coast had been left unprotected except for garrisons at the major ports. The Southwest offered this positive advantage: the people there were believed to be less favorably inclined toward the King than those in any other part of the country.[29] The only drawback was that the reprisals taken after Monmouth's rebellion had been so severe that many might hesitate to expose themselves to any comparable danger again. It is improbable, however, that William was willing to admit much likeness between his own well-organized and well-equipped expedition and Monmouth's harum-scarum venture. There is also this possibility that should be considered, although it can rest on nothing but conjecture: the very fact that no plans to receive him were afoot in Devonshire may have made that region more inviting to William than York and the midland shires where Danby, Lumley, Wiltshire, and others were busy raising troops and preparing to take over strategic places. If he landed in the Southwest he would be on his own, aloof from the intrigue and inter- and intra-party squabbles which were sure to trouble the North. That locality would have to come to his aid once he had landed. He himself could take the South independently of them. That done the rest of the country would have to accept the *fait accompli.*

He set sail on October 20/30, but a storm drove him back, scattering his fleet and killing hundreds of precious horses. James was not surprised. Had not the Host been exposed for several days? Contemporary writers would have us believe that exaggerated rumors of damage were deliberately fostered to make the English think that the expedition would have to be abandoned [30] but the wildest reports that reached London were no more overdrawn than those which flew about the fleet itself, and indeed it was several days before the true extent of the harm done was known. Many, including some of the Dutch in the Prince's closest circles, thought that the enterprise could not be carried out in the face of the loss of the horses and the difficult season. The Prince himself was melancholy, and with good reason.[31] Nevertheless he refused to give up. The countryside was scoured for replacements of horses. New provisions of food were secured. Within a few days all was in readiness and only the continuance of unfavorable weather caused delay. At last, on the evening of October 29/November 8, Huygens, looking out of his window, noted that the wind was from the East. Once more embarkation orders were given. On the next afternoon the Prince set sail.

For a moment after it reached the open seas the great fleet paused, in what may have been indecision. Then, whether guided by the chance vagaries of a wind or by considered judgment, it headed to the Southwest, an imposing spectacle of sixty-one men-of-war and more than two hundred transport vessels.[32] The colors which flew from the frigate carrying the Prince were English. So were the words on the banner at the masthead: "The Liberties of England and the Protestant Religion." But under them, in letters three feet high, the proud defiant motto of the house of Orange Nassau flung its challenge. *Je maintiendrai.* I WILL MAINTAIN.

When the Straits of Dover were reached the fleet halted to close ranks. In that moment of rest it stretched from the French to the English coast; people gathered on either shore could hear the shrill music of the fife and drum corps. Then it continued on its way. Sunday it was observed by watchers on the Isle of Wight, some distance from land, and proceeding so slowly that the onlookers conjectured that the men-of-war were waiting for the heavily laden supply ships. Actually the delay was occasioned by religious devotions and grave celebration, for it was not only the Sabbath, but also the Prince's thirty-eighth birthday and the eleventh anniversary of his marriage. Before the devotions were over a heavy fog came up and under its cover the expedition continued on its way. During the night that same fog and a strong wind carried the invaders past Torbay where they had expected to land. The only possible alternative, for Plymouth was too heavily garrisoned, was Falmouth, far down on the bleak coast of Cornwall. For a moment disappointment ran so high that Admiral Russell told Burnet to get to his prayers for all was lost. Then once more the wind shifted, the Protestant wind, blowing now from the south, the only quarter of the compass whence it could take the invaders back where they wanted to go. Shortly after midday they reached their destination on the southern arm of Torbay: the fishing town of Brixham whose streets are banked on low bluffs that guard the deep V of an almost landlocked harbor. Once there, William's cousin, Count van Solms, was sent ashore with a reconnaissance party of ten or twelve dragoons. When he reported that there was no opposition, the Prince followed him, carried ashore from his small landing boat on the back of an old man of Devon. Some hours later, meeting Burnet, he called out to him with something as near to hilarity as he ever got in his life "Well, Doctor, what do you think of predestination now?"

Let us leave the story of the Prince's landing, his march through Devon, and his entry into Exeter, to Macaulay, who has brought all the power of his magnificent prose to tell of the impressive sight of the army and of the cheering crowds who greeted it along the way and into the streets of the city itself, but makes scant mention of the drizzling, chilly rain, the mud, the steep hills, and the narrow, rocky roads that were little better than footpaths; or of the grim undercurrent of fear that gripped a people caught between a powerful invading army and the orders of their King that any communication or commerce with it were treason and death. The days of high excitement were over. There was work ahead.

CHAPTER **5**

The March to London

Exeter was one of the largest towns of Restoration England and one of the oldest in the realm. Since that time, more than forty years before, when Henrietta Maria had been sheltered there during the last days before her flight to France, the placidity of the town's life had been broken only by the brief flare-up of the Monmouth rebellion. Now, in November of 1688 the old cathedral city suddenly became the political and military center of the country. Baggage wagons came in seemingly endless train from the nearby estuary of the Exe River where provision ships of the fleet were unloading their cargoes. Outlandishly garbed foreign troops swarmed the streets; Dutch officers and aides vied for space in the inns with those of the English gentry and nobility who were of insufficient importance to share the more spacious quarters provided for the Prince and his party at the Deanery. Nevertheless, as far as the inhabitants of the city were concerned, from the highest to the lowest, the prevailing mood was excitement rather than enthusiasm. One man was arrested for saying that he had a bullet for the Prince and knew well how to use it.[1] The Bishop and the Dean of the cathedral had fled. Several others had followed their example, including even a good number of the lesser tradesmen, who preferred to withdraw into obscurity by visiting friends nearby rather than to stay in the city where, although their business might flourish, they would have to commit themselves either for or against the invader. There was some difficulty in getting quarters for the troops, and not a few complaints were heard from both hosts and unbidden guests.[2] Most noteworthy was the fact that none of the gentry from the surrounding country came to offer their services or even to pay their respects. Where were those men who, according to the promise of the "Invitation," would join the Prince as soon as his presence in the land became known?

A passage in Burnet[3] has led to speculation as to whether or not William, angry because none of the Devonshire leaders came to him immediately, threatened to return to the Netherlands and turn over to James concrete incriminating information on the members of the conspiracy. It is certainly possible that the threat may have been made, for on other occasions, Zuylestein's mission of the preceding summer, for example, he seems to have brought just that kind of pressure on his followers, but it is hard to believe that he meant it seriously at this time. His own letter to Admiral Herbert in which he mentions the missing gentry gives no indication that he was greatly concerned about their absence. Moreover, in that same letter, written the day after his arrival in Exeter, he announced his intention to send all the transport vessels back to the United Provinces as soon as the artillery and baggage had been unloaded.[4] Two other letters to the admiral written during the next ten days make references to that intention with no hint that it was being reconsidered. It is improbable that William would have held to such plans if he was thinking of leaving. The length of his stay in Exeter can be much better explained by the need for the debarkation of the army and by the necessity of securing Plymouth and Bristol before he advanced toward London, than by discouragement over a seeming lack of enthusiasm.

William in fact had other problems which were more pressing. Briefly stated these were: first, financial difficulties; second, the organization of resistance to the King in the area under his control and its coördination with similar movements elsewhere; third, the prospect of actual combat with the loyal army; and fourth, the maneuvers whereby authority could be transferred from the lawful head of the government to himself, a step which would have to be taken even if nothing more than the declared purpose of his invasion were to be achieved. The solution of these problems went on concurrently. They were influenced by each other, by the actions of King James, by the general attitude of the populace, and by rivalries and differences of opinion among those who sided with the Prince.

Most immediately pressing was the need for money, for, as Japikse has pointed out,[5] the weakest point in William's position was the scantiness of his financial resources. Demands upon his treasury were many and heavy. His soldiers had been given strict orders not to pillage, and favorable as was the effect of this upon the English, it meant that the army could not live off the land as those of that day were wont to do, but that their leader had to pay his way in cash to make necessary additions to the supplies he had brought with him. As soon as he came ashore he commanded some of his officers to scour the country for more horses to make up for those he had been unable to replace after the recent storm. His own troops had to be paid, and funds must be available for the regiments being raised from the surrounding country and for those soldiers who were expected to come over to him from the King's army. Neighboring merchants and artisans received large orders for cloth and shoes.[6] For all of this William had very little ready money, for most of what had been placed at his disposal by the States General, together with the contributions of the English and the Huguenots and the sums he had drawn from his own private fortune, had gone to pay for transportation and for equipment purchased before he left the United Provinces. By the time he reached Exeter his treasury had sunk to four hundred thousand florins in general funds and seventy thousand florins of his own.[7] At that time it was planned to pay the foreign and Dutch troops with scrip after December 31.[8] Such promissory notes, however, could not be used to remunerate those from whom horses and other supplies were being purchased; nor was it likely that they would be satisfactory to the English seamen and soldiers who were being urged to desert their King with promises not only of

prompt payment of their wages, but even of cash in advance.
The fact that William risked his expedition on such a slender
margin is indicative not only of the extent to which he was
gambling his whole life on success, but also of his calm confidence
of obtaining it. The way he met the problem illustrates the manner in which he arrogated to himself the rights of the head of the
government and involved in his cause people who had no idea
of making him king. Supplies for his fleet were obtained by the
seizure of large stocks of goods kept at Plymouth to provision
the English navy. Such a step was not incompatible with the
right of conquest, but William did not assert that right. He
claimed to represent the true authority of the country. Bolder still
was his taking over the tax machinery of Exeter and the surrounding territory whereby he turned that source of James's revenue to
his own use. All money in the possession of the receiver of customs
was seized and officials who protested were dismissed.[9] William
Harbord, a former Exclusionist and perennial malcontent who
had joined the expedition shortly before it left the Netherlands,
was made paymaster of the forces, and an order was given that
all revenues were to be paid to him.[10] Three other Englishmen
were set to supervise the collection of the excise.[11] Should William be defeated these men, together with Harbord, would be
hard put to it to explain their actions to their lawful sovereign. It
became their interest, therefore, to see to it that William did
not lose. Even before the army set out on its march toward
London, Bentinck was discussing the possibility of another source
of money: that all those who signed the Exeter Association*
should make contributions in proportion to their wealth.[12] Such
a device, if it was proposed, must have met with some opposition or objection, for it was never put into practice. Not until
two weeks later was an alternative adopted. This was a voluntary
loan, backed by some of the men who had by that time come to
join William, notably Sir William Portman, one of the most
influential leaders in the Southwest. The sums thus gathered
served the double purpose of filling the treasury and of giving
their donors additional motive for desiring that the venture they

*For the nature and importance of the Exeter Association see *infra* pp.
172–173.

were financing should be successful. With these resources William made his way toward London.

But not before he had given a due share of his attention to those other matters with which he must cope. Although money was needed immediately, and the success of the expedition was to some degree contingent upon finding it, this problem was in many ways the easiest to solve; it could be dealt with forthrightly and any opposition could be overcome by force. That was not so of the others. They called for tact, cleverness, and patience. Inchoate resentment must be welded into effective opposition at the same time that those who were reluctant to coöperate must not be antagonized to such an extent that they would become active supporters of the King. The assumption of political authority meant also the delegation of that authority to followers in whom jealousy and bitter partisanship of several years standing lay just below the surface of a temporary unanimity. To meet and conquer the royal army would put William in the role in which he least of all wanted to appear, not only before England, but also before his continental allies and friends: that of an usurper. Here were contradictions and complications: a commander-in-chief with an excellent army that he would not use in the field if he could possibly avoid doing so, but upon which he relied for the effectiveness of his civilian activities; a political tactician who based his maneuvers on a display of military strength; a leader of a movement who forced his followers into line by compelling them to focus their sights on an objective so limited that they could not see for the moment that other and less desirable ends must be gained at the same time. Anyone studying the Revolution of 1688 cannot but be impressed with the way in which previously made plans for insurrection and desertion went into operation throughout the country, but he must reserve his true amazement for the way in which everything that happened, whether in his own immediate vicinity or in distant Yorkshire or Derbyshire was, ultimately, in the control of the Prince of Orange, who used what he wanted to use, discarded what he wanted to discard, and ignored, when it suited his purpose, even such old friends as the Earl of Danby himself.

William had never been foolish enough to believe either the unconsidered prophecies of enthusiasts that the whole country would rise for him as soon as he appeared, nor the more cautious half-promises of the writers of the "Invitation" that he would find sufficient support and little opposition on his arrival. By chance or by choice he had landed in that one section of the country where there had been no organized preparation in his favor either among the upper classes or the common people. Neither, of course, had any measures been taken to provide for defense against him, for the King had this, at least, in common with the Orangists: he did not expect an invasion in the Southwest. Those two features, however, did not cancel each other. William took full advantage of the absence of resistance, but at the same time he knew that he must not neglect the local gentry and nobility, nor ignore the opportunity to draw upon the rest of the populace for the rank and file of his army.

Within twenty-four hours after the debarkation at Brixham, letters had been sent to several of the more important landowners of southern Devon and Dorset, calling upon them as "true Englishmen and good Protestants" to join the Orangists. Enclosed in the letters were copies of the Prince's Declaration. Many of the men thus singled out were anything but pleased by the distinction, for in this last outpost of the Royalists of the Civil Wars and present stronghold of Toryism, James might be unpopular, but the tradition of Divine Right was still powerful, and the desire to keep out of trouble was even more so. A good number of the letters were sent, some of them unopened, to the King.[13] Not until William had been in the country a full week did one Burrington, a Devon gentleman who has only this claim to be remembered in history, come to join him. A mixture of motives in which political principles were mingled with a desire to climb on the band wagon and with sheer curiosity, brought in a few others. But if William had had to rely solely upon the support he received at or near the scene of his landing he would never have been able to go very far. Fortunately for him he did not have to do so.

The reaction among the common people was similar to that of those who considered themselves their betters. True enough, the march of the army brought out crowds of onlookers, for it was a spectacle that attracted even the mildly curious. True, too, there were some among them who honestly and with deep conviction hailed William as their deliverer. Then came the call for recruits to join the army, enough of them to form eight new regiments.[14] At first the response was fairly good, but even William's personal secretary, Constantijn Huygens, has attributed that more to hope for revenge for the cruel punishments of Monmouth's time than to positive enthusiasm for the new venture.[15] After two or three days the number of enlistments fell sharply, only to show a temporary increase when the ever-present dread of Papacy was aroused by a rumor that a French ship laden with cruel knives and other weapons to be distributed among English Catholics, had been captured off the south coast, a story which seems to have mushroomed from the fact that two small French ships had been driven ashore by the Dutch fleet.[16] When the temporary stimulus it provided had passed there were found to be enough new recruits for only about half of the companies that had been planned for originally.[17] Sir Rowland Gwin, one of the sanest and most judicious of the lesser Englishmen who were members of the expedition, attributed the lack of enthusiasm to William's lack of money.[18] It is nowhere apparent that William was much disturbed by the lack of recruits. Raw and untrained, their principal value to him would have been to provide commissions for the would-be officers among his English followers who were themselves too inexperienced to be trusted with the crack continental regiments.

His own army, it is true, was smaller than that of his adversary, but he was expecting the latter to be weakened, and the former to be proportionately strengthened by desertions from the royal standard. To accomplish this he depended somewhat upon those treasonous associations which he knew had been formed among the high officers such as Churchill, Kirke, and Trelawney, but he relied still more on his own appeal in which, as had been pointed out earlier, he stressed the duty of all true Englishmen to come to his support. "We shall ever" he declared

remember the service you shall do us upon this occasion, and will promise you that we shall place such particular marks of our favor on every one of you, as your behavior at this time shall deserve of us and the nation in which we shall make great distinctions of those that shall come seasonably to join their Arms with Ours.[19]

This inducement carried the tacit threat that those who did not heed it might later on have reason to regret their delinquency.

Desertions from the royal army began almost immediately. The day after the entry into Exeter a handful of guards came over to the Prince under the leadership of Lord Colchester. Three days later the next contingent arrived with Lord Cornbury, son of the Earl of Clarendon and hence a cousin to the Princess of Orange. An undependable young scapegrace who held an important command mainly by virtue of his close connections with the King's family, he had led four regiments west from Salisbury on the pretext that he was going to fight the invaders. By the time he made contact with the advance guard of William's troops at Honiton only a remnant of his followers were still with him for, the ruse having been discovered, most of the men and several of the officers had fled to rejoin the royal army as soon as they learned the truth.[20] The pattern set here was followed elsewhere. Officers deserted; the men did not. The Irish, although loyal to James, were terrified by rumors of heavy reprisals to be taken against all Papists, and wandered about a hostile country in abject fear. The Scots were unafraid, but they were also uninterested. They refused to fight for either James or William. In the remainder of the army those who did not follow the example of the Scots were left without officers to command them. The effect of the desertions, therefore, was not so much to increase the size of the one army as it was to disorganize the other.

In the last analysis, of course, William was depending very little on either recruitments or desertion, and almost entirely upon the strength and efficiency of the army he had brought with him from the United Provinces. It is interesting to see how he used this army, for his disposition of its forces reveals at least as much of political as of military strategy. The bulk of it was made up of Dutch and other continental troops, including, ironically enough, a goodly number of individuals who were Roman Catholics. Added to it were the six British regiments about whom

there had been so much controversy during the past three years.
Not on a par with the others in experience and training, they
had the virtues of enthusiasm and of being native rather than
foreign to the country where they were now employed. Even
before William left Exeter it was apparent that he was keeping
the European troops close by his side, sending the others ahead
to be advance guards or into the surrounding territory to take
over posts where resistance was either negligible or completely
lacking. Mordaunt had been sent as an advance herald to Exeter.
Shrewsbury and Sir John Guise secured Bristol. Russell was commissioned to negotiate with the Earl of Bath for the surrender,
and then the support, of Plymouth. By following this procedure
William gave adherence to his cause in those places the appearance of joining forces with other Englishmen rather than of
surrendering to or coöperating with a foreign army. He also gave
those officers themselves the opportunity to feel the glow of easy
victory. When there was a prospect of fighting or of serious
work William used men from the Netherlands. With one or two
minor exceptions the few skirmishes which occurred on the
march were fought by those troops. It was Zuylestein who was
sent to guard James after his capture at Feversham, and from
then on until his ultimate escape the King was in the custody of
continental soldiers. The Count van Solms, like Zuylestein a
blood relation of William's, commanded the first troops to enter
London. The over-all view shows very plainly that William
used the English, both those who had come with him and those
who joined him soon after his arrival, for relatively easy assign-
ments and in situations where it was to his political advantage
to use them. The others were kept in the background — if an
army of some ten thousand can be kept in a background — but
they were present in case of need.

Although he was willing to use the English who joined him
after his arrival William very probably preferred to rely for
success upon his own men. Support for this belief is to be found
in his refusal, three months earlier, to keep his land forces small;
and in his insistence at that time that he must take with him an
army competent to meet anything that James could collect.
Further strength is given to the contention by the fact that from

the time he landed until James's first flight had given an indication that all was over, William maintained almost no communication with those men whom he knew were preparing to rise or had already risen in the northern and central parts of the country. Apparently he appealed to the Northerners shortly after his arrival for mounted troops to supplement his damaged cavalry,[21] but beyond that they heard nothing from him. Danby especially was first concerned, and at last angry, because his repeated letters to William brought no replies.[22] William himself did not receive direct information from the rebels until he reached Axminster on November 23.[23] From then on letters were frequent, and the repeated requests for orders which they contain indicate that their writers had had no news of what was going on in the Southwest. For a while it had been expected that the invading army would make contact with some of the English rebels at Oxford, toward which the forces of Delamere, Northampton, Manchester, and Grey were converging, and where William himself headed after his conference with the royal commissioners at Hungerford on December 10. The moment, however, that he received word of the King's flight he changed his plans and headed for London alone, without having established communications with any of the English except those that had come directly to his camp.

Although we can note an absence of correlation between William's own march and the risings throughout the country, it would be well to stop at this point to see how those last were operated. They are significant not only because of what they contributed to the accomplishment of the Revolution, but also because of the way in which they illustrate factional quarrels and the use of propaganda and last but not least because of the wounds they left to cause dissention among the victors after the Revolution was over, dissentions that in some instances led even to conspiracies with James. Before going into them in detail it is important to emphasize once more that the men who had gone to the United Provinces to join William were almost without exception Whigs, or at the very least, men of no particular party affiliation. This may have contributed to the relative unanimity of purpose that seems to have prevailed in his immediate following. But only in part: William's own strong leadership must never be forgotten. The unanimity did not prevail in other parts of the country where old bitternesses between Whig and Tory flared up, and where new bitterness appeared between rival branches of the Tories.

The best illustration is to be found in the Northwest in the irregular triangle formed by Cheshire and Lancashire. Here for centuries the earls of Derby had been the most powerful nobles. A Derby had ridden with Charles I in the Civil Wars. The present earl had been Lord Lieutenant of the two counties until replaced in the general turnover of 1687 by the Catholic Lord Molynieux. With a few exceptions the region had been loyal to James, perhaps in part because there were a fairly large number of Roman Catholics living there.[24] Monmouth's futile attempt to seize the crown had caused the people of these shires, on their own initiative, to draw up a formal expression of abhorrence of his act. Their response to the three questions on parliamentary elections had been mixed, but generally favorable. It was in Chester and in neighboring towns that James had been most enthusiastically received during his progress in the autumn of the previous year, and not even the combined efforts of Macaulay and Burnet can prove that enthusiasm to have been completely sham. Nevertheless, there were intimations of trouble. Lancaster was the home of the violently Whig Lord Delamere, and certain others of that party scattered about the two shires were deeply involved with him in the Orangist movement. Fuel was added to popular emotion by the passage through this area of Irish troops after their landing in Liverpool.

The conflicts came to a head soon after William landed, but the ground had been prepared for them some weeks earlier. When James began his frantic attempt at reformation in October, Derby was restored to office. Having long since been approached by the Orangists, he consented to resume his duties not because he intended to be loyal to James, but because he could use his position as Lord Lieutenant to control the militia. In common with reinstated officers in many other places, he wasted several precious days by questioning the validity of his own appointment and those of the deputies who were to serve with him. On

November 1 he arranged with Delamere to use in the service of the Prince of Orange the troops he was gathering supposedly for defense of the King. For some days after he knew that the Prince had landed and that action was important Derby continued to stall, thereby arousing the suspicion of many of the people who were to serve with him. Probably the game he was playing was more than double, or maybe he himself was double crossed. At any rate, on November 15, Delamere called his tenants together, announced his adherence to the Prince, and ordered them to follow him, declaring that the Earl of Derby was doing likewise. Derby was furious, with good reason, for he knew that many of those whom he had been able to gather into the militia or to induce to take office as deputy lieutenants had come to him because they expected him to remain loyal to James. Delamere's premature announcement now frightened them off. For the next three weeks, although there was no bloodshed, the squabble between Derby and Delamere occupied more of the attention of both men than did the Glorious Revolution that was taking place elsewhere. Delamere accused Derby of deliberately leaving the Delamere estates to the mercy of the Irish and the Papists, and Derby retorted that there were no Irish or Papists in the neighborhood. Whether Derby was right or wrong on that point Delamere seems to have had no real cause for complaint as his estate was unharmed. In the long run all that Derby accomplished was to get himself thoroughly in bad with everyone, for those who were loyal to James had discovered his double dealing and he had not acted quickly enough to win the approval of the Orangists. After the Revolution was over the Lord Lieutenancy of Chester went to Delamere and that of Lancashire to Lord Brandon. It is hard to say which appointment would have stung Derby more deeply. Delamere had obviously done his best to discredit his Tory neighbor. But Brandon, loyal to the crown when so many others were deserting it, had worked with Roman Catholic officials throughout the reign of James. He had, however, the advantage of being the son of one of the leaders of the expedition, the Earl of Macclesfield.[25]

The counties to the North and East were scenes of similar squabbles, although in them the difference was not so much between

Whigs and Tories as between rival sections of the Tories. Danby was leader there, with the widespread Bertie family, of which his wife was a member, to back him. Catholics were still in charge of the garrisons at Hull and Carlisle, but the Protestant Reresby was governor of the city of York and the Duke of Newcastle had been made Lord Lieutenant of the county. Here as elsewhere, when James restored the officials that had been dismissed a year or so earlier their reinstatement was delayed by the refusal of the appointees to recognize the validity of commissions from Sunderland or, after the latter's departure, of Lord Preston who replaced him. The obstructionism was deliberate, motivated almost equally by a desire to snarl the government and by unwillingness to accept responsibility, for a smooth exercise of authority might have calmed the people and perhaps might even have made some of them think that James was sincere in his promise of reform. Soon, however, several of the newly appointed deputy lieutenants forgot their scruples about the validity of their appointments to the extent of beginning to raise troops, for although they wanted delay, they also wanted the militia under their own control.[26] When word came of William's arrival in Devonshire, Newcastle unwittingly and stupidly played right into the hands of the conspirators by declaring that the distant scene of the landing made it unnecessary to keep the North in a posture of defense. Sir John Reresby expostulated with him, and did his best to maintain the troops around York, for he realized that there was just as much danger from local conspiracies as from the invasion. He was ably assisted by several of the deputy lieutenants, but their purpose was far different from his: they were deep in Danby's plans, and Newcastle's actions had given them a wonderful opportunity to pretend that they were taking over the defense of the area. The true aim of their activity began to come out when they proposed to issue a proclamation which would not only declare their loyalty to the King but also call for a free parliament and the Protestant religion. Although the declaration sounded innocent and could be accepted by any decent subject as easily as by a would-be revolutionary, Newcastle was furious. Already involved in that traffic in boroughs which was to make his family notorious in the next century, he was not astute enough to see that lip-service to the ideal of a free parliament could accompany plans for the manipulation of the electorate. Even Reresby believed that in this crisis a declaration of loyalty to the King was enough. The other points paralleled all too closely the Prince's Declaration which he had read and disapproved.[27]

The Danbyites, however, insisted on their own declaration, and their fervor spread to the men in the militia. In spite of that, it would probably have been difficult to secure York by aboveboard tactics, for it should be remembered that most of the men in the ranks and several of the officers had responded to the call to arms in order to repel the invader, not to assist him, and they saw nothing disloyal in the above declaration in which loyalty to the King was emphasized. York fell by a ruse which had been planned well in advance. About midday of November 22, while the county officials, including Danby, were gathered in the town hall to discuss the nature of their proclamation, their meeting was disrupted by the excited entrance of one Colonel Tancred who called out that the Papists were in arms and had fired on the militia. Swearing loud oaths and brandishing their trusty swords, Danby and his henchmen rushed into the streets to defend themselves against the windmills. When the ensuing turmoil ended the city had been seized for the Orangists, and Reresby had been taken into polite but implacable custody.[28]

The Lancashire-Cheshire uprising furnishes an example of factional strife. The York incident shows us how an area that might have remained loyal to James was brought over to the opposition through a hoax which operated not only among the men in the ranks of the militia, but also among the officers, many of whom were uneasy over the steps they were taking. It is possible that even among the Orangists there were several, including Danby himself, who were partially sincere in their protestations of loyalty to the King and who did not foresee or else placed no stock in the possibility that he might be dethroned. Lord Willoughby told Reresby that "it was the first time any Bertie ever engaged against the Crown and it was his trouble, but there was a necessity either to part with our liberties or do it." [29] Some weeks later he voted, in the House of Commons, against offering the crown to the Prince and Princess of Orange. So did the three other Berties who sat in the Convention. So also did Dumblaine, Danby's son, who had taken part in the Yorkshire hoax, as well as that very Colonel Tancred whose outcry had been the signal for action. As for political principles, Danby, the purveyor of boroughs, the dispenser and receiver of bribes, the willing and even overzealous manipulator of shady deals with France, Danby had from the very beginning taken his place in the front ranks of the Orangists not from constitutional scruples but from the hope of regaining political eminence. He was to see the major rewards go to others no more scrupulous, but probably even less so, than himself.

Elsewhere in the North there are indications that convictions either for or against King James were not the paramount issue in determining the course of events. On November 30, Danby wrote to Sir John Hanmer, the governor of Hull, offering him five thousand pounds if he would surrender the city.[30] Hull came over to the Prince four days later. In Cumberland the Tory Sir John Lowther, deep in communication with Danby, began to urge the raising of the militia about the time York fell, but was opposed by the even more staunchly Tory Christopher Musgrave who finally gained control of the strategic city of Carlisle two weeks later, much to the disgust of the Lowthers. The root of the trouble here was that both men wanted to sit in Parliament for the borough of Carlisle. Musgrave eventually won the seat, but his opponent was chosen by both Cumberland and Westmoreland. Similar stories could be told of many other instances where personal rivalries were much more important than support of or opposition to the Crown. Nevertheless, in general there was a good deal of pro-James activity in the North, and it did not come to an end until the Irish panic of December 13 to 15 diverted the attention of both the loyal and the disloyal. By the time the true nature of that panic had been revealed, James had fled for a second time and the Revolution was all but over.

An examination of events throughout the country reveals the combination of well-thought-out plans and organization on the part of a few men with the disorganization of a people who were under the influence of propaganda so thoroughly that they were unable to think clearly. The leaders had laid their plans well in advance. Their grievances were definite, and to a large extent personal, although they were, in many instances, projected into more altruistic ideals of government. Their objectives were fairly clear. Lack of unanimity among them came from difference in purpose rather than from the absence of it. During the days of the Revolution itself the lack of agreement on long-term objectives receded into the background, pushed there by the common necessity of immediate victory for the Prince of Orange. Once he had left the Netherlands, those men in England who had prepared the way for him had no choice but to put their plans into action. Many of them were well aware of the differences of opinion in their own ranks, but each believed that his purpose or the purpose of his cause could be best served by the amount of the strength he could show to the Prince. This was especially true of the moderate Tories who, with the Whigs rising all around them, could not afford to let their rivals claim sole credit for the triumph that was to come. For the moment, then, differences were either forgotten or channeled into rivalry over who could obtain the loudest and strongest support for William.

The organization and well-defined purpose of the leaders stands out in sharp contrast to the lack of it among the people. Except in the Southwest, where the memory of reprisals for Monmouth's rebellion was only three years old, few of the latter had any personal grievances against the King. It was probably for this reason that the outbursts of the "mobile" throughout the country stopped, in most cases, short of bloodshed, for while the excitement of a moment, fired by deliberate agitators, can lead to pillage, burning, and destruction of property, it is hard to push the average man to the point of slaughter except in self-defense or for vengeance for an act done to himself or to someone he loves. Nevertheless, these people had been led to believe that the solution for everything lay in a free parliament. They responded eagerly to the slogan "The King, no Popery, a free parliament." Their energies were directed against the King because they were under the control of leaders who had already betrayed him.

The insistence of the Prince on a minimum of well-defined points, first: no repeal of the Tests, and second: the decision of a free parliament, had a tremendous value, for it concentrated attention on immediate problems and left the nature of their ultimate solution in abeyance. The Whig, the Tory, and the man with no party affiliation could all join a leader with those objectives. At some point, however, there had to be a transfer of authority from the King to his opponent. This had to be done whether or not the intention was to dethrone James. It had been evident since the middle of October that no reforms or promises of reforms were going to satisfy William. He was determined that everything that was done should come as the direct result of his actions, in his presence, and as far as possible, under his direction. He claimed to represent the legally established sovereign power of England which in theory could be interpreted as capable of demanding the obedience not only of the people of the country but even of its king. Whatever James II did, therefore, could be treated with contempt unless it was done under the aegis of the Prince. Yet it was hard for most men to separate king and nation in their minds, in spite of, or perhaps because of, the Civil Wars and the Interregnum. King and people must act together. Neither was complete without the other. Only the most fanatic Whigs and those who were touched by the lingering ideas of republicanism felt otherwise. When William claimed to represent the country he was also claiming that the King must act with him. He was not deposing the King unless or until the latter refused to recognize the intangible fusion. He was merely refusing to admit that James had any authority, and opening a way whereby men, even those of rather strong Tory principles, could render obedience to himself without violating their consciences,

William had begun to take steps toward the assumption of authority before he left the United Provinces, although he did not put any of his plans into active operation before the expedition set out. First of all, there was the Declaration with its demand for a "free parliament" elected on his terms. Added to this was the postscript or "additional declaration" with its reiteration of references to a free parliament and admonition to the people of England to place no faith in the reforms that James had granted. William's orders to Herbert to treat any English seamen who tried to stop the Dutch fleet as enemies of Great Britain should also be placed in this category, although it was never necessary to put them into effect. Another action of major importance was the making of a great and a small seal bearing the English arms which were given to William's secretary, Constantijn Huygens, to use for the validation of all documents concerning English affairs.[31] Huygens received these seals a few days before the first, unsuccessful, departure of the fleet, and retained custody of them until after the New Year when he was forced to yield them to the English William Jephson.

Immediately upon his landing William began to use the authority he was claiming to possess. Although his actions could be construed as those of a successful leader either of a belligerent foreign power or of a group in rebellion against legitimate government, it should be noted that he never for one moment referred to them as such, but persisted throughout in his assertion that he represented the lawful sovereign power in the nation. Upon that assumption he took actions that were normally reserved to the king. One of these was his order, conveyed through Burnet, to the clergy of the Cathedral of Exeter to omit prayers for the Prince of Wales. This, of course, was tantamount to ordering them to proclaim that they did not recognize the child's rights as heir to the throne. The clergy objected, but were forced to yield.[32] The seizure of the tax machinery followed. One of the king's officers who demurred was placed under arrest.[33] Commissions for new regiments were given out, not for a foreign army or for a rebel force, but as lawful acts validated by Huygens with the English seal.[34] Orders were given that anyone who attempted to stop the raising of regiments by arresting men who were on their way to join the Prince should themselves be arrested and brought before Sir Robert Atkins who was commissioned by William as a justice of the peace.[35]

These steps were taken immediately after the landing, without much reference to the English in the expedition. As the latter increased in number, and as political, as opposed to military affairs, became increasingly important, it was necessary to set up some kind of machinery of government for which the English themselves would share the responsibility. The first move in this direction was the formation, on or before November 17, of a Privy Council for English affairs composed of fourteen members all but four of whom had come from the Netherlands with the Prince. Most of them were Whigs, as was to be expected of any group drawn so largely from the original expedition. These men continued to be William's closest advisors on his march to London, and although others of note joined him there is no record of their receiving the status of Privy Councilors.

In spite of claims to a *de jure* basis, this machinery of government was in reality only *de facto*, and must remain such until further measures could be taken to regularize it. Moreover, it overtly committed to the Prince's cause only a small minority of those who were with him. The need for some device or procedure whereby the remainder would show their colors and at the same time indicate that they recognized that William's temporary exercise of authority was lawful, was supplied by Associations or statements which were drawn up by the Orangists in several parts of the country and submitted for signature to those who came to offer their services. The most important of these, the model on which the others were more or less based, was the one which was adopted at Exeter. The background which produced it was both significant and interesting.

That trickle of gentry coming in to join the Orangists, which had started so tardily and had been so small, began before another week was over, to take on much larger proportions. On November 15, William addressed these newcomers in a speech that was a masterpiece of double meaning. Opening his remarks with an apology for not knowing them all in person, he added quickly that he had a list of their names. He had come, he went on, according to their invitation. This introduction was at once specific and general. His reference to an invitation, especially before this particular group, was pure buncombe, for no one had invited him, and among his listeners there were only a very few who had taken part in that careful and noncommittal interchange of suggestions which had built up the conspiracy. Nevertheless, by the very act of coming to him, all who were there had made themselves a part of that body of the English nation in whose name William claimed to be acting and he was careful to let them understand that the responsibility for his presence belonged to them. Lest any might seek later to submerge into the anonymity of a crowd, he subtly informed them, by what might seem to be a rather diffident apology for not being able to call each by name, that their presence was a matter of record. After these opening words he told them that his duty to God had obliged him to protect the Protestant religion, and that his love of mankind had brought him to the defense of their liberties and properties. Then he rebuked them mildy for not having joined him sooner. These words were followed by a grim reminder that he did not need their armed assistance for he had brought a large fleet and a good army with him. What he did desire, he said, was that by their presence they should give countenance to his design. The total impression given by the address thus far was that the expedition had as its objective the establishment of the true laws of England, and that although this would be realized without the adherence of the local gentry, these last would be measured as true Englishmen in accordance with the extent to which they lent support to the cause. The concluding words were intended to remove any apprehension that the Prince might be deflected from his purpose, for, he said, although "we might have had a bridge of gold to turn back" [36] he intended to remain. Noble as those words sound one cannot but question their veracity. Where was the gold to come from? Certainly it would not come from James, who would have paid no Danegeld to his nephew, even supposing he had had it to pay.

The delicate suggestion that those who were flocking to Exeter might well think twice before they deserted, bore fruit, two days later, when Sir Edward Seymour appeared. His coming was considered a distinct triumph, not only because of the high esteem in which he was held throughout the Southwest, but also because he was believed not to be particularly well inclined toward the Prince. [37] Immediately upon his arrival he pounced upon the fact that although the new arrivals were to some extent implicated by their very presence, there was no device whereby they publicly bound themselves to the cause and declared their determination to see it through. They were tied together, he said, merely by a rope of sand. The outcome of his protest was the Exeter Association, drawn up by Burnet, and approved by William.

We, whose names are hereunto subscribed, who have now joined with the Prince of Orange for the defense of the Protestant Religion and for maintaining the ancient government and the laws and liberties of England, Scotland and Ireland, do engage to Almighty God, to His Highness, the Prince of Orange, and to one another, to stick firm to their cause and to one another in the defense of it, and never to depart from it, until our Religion, Laws, Liberties are so far secured to us in a free Parliament that we shall be no more in danger of falling under Popery and Slavery; and whereas we are engaged in this common cause, under the Protection of the Prince of Orange, by which in case his Person may be exposed to danger and to the desperate and cursed attempts of Papists and other bloody men, we do therefor solemnly engage to God, and to one another, we will pursue not only those who made it, but all their adherents and all that we find in arms against us with the utmost severity of a just revenge to their ruin and destruction. And that the Execution of any such attempts which God of his infinite mercy forbid, shall not divert us from Persecuting this cause, which we do now undertake, but that it shall engage us to carry it on with all the vigour that so barbarous a practice shall deserve.

This Association could be signed with a reasonably clear conscience by any man who believed in the obligation of the King to govern according to certain established forms; a belief which would be shared by most of the moderate Tories as well as by all of the Whigs. Nothing indicated any intention to dethrone the King or, what is more important, to question the existing rights of succession. Many copies of it were printed on the press which the Prince had brought with him, and through the distribution of those copies the Association became the formula for the recognition of William's authority, thus identified with "the ancient government" throughout the South and West. The Earl of Bath used it when he took over Plymouth. Ormonde read it at Oxford. It was placed, as we shall see later, before the members of the brief rump parliament in London in December. Significant of the moderate character of its wording is the fact that many who signed it, including Seymour himself, were among those who refused to vote for offering the crown to William and Mary.

Meanwhile other declarations, some of them more immoderate, were being drawn up in other parts of the kingdom. Those who constructed most of them seem to have been ignorant of the action at Exeter. There are indications in a letter of Danby that some of the declarations had been prepared well in advance of the invasion.[38] While they follow the general formula, not only of the Exeter Association but also of the Prince's Declaration, two of them go much further in their statement of principles. The one given by the Earl of Devonshire to the Mayor of Derby deplored the landing of a foreign army but still more "the occasion given for it by so many invasions of late years on their Religion and Laws." Unlike the Exeter Association, it recognized that the interest of the Prince of Orange might be other than purely altruistic by lauding his willingness to submit his own pretensions to the decision of a free parliament. The writers "heartily wished and humbly prayed" that the King would call such a parliament, but if he refused to do so they declared themselves ready to defend their religion, the laws of England, and the liberties of the subject. The absence of an explicit oath of adherence to the Prince is insignificant, for Devonshire had been one of the earliest to be involved with him and had attached his cipher to the letter of June 30. A paper subscribed to by the nobility and gentry at Nottingham about the same time openly identified the signers with the Prince by stating that they were joining with him "for the recovery of their almost ruined laws, liberties, and religion." Calling upon all true Protestants to do likewise, this manifesto contained a hint that the King might be dethroned by dwelling at some length upon the principle that resistance to a tyrant was not rebellion. As it came from the most decidedly Whiggish group of those who were in arms, there is at least a possibility that those who wrote it were thinking in terms of a change of dynasty and were seeking by this means to justify transference of their allegiance from James to William.[39]

Other declarations throughout the country were less specific. Danby issued some sort of manifesto in York, as did the Duke of Norfolk in the eastern counties.[40] They seem to have omitted reference to William and to have stressed a free parliament. But with or without specific references, all of the declarations formed a basis of transfer of authority by explicit demands for a free parliament and by implicit insinuations that so long as James refused to call one he had no right to the allegiance of his subjects.

In the meantime William continued to extend the authority which the Association of Exeter had only strengthened and had certainly not originated. Upon his departure from Exeter he installed Seymour as governor of the town, thereby taking upon himself the right to make civil appointments. Parenthetically it might be added that this appointment not only catered to the vanity of a welcome ally, but also removed from the immediate circles of the Prince a High Tory who might conceivably prove troublesome. The commission of the Earl of Bath as governor of Plymouth and of Pendennis Castle was given under the authority of the English seals in the custody of Huygens.[41] It is true that these and other similar acts kept the normal wheels of local government in operation and prevented the turmoil which might have come from their disruption. It is equally true that William was acting as the head of the state and denying the validity of any orders which emanated from James. But eventually, and regardless of whether or not the issue was put to the test of armed combat, he would have to come to some kind of terms with the existing *de jure* government in London, either to make an outright denial of its authority, or to treat with it for a settlement. To see how this point was reached it is necessary to review the steps which James was taking to cope with the encroachments upon his sovereign power.

How is one to explain James Stuart during these crucial weeks? The easy way is to brand him as a coward and a fool, but he was neither. That rejected, it is possible to mention the state of his health. He was in misery, unable to sleep without opiates, and subject to nasal hemorrhages which weakened him pitiably. But he stands in opposition to his nephew who had never in his life known what it was to possess a strong physique, and whose chronic asthma was now aggravated by the generally damp English climate and by the cold rainy weather through which he pushed his march toward London, so that he coughed constantly, was feverish, and slept little. Each of the opposing forces was led by a sick man. All that can be said in the defense of the one is that he was not accustomed to illness, whereas the other was.

We are forced to go back to obscure psychological forces operating in a middle-aged man who, before he was an adolescent, had known the shock of flight and of imprisonment and of his father's tragic death. He seems to have had one fear and two sources of strength. The fear was that he might meet the same fate as his father. One source of strength was his elder brother, Charles. Few people can recognize James in portraits of him as an adult, but whether they realize it or not, a great many are familiar with his face through the well known "Baby Stuart" of Van Dyke. Ironic symbolism, for James never really grew up! Throughout his life, until he became King, there had been no need for him to rely solely on himself. Always, when his irresponsible actions, and there were many of them, had pushed beyond the limits of acceptance, his brother had been there to pull him back to safety and to soften the blows of retribution. The very constancy of that support had made him unaware of its importance, had even led him to look upon it as an irksome, rather than as a needed restraint. Bereft of it he had turned completely to his other source of strength, religion. James accepted Roman Catholicism with the fervor of a man who had seen one thing after another in which he trusted give way, and in this time of crisis his devotion deepened.

The fear and the one remaining strength seem to have guided his actions during those last days of his reign to the exclusion of anything else. The thought of death was probably no more awful to him than it is to any mortal, but the ignominy of a public execution was something he could not face. A fatalistic foreboding that, given a chance, the English people might turn on him as they had turned on his father crops up again and again in his letters from the time of the Exclusion Controversy up to the Revolution. The only ways he could see of evading that almost certain disaster were either to deny his religion and throw his fellow Papists to the wolves, or to take flight. Because he would not accept the one alternative he is called bigoted. Because he chose the other he is branded as a coward.

This was the man on whom those in England who did not welcome a change in rulers had to rely, the bough on which the dynastic cradle hung so precariously. He is not a tragic figure;

it is difficult either to pity him or to despise him. Therein may lie his tragedy. The constitutional issues at stake meant little to him, yet it was on those issues that the overt battle was being fought. If he had been willing to call a "free Parliament" he *might* have saved his crown. The cost would have been to permit the "evil councilors" to be punished, and to allow the old laws to be applied with unmitigated or even more stringent rigor against the Roman Catholics. Much as it would have violated his conscience James might have consented to pay that price if he could have convinced himself that to do so would obtain the desired end. But he could not. From the moment he was forced to admit to himself that William was coming he was sure that his nephew meant to dethrone him. At first he took refuge in a belief, inconsistent with his general suspicion of them, that the people of England would never allow that to happen. This belief received its first blow when he read the Declaration with its statement that "a great many lords — both spiritual and temporal and many gentlemen and other subjects of all ranks" had invited the Prince to come. It was completely shattered before another month was over. James trusted no one.

Fatalistically, with a growing conviction that flight was his only solution, James met the challenge of the self-styled champion of the Protestant religion and the laws and liberties of the Kingdom over which he himself ruled as "Defender of the Faith." Many of the political leaders of the country were in arms against him, their number increasing as time went on. He could turn for counsel only to a fast-diminishing group in London that fell into several factions: Catholics who advised him to intransigence; loyal Tories who would have liked to see him compromise but were willing to stand by him to the point of exile; sober statesmen like Nottingham and Godolphin who disapproved of the course he had taken but sought earnestly for a viable solution that would save his crown; and the self-seekers who stayed with him while they thought he might win and deserted him at the first inkling that he could not do so.

On October 31 a Colonel Langham, one of the men who had been sent from the United Provinces with orders to distribute the Declaration after they were certain that William had landed, was arrested and several copies of the paper were taken with him. One of them was delivered immediately to the King who read it with consternation. Up to that time he had believed that the Prince was acting upon his own initiative, or at most, with the support of only a handful of English malcontents. Here, however, was the assertion that a great body of temporal and spiritual peers had *invited* the invader to come. To prevent this information from reaching his people James issued a proclamation warning them that distributing the Declaration or any like papers would be considered a crime. The effect on the public, according to one observer,[42] was to stir its curiosity as to the content of the forbidden pamphlet. The Spanish ambassador in London obligingly handed out copies of it to anyone who asked for them.

James might try to keep the Declaration from the people, but he could not keep them in ignorance of the Prince's landing. That was countered by another public proclamation issued on November 5 wherein James asserted that despite pretences to the contrary, William's designs were nothing less than usurpation of the crown, toward which steps had already been taken in the demand that all of the people of England should come to his assistance. The proclamation continued with what was, in essence, a rebuttal of the Declaration. It maintained that the legitimacy of the Prince of Wales, upon which William had cast doubts, had been attested by "witnesses of unquestionable credit." The demand for a free parliament was answered first by the accusation that William himself was the prime obstruction to it, for no parliament could be free so long as there was a foreign army in the land, and second, by the promise that one would be called as soon as the invaders had been repelled. This parliament would indeed be free, for the ancient rights and privileges had already been restored to the electoral bodies. In conclusion James promised that he would listen to all the complaints and grievances that this parliament might have to make, and he repeated and reaffirmed the assurances he had already given of his intention to maintain the religion, liberty, and property of his subjects.

These were the first acts by which James sought to hold his

people together. When he tried to supplement them by others of a more positive character he ran into difficulties. His earnest desire that all lay and ecclesiastical magnates whose continued presence in London seemed to betoken loyalty should publicly repudiate William's declaration, was met with cautious refusal. The bishops, led by Canterbury, excused themselves on the ground that to do so would be a civil act for which they as clergy had no authority — a far-from-subtle reminder to the King of the stand he had taken at the time of the trial of the preceding summer. The temporal peers, for their part, hemmed and hawed, and finally raised the objection that the authenticity of the Declaration had not been established, although many of them must have known that there could be no doubt on that score.

James was no more successful when he called upon his peerage for advice. A sharp conflict between his views and theirs was apparent at once, growing out of difference in opinion as to the purpose of the discussions. James wanted counsel on how to repel an invasion and put down rebellion among his own subjects. The peers suggested methods of compromise. James felt that it was both too late and too early for such measures. The reforms he had already made seemed to have done no good. Any further concessions should come after victory, not before it. This disagreement on the ends to be attained was complicated by the unwillingness of any group except the extreme Roman Catholics to take a bold stand which would place it in unquestionable defiance to William. Clearly many of the peers, whether or not they were numbered among those that had been dealing with the Prince, were sure enough of his ultimate success not to wish to be marked as his opponents. Many of them were playing for time. This lack of wholeheartedness among the peers is at least as responsible as James's hesitancy and vacillation for the London government's failure to adopt any definite policy.

Even when left to themselves the peers quarreled. There was a general feeling among them that a parliament must be called, although some were in sincere doubt as to whether or not this was the right time to do so. Yet no sooner was there agreement on petitioning the King to order an election than another and more specious objection was raised. Halifax maintained that such men as Jeffreys and the Earl of Rochester must be excluded from any list of signers on the grounds that one of the first demands upon Parliament must be the punishment of the King's "evil councilors" among whom those two would be numbered. This point was reasonably well-taken with Jeffreys, but it is hard to see its applicability to Rochester who, although he had been a member of the Court of Ecclesiastical Commission, had certainly not been in James's good graces for the past two years. It is, therefore, reasonable to assume that political rivalry moved Halifax, and Nottingham who supported him, much more than sincere conviction. At last, after ten days of squabbling, a petition was presented to the King. Signed by Canterbury and five of the bishops, and by ten temporal peers, including both Clarendon and Rochester, but lacking the names of Halifax and Nottingham, it reached the King on the night of November 16 as he was preparing to join his army. His answer was a reiteration of his refusal to grant the request so long as William was in the kingdom. In his eyes a state of war existed, and he still retained enough confidence in victory to refuse to parley.

What happened in the next ten days is well known. Just before he left London, James, having heard the news of Cornbury's desertion, had called together the officers who were nearby and had offered to take back the commissions of any who did not wish to fight for him. For answer he received loud protestations of loyalty, even from Grafton, Kirke, Trelawney, and Churchill, all of whom had long been plotting against him and were planning even now to go over to William as soon as conditions for doing so were favorable. His confidence bolstered by these avowals, the King went to Salisbury, and it was while he was there, incapacitated by severe nosebleed from taking personal command, that the great wave of desertions among the officers took place. The army was now so disorganized that combat was out of the question for the moment. James returned to Whitehall, ill and discouraged, to find that his daughter Anne had fled the night before.

Three courses were open to him: to barricade himself in his capital, to compromise, or to leave the country. He resolved on a combination of all three. The unpopular and Catholic Hales was removed from the command of the Tower, and Skelton, so recently a prisoner there himself, was put in his place. Preparations were made to send the Queen and the Prince of Wales to France, and James promised his wife that he would follow her. The peers were once more called into council. Although the thought of flight was undoubtedly present in his mind at this time — he even mentioned its possibility quite openly [43] — its desirability was strengthened by the unpalatable advice which the peers, now brought to some show of unanimity through desertions and through the exigencies of the occasion, had to give him.

James opened his first meeting with the peers by referring to the petition for a parliament which, he said, he was now willing to grant. Several of the lords who had signed the petition seemed to think that that was enough, but others warned the King that he would be compelled to do many things that would be distasteful to him. Their leader, Halifax, again backed by Nottingham, further insisted that calling a parliament and opening negotiations with the Prince of Orange would not be enough. The King must also denounce all relations with France, dismiss all Roman Catholics from office, and publish an amnesty to all those in rebellion against him. During the next few days the King yielded to some of these demands. He did not dismiss the Roman Catholics, although only a few remained, nor did he publicly renounce any reliance upon France. In view of the fact that he had never relied very heavily upon France it was unfortunate for him that this should have been made an issue just when he was planning to send his wife and son to that country and seriously considering going there himself. He did, however, begin the process of issuing writs for a parliament to meet on January 15, and he published a proclamation of amnesty to all those in arms against him. Most important of all, he arranged for a commission, to be composed of Halifax, Nottingham, and Godolphin, to go to the Prince of Orange. Simultaneously he continued to plan for his own flight, stimulated thereto by repeated warnings from Halifax that, considering the state of affairs, "he could not expect that the Prince would accept of any concessions than such as would put it out of his power to do such things as he had done heretofore against the laws." [44] Just how far he was pushed in his decision to leave the country by increasing discouragement over the fact that each concession seemed to bring new demands and complaints, and just how far his concessions were insincerely granted in order to stall for time, it is impossible now to determine. It may be that James himself never knew. In singleness of purpose and in rigid determination to see what he had started through to its end he was no match for his nephew.

The Prince received the first word of his uncle's willingness to treat with him on December 1 when a herald arrived with a formal request for passports to permit the visit of the royal commission. By that time his march had taken him to Hindon, only a few miles from Salisbury. Although the journey thus far had been highly successful, William was nevertheless under a tremendous strain. He slept badly, and was severely troubled by his constant ailment, asthma, which was undoubtedly as much aggravated by the damp cold weather as by his anxiety over the outcome of his venture. Those about him complained of his frequent harsh words, for the slightest mishap brought on a storm of abuse to those who served him. With each day's advance, however, the situation had grown brighter as one after another of the English army officers had come over and as word had been received of risings in other parts of the country. The news had been so encouraging that before William was five days out of Exeter the men in his army had begun to speak of the possibility that everything would be settled without any fighting, and that impression had received added strength when it became known that the King had returned to London. The English had been especially exuberant, and had congratulated each other "that now the business is done." [45]

The general optimism was now heightened by the arrival of the request for passports for the Commissioners. Zuylestein laughingly commented that the King sought to capitulate.[46] Van Citters, joining his countrymen two days later, reported that the King was going to give His Highness a free hand.[47] Such high spirits, however, were most prevalent among the Dutchmen of lesser rank. In the highest circles, and among some of the Englishmen of all ranks, they were tempered by the realization that the time had now come when fine words would no longer be enough, that a concrete settlement of the issues raised in the Declaration must be reached, and that in reaching it account must be taken of factional rivalries and of the unsatisfactory character of some of those who had come to join the Prince. The sober Sir Roland Gwin was one of the first to voice doubts. Hearing that a parliament was to be called, he warned that the Prince must be careful to place men of unquestioned integrity in his service or the parliament would do no good, and he pointed out that Roles, one of the men who had been made receiver of the excise, was known for a "false player." [48] There was more to this than petty jealousy, for if the Prince was to live up to the high words of his Declaration, he must work to put the government of England in the hands of men who were above reproach.

Apparently giving little attention to the problems confronting him, the Prince continued his march. At Hindon he was joined by the Earl of Clarendon who only a few days before had been sitting in the King's council, cringingly lamenting the desertion of his son, Lord Cornbury. The next day's journey brought William to Salisbury where he was received by the Mayor and the aldermen who donned their robes of state for an official welcome. Their guest entered the city not as a conqueror but as the ruler, recognized as the representative of the nation's sovereign power to whom the inhabitants owed allegiance. Men and women flocked to watch him as he ate as they flocked to watch royalty. After lingering in the city for two days he marched on and arrived in Hungerford on December 7. It was there that the Commissioners from the King reached him.

Now the issue of what to do was placed squarely before him. This was his problem: how was he to live up to the words of his Declaration, and at the same time gain the objective he so dearly desired, the crown. If he met the King's Commissioners he would be compelled at least to consider the propositions for settlement which they would lay before him. By the very act of treating with them he would be recognizing James's position as legitimate head of the government, something he had hitherto refused to do. If he himself had been unaware of the danger it was clearly put to him in a letter which he must have received at least two days before Halifax and his associates arrived. Written from London by Sir Robert Howard, one of the men deep in the plans of the Whig group, this letter is of utmost importance, for it clears up once and for all any doubts that William might personally have been unaware of plans to make him king.[49] Howard had been visited a few days before by Halifax who, after telling him that he had accepted the task of going to the Prince, had admitted that he was troubled by the assignment. Howard reported that he had replied that Halifax had good reason to be troubled, for his action could give rise to suspicion that he was trying to delay the advance of the Prince's army by holding out for a treaty when none was possible. A treaty suggested compromise and accommodation, but "everything must be built on new foundations." Howard saw the whole procedure as a plot of the Tory-Church party to gain the advantage of being those who had posed as mediators between the King and the Prince and to reach a solution whereby, with James still on the throne, they could hold the balance of power in the kingdom. But, he warned, any suggestion that the Prince was sympathetic toward this objective would dampen the spirits of the people who

so far from having any thoughts of settling things by an accommodation, only fix hopes of remedy by a total change of persons . . . and therefore, as Your Highness has come to redeem us from the threatening miseries of Popery and Slavery, we can never suffer the name or trust of power in any other person.

This message bears a marked similarity to others the Prince had received in earlier years, notably those from the Countess of Sunderland and from Patrick Hume in that under the cover of words that professed loyalty to him, it conveyed the warning that any suspicion that he was willing to compromise with the King would cause defection of many of his followers. Yet those who held such sentiments were Whigs, and with them William was never entirely at ease. He knew that they were a minority, and, in comparison with the total population of the country, only a small one. Moreover it was the Tory following that William wanted, for it was that following which would maintain the valuable royal prerogatives once the "change in persons" was

THE MARCH TO LONDON 185

accomplished. To keep in the good graces of this latter group he had to go through the motions of negotiating with the King.

This letter also shows us the dilemma faced by many an English politician of the day. If James had a chance of remaining on the throne those who were prominent in working out an accord between him and the invader who claimed to represent his people, stood, if they were successful, a good chance of capturing the prominent offices in whatever new government would be formed. If they failed they were open to the displeasure of each of the two parties between which they sought to make a compromise. The Whigs, for their part, resented any suggestion of a compromise, for they formed the majority of those who, through taking up arms, had laid themselves open to charges of treason, and even if such charges were not pressed, they felt that the risk they had taken warranted victory for their policies and rewards for themselves. The less violent extremists on the opposite side, which means for the most part those who were not Roman Catholics, saw little chance for complete victory for the King. Many of them pressed for an accommodation not so much because they believed in it as because they thought it was the only way of salvaging anything. This widespread belief that James could not win accounts for many of the desertions in higher circles, for example: that of the Earl of Clarendon.

William faced the situation with the same clear realism that he had shown all his life. That he was feeling the effects of the nervous strain and of the physical rigors of his march we already know, but he was too accustomed to ill health for the weakness of his body to lessen the vigor of his mind. Although what he faced now was the climax of his design, the situation was not markedly different from that which had confronted him ever since he first determined to act. Halifax, commenting on him less than a month later, wrote "Note, a great jealousie of being thought to be governed. . ."[50] This characteristic was one of the most striking in the man's make-up. Combined with it was an even greater aversion to being made the tool of others. From the moment that he responded to the first overtures of the English he had been aware that he might be used, that his and his wife's pretensions to the crown were of less significance than hunger for offices and their emoluments, if one takes the worst view, or ideals of government, if one takes the best. Already we have seen how carefully he planned his actions so that he took no irretrievable step until the majority of the English who supported him had committed themselves so far that they could not turn back. He had so maneuvered matters that the responsibility for his actions was theirs, not his. He knew that most of them could not, and that the others would not, retreat now. It was up to them to decide the process by which final settlement should be reached.

An incident recorded by Huygens is worth noting in this connection. The day after they had heard about James's desire to send commissioners some of the Dutchmen in the Prince's camp fell to discussing how difficult it would be to reach an accord, especially with reference to the Prince of Wales. Bentinck, who was present, brought his comrades up sharply with the warning that this was none of their affair, that all problems must be examined by a free parliament, and that His Highness must abide by his Declaration.[51] These words, and we know that as always, the man spoke the thoughts of the master, provide the keynote for subsequent action. William was scrupulous throughout, not only in insisting on the observance of legal forms, but also in compelling the English to handle affairs themselves.

Hungerford, on the Kennet River, is somewhat more than half way from Salisbury to Oxford. It is a gentle town today, a favorite spot of anglers, many of whom find their lodgings at the old Bear Inn once a part of Henry VIII's dowry to Anne of Cleves. The present host takes pride in the fact that Queen Elizabeth never slept there. On December 7, 1688 *The Bear* suddenly found itself the headquarters of the Prince of Orange and his staff. Every available bed chamber was taken. Public rooms were soon so overcrowded that Huygens complained he could scarcely breathe. After one night the Prince himself left for the more spacious manor of Littlecote, two miles to the west. Before his departure, in the long low dining room, under beams already black with many years of smoke, William had held his first meeting with the King's Commissioners.

All three of the Commissioners were men with whom the Prince had held correspondence before. He was personally better acquainted with Halifax and Godolphin than he had been with most of the Englishmen who actually joined him. As old friends these men would have been justified in thinking that they might have a private interview, and there is reason to believe that they hoped for just that. They were disappointed. Not only unwilling to lay himself open to the charge of private negotiation, but also determined that none of the English should be able to evade their responsibilities and that he himself should appear, not as a foreign invader, but as the representative of the country, William received the King's emissaries surrounded by leaders of the English nobility. For a moment his poise was shaken. When the cold, formal note of the King, inscribed by a secretary in French, the language of diplomacy, was handed to him, William remarked that it was the first letter he had ever received from his uncle which had not been written by the latter's own hand in English. This is the only evidence we have that he was conscious of the poignant overtones of his act, that he remembered the time when his mother's brothers had given him a great part of the little warm personal affection his childhood had known.

The emotional interlude was short-lived. William told the Commissioners that they had seen his Declaration and knew from it that he came in response to the call of the English people. What happened was properly their affair, and he would do nothing without their agreement. He asked that their propositions be put in writing. With that he left them. Requests from the Commissioners for private discussions with some of the English in the Prince's party, particularly that of Halifax to see Burnet, were refused. William was too canny to give the wily marquis an opportunity to draw out the garrulous divine, and moreover he was not going to stimulate the already growing jealousies in his own ranks by permitting any of the latter to make private propositions to the King's representatives. Halifax and his two companions were excluded from the private discussions of the Orangists, and whenever they were present at any large gatherings, were condemned to the isolation of the crowd.

The proposals which had to be considered were summed up in the following memorial of the Commissioners:

Sir: The King commandeth us to acquaint you that he observeth all the differences and causes of complaint, alledged by Your Highness seem to be referred to a free Parliament.

His Majesty, as he hath already declared, was resolved before this to call one, but thought that in the present state of affairs it was advisable to defer it till things were more composed.

Yet seeing that his people still continue to desire it, he hath put forth his proclamation in order to it, and hath issued forth his writs for the calling of it.

And to prevent any cause of interruption in it, he will consent to everything that can be reasonably required for the security of all that shall come to it.

His Majesty hath therefore sent us to attend Your Highness for the adjusting all matters that shall be agreed to be necessary for the freedom of election and the security of sitting, and is ready to enter immediately into a treaty in order to it.

His Majesty proposeth that in the meantime the respective armies may be restrained within such limits, and at such distance from London as may prevent the apprehensions that the Parliament may in any kind be disturbed, being desirous that the meeting of it may be no longer delayed than it must be by the usual and necessary forms.[52]

During the next day and a half, while the Orangists were considering what answer should be given to this message, Halifax and his two fellow Commissioners had a chance to look about them. What they saw gave no cause for reassurance. One glance about the crowded streets of Hungerford was enough to erase the impression given by optimistic newsletters recently circulated in London that the invading army was untrained, poorly equipped, and badly led.[53] Although all three were familiar enough with English politics to be aware that gathered in this little town were individuals of all shades of opinion, their lack of contacts kept them from realizing the potential danger to the Orangists themselves inherent in those differences. William had been wise in compelling isolation. So far as the Commissioners could observe the atmosphere was triumphant, fearless, pungent with refusal to brook the least suggestion of compromise.

In the frame of mind induced by these circumstances these men made no effort to soothe the King with false hopes. A short time after their official reception they reported that they saw no disposition to stop the march of the army, but rather a determination to go ahead so strong, especially among the English,

that not even the Prince could hold it in check. Basing their
assumptions on what they had been able to gather from common
discourse, they tried to give the King some forewarning of the
response his advances would meet and of what he would be
expected to do. The old familiar insistence on the dismissal of
all Catholics from civil and military offices, which they themselves had advocated unsuccessfully, was repeated with the
emphasis of a probable *sine qua non*. Only faint promise was held
out to James that the concessions he had already made would
be accepted. His pardon of all those in arms against him had
been to no avail, the insurgents refusing to accept it on the ground
that by doing so they would admit guilt. Instead they expected
a declaration from the King that they had been acting in defense of the laws and therefore needed no pardon. Even the
hope of solution through Parliament was shadowed by the suggestion that it must not be dissolved without the consent of
its members.[54]

Although the Commissioners did not know it, in the conference of the English nobility and gentry which William had called
to draw up an answer to the King's message a spirit was becoming
manifest that was even more threatening than what they had
observed. The stated objective of the Orangists — the convocation
of a free parliament — seemed, it is true, to have been attained,
with only the working out of details still in need of consideration. At this point the reluctance of many of the disaffected to
submit to that very institution in which they claimed to place
their trust came openly to the fore from a background where
it had been observable for some time. Before the Commission
reached Hungerford a newsletter had announced that "Small
regard is given by the King's enemies to the intended calling
of Parliament, such imagining the great business will be over in
half forty days."[55] In the Prince's own camp the astonished
Huygens had heard Burnet declare that the people of London
laughed at a free Parliament so long as any Papist remained in
England or any Irish troops in the armies of the three kingdoms.[56]
Talking to Clarendon that same day Burnet was even more outspoken. "It is impossible," he cried. "There can be no Parliament!
There must be no Parliament! It is impossible!"[57]

Burnet was far from expressing a sentiment peculiar to himself. Moderate newcomers to William's circle were disturbed over the views they heard on all sides.[58] Having taken the Declaration at its face value, they had joined the triumphal progress toward London in order to compel the King to submit to the familiar mechanism of parliamentary discussion. Now they were called together, or so they thought, to agree on terms whereby that stated aim could be realized. The only questions that seemed to call for immediate solution were first, how to provide for the safety of any men now in arms against the King who might be members of the House of Commons; and second, how to dispose of the two opposing military forces so that there should be no clashes between them. The terms which the Commissioners brought indicated that the King would be reasonable on both points. To the dumbfounded amazement of men like Clarendon and Abingdon, and even of Shrewsbury, the majority of the English whom William had asked to confer among themselves insisted that any negotiation with James must be conditional upon his having first recalled all writs for parliamentary elections. Overriding the futile and outraged protests of the moderates, they got their way.

But they did not keep it. When the statement drawn up at the conference was brought to Littlecote for approval, William struck out this surprising demand. The next morning at another, and still more heated meeting at *The Bear*, it was reasserted, and the terms in their original form were returned to William. The messengers charged with the task of informing him what had been done found that the hotheads had reached his presence before they were able to do so. William consented to listen to the views of the majority group, but after he had done so he calmly deleted the controversial words once more, without bothering to answer the arguers.[59] The latter were as helpless as they were furious. If William insisted upon abiding by the Declaration there was nothing they could do.

That is the bare outline of the story. Its meaning is fairly clear if it is considered in conjunction with the whole course of the developing opposition to James. These men were far from being opposed to calling a parliament eventually. It was one called by

James at this time to which they objected, for it suggested a compromise, for which they were in no mood. They wanted to be absolutely certain that James was beaten and that he, together with the more or less wavering Tories, understood that he was beaten. Only then should there be any move toward working out the problem of reconstruction of the government. The King would be called before a parliament only for judgment, not for negotiation. Parliament itself was desirable or acceptable more because it was the only known mechanism by which the political, as distinct from the military, aims in view could be realized than because it stood for a continuation of legal government. These men were asserting a basic principle of revolution ". . . that whenever a government becomes destructive of these ends it is the right of the people to alter or abolish it." In the end, not only at Hungerford, but also in the subsequent Convention, their ideas lost out, with the result that this became a revolution in defense of law, not a revolution against law.

Once that is understood, William's position is no longer puzzling. He had no desire whatsoever to attack the existing principles of English government or to help others to do so. The laws as they existed were satisfactory to him, if he did not indeed believe that they placed too much, rather than too little, restraint upon the king. Moreover, unlike the noisier Whigs among his adherents, he was keenly aware of several facts. One was the necessity of not antagonizing the Tories; another, that it was the politic way to go through the form of accepting negotiation when one knew that he held the upper hand and could be reasonably sure that his opponent would not accept the counterproposals made in answer to a request for terms. There was also the matter of calling a parliament based on such firm legal footing that its decision could never afterwards be called into question. So long as James remained in the kingdom he, and only he, had the right to convoke such a body. If he left the country, well and good. Then the claim could be made that his absence imposed on others the obligation to act in his stead. "We may drive away the King," William insisted, "but perhaps we may not know how easily to come by a Parliament." [60]

It might be claimed that in overruling the decision of the conference William was going counter to his principle of forcing his adherents to accept all responsibility. To a certain extent that is true. He could not, however, permit them to take such a step, for to do so would make him false to his published Declaration. That, he knew, would be unwise if not, in fact, disastrous, because of the impression it would make both in England and among his allies and friends on the Continent. It was also unnecessary, because the terms which he offered were hardly such that James could be expected to accept them. "You will find a letter of credentials which the King has given these commissioners" wrote Bentinck to Herbert, "with the proposition of the said commissioners and the response which his Highness had made, *but I do not believe that it is possible that the King will accord these points.*" [61] (Italics mine.) Do we need to add that he was undoubtedly voicing William's opinion?

Drawn up by the English nobility and gentry, but given final form under William's supervision, the answer submitted to James through the Commissioners required in the first place "that all Papists and such persons as are not qualified by law be Disarmed, Disbanded, and Removed from All Employments Civil and Military." Whether or not he knew from Clarendon, whom he had questioned closely a day or so before, that the assembled peers in London had pressed James to do just this and that James had been unwilling to yield, William could still be certain that James would consider compliance on this matter not only as the abandonment of everything for which he had stood throughout his reign, but also as a dishonorable desertion of his fellow Catholics. The second demand would be equally hard to meet: "That all Proclamations which reflect on Us or on any that have come with Us, or declared for Us, be recalled, and that if any persons for having assisted Us have been committed, that they be forthwith set at liberty." James, in other words, must not only cease to refer to rebellion but must also recognize the justice of the cause of those who had risen against him. In doing so he would have to admit himself a tyrant. Maybe he was one, but he could hardly be expected to agree with those who thought so. The next points were reasonable enough suggestions for disposal of troops pending a final settlement in accordance with James's own suggestion that both armies be kept some distance from the vicinity of London. Then followed a provision that "to prevent the landing of French or other Foreign Troops, Portsmouth may be put into such hands, as by Your Majesty and Us shall be agreed on." The last demand: "that some sufficient part of the public Revenue be assigned Us for the Support and Maintenance of Our Force till the meeting of a Free Parliament" was by far the most arrogant. James was not only called upon to recognize that those who had rebelled against his rule were justified; he was asked to provide for the expenses they incurred by that action. This was not negotiation. It was a statement of terms preliminary to complete submission.

What form that submission would have taken we shall never know. While the discussions at Hungerford were only the penultimate step in the transfer of authority from James to William, they made the ultimate transfer inevitable. James could, of course, have accepted the terms then offered to him. It is tantalizing to conjecture what dismay would have prevailed among the majority of the Orangists had he done so. But the emotion would have been dismay, not consternation. There would have arisen merely the necessity for devising new means to achieve the desired end: "nothing less than a complete change in person." Those who today write pontifically about what James could or should have done to save his throne are no less short-sighted than the men who were still unable, in mid-December of 1688, to admit the inevitable. Statements of what ought to have been done are pointless unless equal attention is given to the possible consequences of such deeds. No good chess player fails to consider his opponent's next move; if he is really good he looks still further ahead. Considering the situation merely as an abstract problem in which no counteraction need be thought of, James probably should have dismissed all Catholic officials, not only because it would have been expedient to do so but also because he had kept them there in defiance of statute law even though the courts had upheld him. Aside from consenting to submit the validity of his son's legitimacy to parliamentary investigation, that was the only demand made upon him that he had not at some time tried to meet. Had he gone thus to Canossa, James would have forced his adversaries either to admit the sincerity of his concessions or to come out in the open with a demand for his abdication. It might have been a wise move, but James was not as clever or as unscrupulous as the Emperor Henry IV, nor were his opponents as honorable as Gregory.

Let us leave conjecture for reality. Under the protection of a crowd Halifax had at last managed to have a few words with Burnet. "Did they have a mind to have the King in their hands?" he asked. "By no means" was the answer, "for we would not hurt his person." "What if he had a mind to go away?" the Marquis queried next. Burnet replied that "nothing was so much to be wished for." [62] This, of course, was the easy, the obvious solution, one that William was hoping would be reached, as is shown by his above-quoted statement "We may drive away the King." Whether he based his assumption on his own analysis of his uncle's character, or whether he had positive information is not clear, but it is probable that the one supplemented the other.[63]

Be that as it may, the fact remains that, before the Commissioners returned to London, James did go, impelled not so much by fear for his own safety as by the desperate hope that his subjects, left to confusion, would be compelled to call him back on his own terms. He was disappointed. And as if to climax the ineffectual nature of his whole life, he was denied success even in flight, for he was captured and recognized before he could get out of the country.

The Revolution seemed now to be over. Not only was James making little if any bid for the allegiance which he had essentially, if unwittingly, renounced by his departure, but any attempt to return it to him after his capture met with prompt and effective discouragement. The peers in London, for their part, could claim authority as the old Great Council of the realm. They did not, however, by any means constitute the whole of the peerage, for many of the members were either in the immediate following of the Prince or working for him elsewhere. Moreover, while it is true that they came nearer than any other body in the country at that time to having a historical constitutional basis for their authority, and while the Prince was aware that he would have to respect their jealousy of birthright, any suggestion that they could have asserted their claims in opposition to the advancing Orangist army is unacceptable. The real government of England was in the camp of the Prince of Orange; the exercise of it, already established in the localities through which he had passed, was soon to spread throughout the country.

Word of the King's flight was received with joy in the head-quarters of the Prince. It also brought about a change in plans, for William realized that it was imperative that he should go to London at once. Without waiting for any official invitation from the City itself or from the peers, he turned away from Oxford, whither he had been heading, in the direction of the capitol. That same day he at last acknowledged Danby's increasingly irritated communications with two letters, by the first asking the earl to come to him that he might have the benefit of his counsel now that the King's retirement had so greatly changed the aspect of affairs; and by the second urging that all those who had risen in his cause be sent home, for the common soldiers would but be an expense to the country and their leaders could better occupy themselves by securing their elections to Parliament.[64] These letters are only two of many indications that William thought the struggle was over.

That opinion was shared by a good many people. Within a short time after he had turned toward London, William began to receive word not only from his friends in the capitol or from those who were still undecided, but also from his recent opponents. The morning of December 11, Feversham, commander of the King's army, wrote that, His Majesty having left England, he had informed all the troops under his command that they would receive no further orders from him,[65] which was the equivalent of telling them to disband. The same day officers of the Irish troops sent word that their men were ready to submit, and requested that William take measures for their safety.[66] The officers of the Scottish regiments wrote in much the same terms except that they did not have to worry about reprisals taken against their men.[67]

All this strongly resembled military surrender. Meanwhile the civil landslide, too, was taking place. To the Prince at Henley came a delegation from the City of London [68] to present him with an address, drawn up the morning after James left, from the "Lieutenancy" of the City expressing their great gratitude for his undertaking and urging him to come to London "with what convenient speed you can, for the perfecting the great work which Your Highness has so happily begun to the general joy and satisfaction of all." [69] Surely no victor could ask for a more wholehearted welcome. This delegation had scarcely withdrawn from the princely presence when another turned up. This one came from the peers, to inform William that he was expected in London, and to lay before him a declaration stating their determination to join him for the preservation of the nation's freedom by calling a parliament. They added that until His Highness should arrive they were prepared to take on themselves the responsibility of giving such directions as might be necessary for the preservation of order. [70] Their lordships were not so fulsome as the men of the City. William's reaction is indicated in his reply: thanking the peers for their declaration he said in conclusion "hee intended to bee in town in a few days, *the City having invited him.*" [71] (Italics mine.)

The next morning William learned that James had been discovered and was being detained. Although Schomberg expressed fear that there might be some trickery connected with this capture, William seemed unworried. [72] Receiving the news with a jeer, he paid no further attention to it that day, but pressed on to Windsor where he took up his quarters in the castle. There seemed to be little enough cause for alarm.* The King was in custody, but Feversham, William knew, had been sent to release him and let him go wherever he wished. It apparently did not occur to William that James might not seize this opportunity to make good his plans for escape but would instead return to London. The following day, however, saw the arrival of two

---

*How little William was disturbed is indicated by the following quotation from Mary's *Memoirs:* "On the 30th of December arrived the news that the King had been arrested. The Prince told me at the same time that I should prepare to come to England." (*Lettres et Memoires de Marie, Reine D'Angleterre,* p. 91.) Whether or not the news of her father's arrest came to Mary directly from William in the same letter in which he told her to get ready to come to England — and the wording suggests that that was the case — he certainly must have been fairly confident that the Revolution, for all practical purposes, was over.

pieces of information which made the situation seem more serious. Official word from London indicated that at least some of the peers who had seemed ready to receive William a day or so before, were swerving back toward James. Moreover the sailors who had captured the King, laboring under the idea that they had done a good turn for the Orangists, refused to release him. Perceiving that he could stand aloof no longer, William sent Zuylestein to find the King and place him in safe quarters in Rochester. He did not know that James, encouraged by the joyous relief shown by many at his discovery, had changed his plans and had started back to London. The uneasiness awakened in William by the hint that several lords were ready to welcome James turned first to sternness on the confirmation of that news, and then to fury when Feversham arrived with official word from the King, whom Zuylestein had failed to find, that he was on his way to Whitehall from whence he would be willing to reopen negotiations with William on the following Monday. Feversham was arrested, ostensibly because he had entered a hostile camp without a passport, but more probably to indicate, to any who had any doubts, that in William's opinion at least, a state of war still existed and that he had sufficient force to show who was master.

Within a few hours, however, William's temporary, but characteristic outburst was over, and he was able once more to direct affairs with the outward calmness just as characteristic and much more constant. Halifax arrived from London, at last and once and for all throwing in his lot with the man toward whom he had blown hot and cold for so long. His arrival was of utmost significance for it indicated that wisdom, and its lesser brother discretion, had decided against King James. There was little chance that the latter, even if backed by the sounder men of his kingdom, could or would reëstablish the firm and stable government which the country, its trade disrupted, its people panicky with fear of Irish bogeys, needed. Sound judgment decreed that those who were able to exercise some control should side in with the stronger contestant, while self-interest dictated that they should do so before it was too late. All but a few of the leaders were now at Windsor. Among those still missing were Nottingham who, perhaps with poorer judgment, but certainly with more altruism than Halifax, remained in London. Danby lingered in the North, as deaf now to William's pleas for his presence as William had been to his own letters a few weeks before. He hoped to be the man whose hands would hold the balance, but in all his long and active political life he never made a greater miscalculation.

Already James's flight had opened the possibility that the object of the Revolution might be attained by the simple process of declaring the throne vacant. Already William's Dutch followers were discussing the relative merits of his making a claim for himself or deferring to his wife's rights.[73] The return to London, however, changed all this, for certainly the fiction of vacancy could not be sustained so long as the King was at hand. To decide what should be done William called together all those peers — by this time a large majority of the whole — who were at Windsor and placed the problem before them.

He was determined not to enter London so long as James was there, nor did he wish to use military force to compel the other to withdraw, as that would mean entering the city as a conqueror, and, worse still, a conqueror who had refused an offer to parley with his foe. In many ways William and his followers were now in the predicament posited earlier in this discussion when the question of what might have happened if James had accepted the Hungerford terms was raised. Viewed from some aspects the situation was better; from others, worse. Earlier the time element, while important, had not been paramount. Now, because of the outbursts of lawlessness throughout the country, and because trade was suffering severely, it was essential that unquestionable authority be established forthwith by someone. James, ostensibly free, but actually a most unwilling captive, had brought discredit upon himself and his cause by leaving. On the other hand, now that he was so completely in their power the Orangists could not escape some measure of responsibility for what happened to him.

In the meeting at Windsor some of the lords were heard to suggest that James should be kept in custody in England or elsewhere. But a king, even if he was a prisoner, still retained his crown. Captivity, too, suggesting tragedy, might win for James, as it had done for his great-grandmother, a measure of loyalty that he had never known as a free man. That solution rejected, the possibility of negotiation was raised. When that happened William was faced at last with the direct issue, for from this offer there could be no evasion in the form of references to broken promises and unfulfilled demands. He refused to consider the proposal. The grounds of his refusal are highly revealing: that is to say, negotiation would mean recognition of James's position which, in its turn, would destroy the fiction of a vacant throne and a deserted people.[74] There remained only one possible alternative: to force James to leave London, trusting to luck that once that was done he would recognize that his situation was hopeless and try again to escape from the country.

That plan, as everyone who is at all familiar with the story knows, was adopted. Familiar, too, is the story of the careless guarding which gave James every reason to understand that his ultimate departure would be welcomed rather than hindered. Nor could he avoid the conviction that it was his nephew who was directing affairs. True enough, English peers brought him the order to leave Whitehall, for William had refused point blank to send the message by some of his own officers,[75] but of the three, Halifax, Shrewsbury, and Delamere, the last two were so thoroughly identified with the Prince that the mere fact of their being English rather than foreign was unimportant. Moreover their clinching argument was a letter, signed by the Prince, desiring the King to leave. Van Solms supervised James's departure from Whitehall; Dutch troops provided the loose guarding through which he slipped so easily — but also so tardily as to awaken a real fear that he had not taken the hint.

Ever since that time there have been rumors that William, by some devious method, managed to convey to his father-in-law a threat that if the latter did not leave the country his life would be in danger. Not only is there no evidence for this, but logic argues against accepting the suggestion. William could scarcely have failed to realize how thoroughly he would be discredited, both in England and on the Continent, if James were murdered. The very possibility of such a thing happening must have worried him for he could not but have known that even if he were able to clear himself of direct complicity, he could never banish doubts from the minds of a good many people any more than he had been able to do in the case of the De Witts. Nevertheless, it should be noted that William never once, as he could so easily have done, sent James any assurance of personal safety. Whether this was oversight or calculated neglect, the generous gesture was never made.

A few hours after James left, William entered London. Deliberately he avoided, by taking another route, the crowds who had braved the cold rainy weather to throng the way he had been expected to travel. The journey in from Zionhouse had been made over slippery, icy roads; perhaps the resulting exhaustion to one whose health was always fragile was as much responsible for his desire to escape the crowds as any aversion to a public ovation. Yet his failure to appear before them struck an unpleasant note among the people who had come out to greet him. While they made their way homeward, not a little disgruntled, the man whom they had hoped to cheer was settling himself in St. James's Palace. The apartments which had been made ready for him were those in which the Prince of Wales had been born six months before.

CHAPTER 6

The Interregnum

At some point after his arrival in London but before he and his wife had been proclaimed King and Queen, William is supposed to have said of the shouting, cheering crowds that milled around Whitehall "They cry 'Hosannah' now, but later on it will be 'Crucify him.' " [1] His almost irreverent words, based as they were on only-too-vividly-remembered experience, are perhaps forgivable. Hailed as a savior sixteen years before in his native city of The Hague, he had lived to see his own countrymen come to look upon him as a potential tyrant. All his life he had distrusted the easy adulation of the crowd. He knew that any position, to be secure, must be founded upon accomplishment, not promise. He knew, too, that if he was to win and keep the crown of England he must persuade the people who were to be his subjects to *ask* him to take it, and to do so in such a way that there could be no question either of their responsibility or of his claim to the title.

Not so much in the crowds that thronged the streets as in those smaller and more elite groups that were inside the palaces or the town houses of the aristocracy were to be found many who would willingly have evaded all responsibility, however much they might desire to see William become their king. In the course of informal conferences held at St. James's and elsewhere during the first ten days after the victors entered London, sometimes in William's presence, sometimes in his absence, the name of Henry VII was heard frequently. Precedents set by this first of the Tudors and ancestor of the present contender seemed admirably suited to the existing situation. Like the Prince of Orange he, too, had landed in England with an army to free the country from a tyrant's rule. Unlike him, however, immediately upon vanquishing his antagonist Henry had seized the crown, claiming it by that most ancient of all rights, conquest. A few years later in his reign a law had been passed which, although somewhat indefinite in wording, was subsequently construed to mean that the rendition of service and allegiance to a *de facto* king was not treason. Here, then, was the ideal way out for those who were becoming uneasy over the prospect of an extended interregnum. If William could be induced to seize the crown forthwith by right of conquest as his forefather had done, those who recognized him had precedent to protect them even if James at some future date should be restored. The process of hedging, never absent from the men who engineered the "Glorious Revolution," was present even in this moment of triumph.

As usual, William was too wise to be caught by such a transparent device. He knew that he was not in the same position as Henry VII, and that the precedents cited were not the only ones that had been established in the intervening two centuries. Not only was his antagonist still alive but, during the first few days of the discussions he was still in England albeit he may well have been muttering "A ship, a ship, my kingdom for a ship!" The crown had not rolled under a convenient hawthorne bush to lie waiting for a new claimant to pick it up and place it, unchallenged, on his own head. The present trial by combat had not been preceded by decades of conflict during which all laws of succession had got so thoroughly snarled that not even the most learned lawyers of the realm were willing to place themselves in jeopardy by pronouncing in favor of one or another of the several contending heirs. According to what seemed now to be the accepted law at least two people had rights superior to William's: his wife and her sister, for among the precedents which had set in the years that lay between Bosworth Field and 1688 was the right of a woman to succeed to the throne.

William refused, therefore, to be hurried. Even the pleas of his followers that he do something to safeguard them against the danger of future prosecution for treason seem to have made no impression upon him. It is perfectly consistent with his earlier actions to assume, although there is no direct evidence, that he acted deliberately. So long as the men about him depended for safety upon his own retention of authority his position was reasonably secure. If, on the contrary, he acted at this early date to shield them, he also relieved them of responsibility that they could never repudiate if they were forced to take the initiative and declare him king. Once that had been done the statute of Henry VII might be invoked to absolve them at law. It could never clear them in opinion.

That was not all. William was keenly conscious of other difficulties that his seizure of the crown by right of conquest might create. Probably of primary importance to him was the reaction of his continental allies, especially Spain and the Emperor who, as we know, had looked askance upon the venture from the outset. His letters to Waldeck during this interval are filled with expression of his reluctance to assume a crown which, he said, he felt was being thrust upon him.[2] Contradictory to his known acts at the time as these protestations appear, they are perfectly logical when one realizes how damaging any impression that he had gone to England primarily to make himself king would have been to his continental projects. For him to follow the example of Henry VII would be to give the lie to his own declarations at the same time that it substantiated the accusations made by D'Avaux and Louis XIV. In addition to the diplomatic problem there was also that of James's daughters. Little as he had to fear from Mary herself she had champions who were already beginning to make themselves heard, and Anne and her partisans constituted a very real threat. Last but not least there was his own Declaration in which he had stated that he would leave all decisions to a free parliament. He had repeated this in the second Declaration issued to counteract the effects of James's gestures toward reform. To repudiate his word would be worse than unethical. It would be imprudent. He could not take the crown and then call Parliament. Parliament must come first.

The first ten days after William's entry into London came as near as anything during the whole revolutionary period to constituting a real interregnum, although technically, of course, the designation continues to apply for some time longer. Sovereignty, says a later theorist, is found in that power to which a group of people habitually render obedience. The habit of rendering obedience to James had been abruptly terminated, and even though we grant that England's monarch was even then to some degree the symbol rather than the substance of sovereignty, the mechanism of government depended upon his authorization for true legal functioning. Nevertheless, because of the very concept, never absent although at times dormant throughout many centuries of national development, that there was a sovereign power which the king represented and administered but did not wholly incorporate within himself, the problem during these days was less that of maintaining order than of finding some group capable of assuming sovereignty temporarily with the objective of restoring it to its accustomed seat as soon as possible.

It is small wonder that from these days have been drawn the classic examples of what happens when a political society, having repudiated its ruler, reverts to a state of nature to find within itself the source of power upon which a new government can be based. But the appearances that have furnished the examples are largely illusions. Although the habit of rendering obedience to William had not been established, authority, in the sense of the ability to command such obedience as distinct from any juridical right to do so, certainly rested in him and foolish indeed would have been those who questioned this fact. Yet, since it was to his advantage that the appearance should seem to be reality, he was content to use his authority sparingly for the time being, exercising it only in those areas that would admit of no delay. Orders he gave for the disposition of the English army showed that he considered himself their commander, but, although superficially premature, the action was necessary. So, too, was his directive to the Mayor and the Common Council of the City of London, newly elected under the restored charter but not yet formally installed, to take office without the customary oaths of allegiance. Somewhat more presumptuous, perhaps, was the command he sent to the stewards of all the royal palaces forbidding them to part with any of the furnishings in their custody without his expressed approval. And Barillon, the detested French ambassador, despite the fact that he had publicly drunk the health of the Prince of Orange, and over his own outraged protests that no one but James had the right to dismiss him, was sent packing back to France on twenty-four hours notice.

Meanwhile, whatever continuity of government there was resided in the body of the peerage, most of whose members were now in London. The arrival of those who either had been with William's army or else had been managing their own more or less correlated uprisings elsewhere, changed the political color of the group in some respects, chiefly by strengthening the anti-James element, but certain fundamentals were unaltered. Less an extension of the Crown than were the administrative, the representative, and the primarily judicial institutions of the realm, this body was, paradoxically, at once jealous of its position and somewhat reluctant to exercise authority. In addition it rejected any concept of a dissolution of government, wishing above all else to preserve a semblance of continuity. Meeting at each others' homes and in informal gatherings at the court, the peers tried in vain during the first day or so after William's arrival in London to reach some working agreement, but their first formal conference with him, on Thursday, December 20, found them still undecided on all points except that somehow a parliament must be convoked. "My Lords," William said on that occasion, "I have desired to meet you here to advise the best manner how to pursue the ends of my Declaration in calling a free Parliament." "On speaking those words" adds the chronicler, "he withdrew and left them to consult together." [3]

Ostensibly the purpose of this meeting was as William had stated it: to decide how to go about calling a parliament. Actually a far graver problem was involved of which the above was only an outward manifestation. It was nothing less than whether or not James was still king. That the group was sharply divided on this issue there can be no doubt, but so long as James remained in

England those who wanted to take the government out of his hands, be it by replacing him entirely or by setting up a regency, could only stall for time. Like William they expected the one-time fugitive to make a second attempt and were disturbed only by his delay in doing so. Consequently the first discussions, formal as well as informal, centered mainly on projects which gave a show of recognition to James as a sovereign. There was some talk of proceeding on the basis of the writs he had issued earlier in the month, but this was rejected because only a very small number of the peers and a minority of the counties and boroughs had received the necessary summons.[4] Rather hopelessly, for they knew they could scarcely expect the royal coöperation, some of the lords proposed that James himself might be induced to take the necessary steps, especially if the request was accompanied by "all the offers in the world which are consistent with safety."[5] Their opponents, who might have been willing to accept the first part of the suggestion, as a refusal from James would have strengthened their own position, declined, of course, to consider the whole plan. Despairing of finding a solution unaided, on the second or third day the peers called in five eminent lawyers, the nonegenarian Maynard, the youthful Holt, Pollexfen, soon to become attorney general, and two others.[6] Asked to give an opinion on whether or not the Triennial Act could be put into effect in view of the fact that more than three years had elapsed since the last session of Parliament, these experts could give only one answer. Vague as the wording of the act might be on what constituted an occasion for its application, it was specific in stating that the writs must be issued by the king. No procedure had been set up to use in the event of his failure to do so. Unable to provide an acceptable solution the lawyers, with Pollexfen in the lead, gratuitously offered another by repeating the suggestion already made that William claim the crown by right of conquest and issue the writs himself.[7] When William refused again a blind alley seemed to have been entered. This was Saturday, December 22. Throughout the morning and afternoon of a gloomy Sunday, lords and commoners, Orangists and Jacobites, Dutchmen and Englishmen hunted in vain for a way out.

As usual William remained calm, and waited with little show of outward impatience for the news that he was confident would arrive eventually. At about four-thirty in the afternoon of that Sunday it came. James had fled again. In the following hours the all-important decisions were made, not in a full conference of the peers, but in informal gatherings of William's supporters and, to some extent at least, in his presence. With the King out of the way William should be asked to take over the administration of the government and to call, not a parliament, but on the basis of the precedent of 1660, a convention which would be the same thing for all practical purposes and could, like its predecessor, eventually be transformed into the recognized body. Apparently the peers were willing to take this step on their own authority but William, knowing that the Commons were no less jealous of their position than the Lords of theirs, insisted that they too, should be consulted.[8] That evening he issued a proclamation calling all members of the Parliaments of Charles II who were near enough London to be reached in time, to meet with him on the following Wednesday in conjunction with certain members of the government of the City of London to decide what steps to take in the existing crisis.

When the peerage met the following morning those of its members who did not know that James had fled were soon enlightened. All of them realized now that they would have to act without him. Inspired by over-enthusiasm, young Lord Paget sprang up to move that Mary be proclaimed queen immediately, but the rush to her colors that might have been thus started was effectively averted by Devonshire and Delamere.[9] Instead the peerage put into solemn resolutions the decisions that had already been reached the previous evening. There was only one change, or rather, an emendation. To the request that William take over the administration of the government, left without a time limit the night before,[10] was added a definite terminus, January 22, the day upon which the convention was to assemble. Whether or not this was displeasing to William, it was too unimportant for cavil. The resolutions were presented to him that day, but he declined to commit himself upon them, saying that his answer must await the decision of the Commons.

On Christmas day, while the weary but hopeful James II traveled over the snowy roads of northern France from Ambleteuse to Paris, the people in the capital he had left behind him waited with the tension that comes from mixed emotions and divided opinions. Their King was gone, and his ultimate deposition seemed inevitable. Now that their actions were irrevocable many were aghast at the consequences, and in the army especially were to be found men of all ranks who felt, with much justification, that they had been tricked into a measure of disloyalty far in excess of anything to which they would have given their assent. Only a minority of the Orangists had intended to go this far, and even among them there were those who now indulged in a sort of futile pity for the man they had driven away, perhaps seeking subconsciously by this device to assuage an uneasy sense of guilt. Those few Roman Catholics still in the environs of London made whatever capitol they could of the emergent disagreements, suggesting to the Dissenters that they were helping to establish Anglican supremacy, and insinuating to the Anglicans that the position of the Established Church would be undermined by William's Calvinism.[11] But the outright Orangists were in the saddle now, with all the forces of propaganda riding with them. Sentiment in favor of James was identified with popish and pro-French inclinations. Rumor said that the apprentices of the City were planning to march on Westminster if the assembly of the Commons failed to show proper spirit.[12] The Dutch army was led by Schomberg of international fame. Vacillating office seekers, looking at all this display of strength, decided that the time for protest had passed. Burnet, shedding metaphorical tears, whether real or crocodile it is hard to say, over the plight of the fallen monarch, wrote to Admiral Herbert that whatever their misgivings, discretion demanded from William's supporters the appearance of a bold and common front.[13]

This was the atmosphere in which a new Rump Parliament met on the morning of December 26. It has frequently been stated that William, in calling to this assembly only those who had sat in the lower house during the reign of Charles II thereby openly and intentionally insulted James, whose only Parliament might have been considered the logical residue of authority.[14] But William, whatever his many faults might be, was seldom moved by pettiness. He was far more likely to act on the promptings of a shrewd and ruthless political acumen, and this must have been what moved him now. Several of his own most prominent followers would fall into the designated category but not into the other. Among them were such esteemed councilors as Henry Sidney, Sir Robert Sawyer, and Sir Rowland Gwin. There also would be hothead Robert Peyton who might cause trouble if he were omitted, and with him would be joined William Harbord and Sir John Hotham, whose vigorous protest the Prince had overruled at Hungerford. In a word, the gathering would be almost solidly pro-Orange as the less-than-three-day-summons left little time for any but those who were currently in London to answer. There was little possibility that the City apprentices would need to go into action.

It is to be regretted that there is so little in the way of an official record of what happened at this meeting, and that even that scanty report is no better supplemented by unofficial accounts. The group assembled, went through the business of choosing a speaker, Sir Henry Powle, and passed resolutions modeled on those already accepted by the peers. At the very beginning of the first session Sir Robert Sawyer's question of by what authority they met was answered curtly by Sergeant Maynard that the authority of the Prince of Orange was all that was needed. A proposal that the group as a whole endorse the Exeter Association called forth what seems to have been the most animated discussion, but it was on minor rather than on major points. As a compromise a copy of the Association was placed on a table where those who wished to sign it might do so. Several, but not all, of the members affixed their signatures. Someone, whose name is not recorded, suggested that the administration of the government be placed in William's hands for a full year, rather than just up to the Convention. Here, perhaps, was a real point of danger, although the perpetrator may well have been motivated only by a desire to express complete confidence in the Prince. However, unlike the original plan of an indefinite term, it retained the element of a time limit but placed it so far in the future that it might well have become the cause of dilatory action some weeks hence. It was dismissed on the ground that the power of the present body did not go beyond the opening of the Convention. Although further particulars of discussions are lacking, there are two good reasons for believing that no serious disagreement arose. One is the very silence on the subject, for disputes usually find their way into some sort of record. The other is the time element. In one day all of the business was done and an agreement on everything but some minor points of procedure was reached. Not many hours could have been allotted to the airing of differences of opinion or to the settlement of those differences.

By the evening of December 26 William had seen and unofficially approved the resolutions of the Lords and Commons but it was not until two days later that booming cannons and ringing bells signaled to the people of London and Westminster that he had graciously consented to take over the administration of political and financial affairs and to issue writs on his own authority and that of the Lords and Commons for the election of a Convention.[15] By this step he had become, for all practical purposes, the ruler of England. The position was at once encouraging and embarrassing to the man who had worked so long to reach it; encouraging because it suggested so clearly what the final outcome must be; and embarrassing because the tenure of authority had a definite *terminus ad quem* which meant that long-term decisions could be made only tentatively and, to some extent, almost surreptitiously, as it would not do for the Prince to pretend to powers that had not yet been confirmed no matter how sure he might be that he would get them eventually. Yet the decisions had to be made; and by the very act of making them William was tightening his hold upon the country which, having theoretically called him to its assistance, could not repudiate him now.

One problem of immediate importance was that of money. The state of the treasury, reasonably good throughout the whole of the reign up to only a few weeks earlier, was now very bad indeed. James had spent heavily to prevent the wages of his army and navy from falling into arrears. The flow of income which would normally have compensated for this withdrawal of funds had been cut off by the breakdown of the tax machinery not only in those parts of the country that William had taken under control, but also, and more disastrously, in other areas where his associates had followed his example by seizing national revenues to help finance their own contributions to the Revolution. The result was a political and financial snarl, with those who held their commissions from the old government afraid to carry out their duties; and with several people, especially the brewers, refusing to recognize the authority of either the old or the new officials. William, now in fact maintaining two military forces, his own, and those of King James, in addition to having assumed responsibility for administering the regular financial affairs of the kingdom, could not allow such a state of affairs to continue even though in order to end it he had to resort to a curious repudiation of his own actions. On January 2, he issued a proclamation "for the better collecting the Public Revenue" which, after stating that "since the fifth Day of November last divers Persons have intermeddled with, and received the Public Money, arising by the Revenues of Customs, Excise, Hearth, and other ways, some by Commissions and Authorities from Us, for the support of those that had taken Arms under them, and for other publick use" went on to revoke all commissions given by himself, and concluded with the order that all former officials should reassume their duties.

A few days were sufficient to show that this action was not going to produce the needed results. Owing to unsettled conditions, trade, both foreign and domestic, had been dwindling to such a degree that the revenues produced from it, even when collected, were inadequate. The already discontented English army listened readily to rumors that their wages would not be paid, and it is true that with the resources at his command William could not have met the obligations that confronted him. He called, therefore, upon financial London for a voluntary loan, to be secured by the future revenue of the country. The response was highly gratifying. Some brought in as much as ten thousand pounds, and many more made contributions of a thousand, while offers of less than fifty pounds were refused. Within a few days more than two hundred thousand pounds had been raised.[16] There is nothing that suggests the presence of any of the characteristics of a forced loan. That the London merchants contributed so liberally can be explained easily enough on the basis of their desire to bring about an end to the existing unsettled conditions, so bad for their business, as quickly as possible. The loan, of course, had the added advantage of making those who subscribed to it more than ever anxious to establish the power of the Prince upon a firm and permanent basis.

In agreeing to take over the civil administration of the realm William had assumed still another vexatious problem, especially as far as local and county government were concerned. After James's first flight the peers had issued orders for all the local office holders who were not Catholics to continue to carry on with their duties: William confirmed their actions by a proclamation issued on December 31. In spite of this, confusion was widespread. Although James had withdrawn most of his Catholic appointments, a few officials of that faith had never been relieved of their duties which, under the terms of the above orders, left the localities involved without any responsible authorities. In several other areas those who were supposed to replace the Catholics had not been formally installed, frequently, as we have seen, because of their own deliberately dilatory tactics. Now these men either hesitated to take on their duties or else failed to command the obedience of the people, while here and there individuals and groups angrily refused to recognize William's authority. Northern and central England especially saw several heated disputes and some rioting. The problem was one that could not, by its very nature, be solved during the Interregnum. Fortunately for William it never assumed proportions which demanded the use of force of any size. The situation at Westminster, where only a handful of officials, such as Godolphin, remained, was much simpler. Men who had come over with William — Jephson and Harbord, for example — were only too ready to take over administrative positions even though they knew that their tenures were supposed to be temporary.

Meanwhile military affairs also needed attention. Intricate and far-reaching questions which they raised involved both foreign and domestic policy over neither of which was William as yet in complete control. The first foreshadowings of his later unpopularity now made their appearance. Members of the English aristocracy who had lands in Ireland, fearful lest Tyrconnel should gain control of that country, clamored loudly that a strong force should be sent over at once. At the moment William did not dare to grant their demand. There were too many indications that the English troops not only might refuse to fight for him, but even that they might desert to the enemy, thereby providing James with a strong and loyal army for an attempt at restoration. Even in England desertions arising from loyalty to James, from fear of overseas service, and from continued rumors that wages would not be paid, grew to an alarming number.[17] Here is strong evidence that it had been the well-planned action of a handful of officers rather than any widespread disloyalty to James that had resulted in the military debacle of a few weeks earlier. Moreover some of the officers who had joined the Orangists at first were now either disgruntled because they had not received desired preferments, or disturbed, as we have seen, at the turn things were taking.[18] English troops had been sent out of London and Dutch guards posted in their place.[19] This not only angered the London tradesmen, who found the new soldiers much more frugal than the old, but also aroused the jealousy of Englishmen in and out of the army. To top off everything else, about this time the English began to remember that one of the complaints against James had been that he had kept a standing army among them, and pamphleteers acrimoniously pointed out that troops were being quartered in private dwellings without the consent of the owners.[20] The new situation did not seem much different from the old.

Under the circumstances no answer would have been completely right. William needed to have his own army by him whether or not he wanted to appear in the role of a conqueror. To satisfy all those who wanted commissions or preferments would have been impossible. Appointments had to be made either on the basis of political advantage or of length and degree of service to the Orangist cause. If the two criteria came into conflict it was the latter which must be disregarded. On January 8, to meet the criticisms concerning quartering of troops William who, to do him justice, appears to have been ignorant of this violation of established right, issued a decree that in the future no one should be compelled against his will to accept soldiers into his dwelling,[21] but critics pointed out that the phrasing of the order made it sound like an act of grace rather than an acceptance of a principle. A week later, reassured by the response to the voluntary loan, William tried to pass his confidence on to the army and navy by proclaiming that the rumors of inadequate funds were false, that wages would be met, and that all deserters who returned within fifteen days would be unpunished.[22] About the complaints of a standing army, and about apprehensions over service on the Continent he could do nothing. He could not disband the army; the apprehensions were all too well-founded.

For, in December, Louis XIV had declared war upon the United Provinces of the Netherlands and the dreaded general European conflict was at last a reality. Now, to the suggestion of his continental allies that they would rather like to have their troops for their own defense, William saw added the pleas of Waldeck and the demands of the Netherlands Council of State, not only that he should send the Dutch army home immediately, but also that he should make good his pledge to supplement it with English forces.[23] He was in a dilemma. He wrote constantly to Waldeck, making promises of what he would do as soon as a settlement was reached which went far beyond any authority he would ever have by making commitments about English troops long before the nation itself had entered the war.[24] When word of this leaked out even his most intimate advisors became uneasy, and were only partially satisfied when the Prince justified his actions on the basis of existing treaties which bound England to furnish assistance to the United Provinces in case the latter were attacked.[25] In the army and navy this justification had no soothing effect whatsoever, but rather stimulated the already alarming desertions and contributed to scattered mutinies which broke out in both branches of the services.[26] The common soldiers and sailors were far from enthusiastic about fighting anyone, even the French.

The military aspects of English foreign relations, serious though they were, did not constitute the only problems with which William had to cope in trying to bring the country into line with the continental policies he had been formulating for the last year and a half. Repeatedly, as we have seen, he had assured his European allies and friends that he favored religious toleration. Yet the tenor of public opinion in England was rabidly anti-Catholic. Pamphlets and broadsheets hailed William as England's deliverer from Popery and Slavery. The first act of the Council of Peers had been to decree that all Catholics, with certain exceptions such as foreign merchants, should be banished from the area within a ten-mile radius of London. From the country came stories of deeds of violence to the homes of the Catholic nobility and gentry. There was no bloodshed, it is true, but there was a good deal of burning and looting of property. In London itself the home of Don Ronquillo, the Spanish ambassador and a person with whom William especially wanted to be on good terms, was sacked and set on fire during the Irish night while, ironically enough, that of Barillon went unharmed. The violence had diminished somewhat, but had by no means disappeared, when the new year opened. William tried to control it, but he did not dare to make any effort openly to curb the opinion from whence it sprang, for he knew that the religious issue was all-important in thwarting any movement to recall James.

Nevertheless he had to do something. Writing of the unfavorable impression the treatment of the Catholics was making on the Continent, Waldeck insisted that countermeasures must be taken.[27] The French recalled William's own criticism of the revocation of the Edict of Nantes and renewed the accusation that he was trying to start that bugaboo of central European diplomacy: a war of religion. Hoffman told William that the Emperor wondered how he could expect Protestants to be safe in Roman Catholic countries if so little heed were paid in England to the precepts of toleration.[28] But the best that William could offer was a mixture of appeasement and denial of responsibility. Fortunately, on the night that Don Ronquillo's house was destroyed the Earl of Mulgrave had taken the ambassador under his protection and had paid him the honor of giving him quarters in Whitehall.[29] To this gesture William now added a financial reimbursement for property damages that was more than adequate to cover all losses incurred.[30] It was undoubtedly intended to be more than adequate. A few days later, when Hoffman and Ronquillo presented a joint protest from their governments, they received a very interesting answer. Although deprecating what had been done, William maintained that he could not be held personally accountable.

It has distressed me very much . . . that the Lords have insisted upon the re-issue of the proclamation against the Catholics. But I ask you yourselves, who have resided so long in this country, to bear witness if I can check these violent passions immediately, *especially as the government has not yet been turned over to me.* I beg you to give me time.[31] (Italics mine.)

Some days later he wrote the King of Spain a long personal letter, expressing regret and again disclaiming responsibility.[32]

Perhaps he was justified. The English may have gone beyond what he had expected. However, he was not entirely without responsibility. The banners on his flagship had proclaimed his championship of the Protestant cause, and how can any cause be championed if it has no enemy — or if that enemy is not attacked? He had reason to know, too, long before he came to England, how fanatical the people there were on the subject of religion, and how they identified his coming with a rescue from "Popery and Slavery." True, his own Declarations had studiously avoided any mention of Roman Catholicism itself, but they had emphasized the country's laws, and William knew well enough how those laws stood on the question of toleration. Nor can he be cleared of having given his continental friends assurances that he must have known he could not make good without running counter to the express wishes of the English people. Here, as in the army, the cause of the Revolution carried its own innate betrayal.

Clarendon and Burnet have given the impression that during this time it was extremely difficult to gain access to William's presence, and because of that the first accuses him of being unduly aloof, and the second praises him for endeavoring to maintain strict impartiality. Their version of his conduct has become a legend which does not, however, stand up when it is scrutinized in the light shed by other accounts, especially those of the Dutch. True enough, he was inaccessible to such men as Clarendon who wished to pester him with self-important complaints and requests. He was extremely busy: his lifelong disinclination to keep abreast of his work had to be mastered for the moment in the presence of urgent demands. The heavy duties he still held vis-à-vis the United Provinces had accumulated while he was more or less out of touch with The Hague during the voyage and the march from Exeter. Above that he was too preoccupied in conferring with men of proven loyalty and political weight to have time for waverers like Clarendon, or even for an old adherent like Burnet whose influence in England was not very great.

Although there is scant record of what went on at the conferences William held with English political leaders, the list of those with whom he is known to have had discussions before the Convention opened is interesting in itself. Mordaunt, Sidney, Shrewsbury, Churchill, Lord Bristol, and Sir William Temple and his son were each received at least once; Halifax, several times. Temple and his son were primarily concerned with affairs in Ireland where the family estates were located. Bristol seems to have come to report on elections, for when he left he announced exuberantly to Huygens that all was going well and that "he believed they would make him king." [33] With Mordaunt, Sidney, and Shrewsbury, all of whom had been with him so long, the conversations were probably no more than over strategy to be used to attain the desired end. With the other two the case is different. What he talked of with Churchill is unknown, but it probably concerned the Princess Anne. Halifax has left us a record of what passed between him and the Prince during one of their frequent meetings: the occasion alluded to earlier when William stated flatly that he had no intention of accepting a regency. [34] Halifax, the laggard, had now gone completely over to William, and he seems to have seen more of him during this interval than did any of those who had come over on the expedition. His prestige and his superb abilities as a parliamentary tactician were too valuable for William to let pique stand in the way of accepting his support.

It will be noted immediately that the name of one of the most prominent instigators of the Revolution is missing from the above list: that of the Earl of Danby who, after having been delayed first by injured pride and then by the Irish fear, finally arrived in London shortly before Christmas. That he is not specifically mentioned does not, of course, mean that he was not received in private audience. On the other hand, he is important enough so that the absence of any reference to such an event, especially by Huygens, who seems to have kept a fairly accurate record, suggests that none occurred. Whether Danby deliberately avoided the Prince, or whether he was not summoned to the presence, cannot be determined. Probably there was a combination of both. The earl was undeniably not only annoyed by the way in which his messages had been ignored, but also disturbed by a dawning awareness of the nature of William's political ambitions. William, for his part, could not have been unmoved by Danby's efforts first to reach some kind of agreement with James, and then, when that was rendered impossible by the latter's departure, to place Mary on the throne alone.

The audiences discussed above were all, as has been said, private. As far as other contacts were concerned, Clarendon himself notes that William held his court daily and mingled freely with all those who presented themselves there, although he does remark on the Prince's habit of taking to one side each person with whom he spoke. Neither did William seclude himself in the palace of St. James. He probably won one friend at this time by losing six hundred guineas to Catherine of Braganza in one evening's game of cards, but he recouped his losses a few days later from the Prince of Denmark! The public saw neither more nor less of him than it did of most royal personages. It was noted that, on December 30, he had taken communion according to the Anglican rites, which should have been a point in his favor. But not even a victorious deliverer can please everyone. Many good Anglicans, knowing perfectly well that he was not of their persuasion, looked upon the act as an indication of a too-Latitudinarian frame of mind. As if to offset this, newsletters commented approvingly on his acts of charity to the poor and to the prisoners during the unseasonably cold weather.

Several Englishmen, it is true, complained that William did not treat them with that affability to which they had become accustomed under the reigns of his Stuart uncles. Some went so far as to urge Dijkveld to use his influence to bring about a more comfortable atmosphere at the court. The reason for William's aloofness, however, stems less from politics than from personality. The old forces which had made him a shy, self-conscious child and a distrustful man were deep-rooted, nor was the prevailing situation one which would contribute to the disappearance or even to the modification of his characteristic traits. Here in full strength was the basic element that had formed his personality: a political group which would use him to advance its own cause. From boyhood he had struggled against similar encroachments upon his sense of himself as an individual. The familiar situation brought the familiar response.

It is no wonder that during these days his Dutch friends and servants found him even more peevish, ill-tempered, and hard to please than he had been on the march from Exeter. Although occasionally distressed and sometimes angry, for the most part these men humored him, for they were accustomed to him and recognized the outbursts for what they were: the signs of a tension which he could exhibit to them without danger but must, if possible, hide from the English. He who so seldom had had to wait for others, who had been used rather to being the one for whom others waited, was now forced into a sort of suspended existence while someone else took the overt initiative. Sure as he might be of the outcome, he could not act decisively and openly, and there were a host of things that needed decisive action.

Nevertheless, although he had to appear to refuse the initiative, the part William was playing was far from negative or passive. Despite his aloofness and his preoccupation with the affairs of the United Provinces he maintained a constant control over English political developments from the time he reached London until he was proclaimed king. This control was more effective in the first than it was to be in the concluding days of the period, but it was never absent, never ineffective. At conferences where tact and political judgment indicated that he should be absent he was ably represented by his lieutenants. In the still more significant and highly informal gatherings of the English where plans for action were made and relative merits of alternative policies and solutions to the existing crisis were discussed, if he himself did not intrude Bentinck was usually present or, after he had become unwelcome, the more acceptable Dijkveld, who arrived in London during the second week in January. The days immediately preceding the Convention did, it is true, see the appearance in London of dissenting groups composed in part of new arrivals from the country and in part of those who either had all along opposed the steam-roller tactics of the Orangists or else were losing their initial enthusiasm. Holding their own informal meetings, such groups eventually became welded into an opposition party. William could not intrude into their sessions nor restrict their activities, but he could and did take measures to counteract their work.

Everything was waiting upon the meeting of the Convention. Writs, validated by the seal that William had brought with him,[35] were sent out with all possible speed. They were very carefully worded. William claimed the authorization of the Lords Spiritual and Temporal, and of those members of the Commons of Charles II residing in or about London, together with that of the aldermen and members of the Common Council of the City. He stated that the purpose of the Convention was to determine how to attain the ends he had set forth in his Declaration. The elections were to go "according to ancient usage. . . before the seizure on surrender of the charters made in the time of King Charles II." [36] According to a later directive, troops were to be withdrawn from all areas near polling places.

The time allowed for elections was unusually short; less than three weeks. However, the people were not unprepared for the event and in several boroughs and counties the decisions already made for the abortive summons of the preceding September and December were merely confirmed.[37] The elections were not entirely peaceful. Newcastle, for example, refused to hold one, but two anti-Orangists were finally validated from the borough.[38] There were a few reports of riots and bribery, especially in the western and central parts of the country, and the order that troops should be withdrawn was not always strictly observed.[39] Much of the trouble, however, seems to have come from confusion arising from the withdrawn and now restored charters which, in some cases, left the boroughs in a quandary to know who did and who did not have the right to vote.

The most interesting conclusion that can be drawn from a study of the members of the Convention is that *no* particularly significant conclusion can be drawn. Stout royalists and near or avowed republicans sat together on the benches. There is this, however, that should be noted. Free as the elections may have been there was a strong invading army in the country. Nor shall we ever know whether or not that small minority of Englishmen who were qualified to vote really wanted the Convention to make William king; the issue was not placed before them in those terms. But from what scant records we have of the electioneering that went on we do know that in some instances at least voters were led to believe that supporting men known to be opposed to the Prince would not be healthy, and many would-be members soon learned that it would be wise for them to sign the Association if they wished to be elected.[40]

Throughout the country and especially in London the talk ran steadily to the subject of what would be done when the Convention met. Gradually there arose a fairly well-defined opinion. The Prince and Princess of Orange would be made king and queen.[41] That this was the current of opinion does not mean that those who held it necessarily favored that solution. There were in the country at least five clearly defined views on what ought, in contrast to what probably would, be done. One group, small but loyal, wanted James brought back. Led by the Dean of St. Paul's, Dr. Sherlocke, they pointed out that all of William's past declarations from the Fagel letter on were inconsistent with any other solution. Another group, also loyal but more aware of the limitations of possibility, suggested a regency. The movement for such a solution probably originated at this particular time with Archbishop Sancroft, but it had been foreshadowed as far back as the Exclusion Controversy. Those who were attracted to it now, men such as Nottingham, Roch-

ester, Clarendon, and Heneage Finch, hoped to be able to preserve some form of continuity of government. Then there were
those who wished to make Mary queen alone. These preserved
the show of legality by assuming that James had abdicated.
Among some of them we find the interesting view that he had
not abdicated, but had *forfeited* the crown by breaking his
coronation oath. A fourth group in the broader factional alignments were for the joint settlement. A few were for the sole
kingship of William.

Although he was too clever to commit himself, William seems
to have been of this latter group. The persons who were most
active — almost the only ones, in fact, in promoting his candi-
dacy were the two men who were closest to him: Halifax and
Bentinck. It is possible to assume that Halifax might not have
been reflecting the Prince's views. It is not possible to assume
that Bentinck was not. The proposition failed, however, to attract many followers. On the contrary, it created a serious antagonism toward William even among some of his earliest and
most ardent followers such as Admiral Herbert and Gilbert
Burnet.[42] Danby, of course, never favored the idea. That Bentinck was known to support it was a drawback rather than
otherwise for already the English were beginning to resent his
privileged position. In general the proposition created enough
antagonism so that it was not pushed very hard. Dijkveld is supposed to have had something to do with persuading the Prince
to moderate his position, and this may well be true, for, shortly
after his arrival, he stated openly among the Dutch that he
thought William had got himself into a mess.[43] He knew the
temper of the English better than either William or Bentinck,
and he had, of course, known their original intentions.

It is interesting to note that at this time no suggestion was
made that William's own hereditary claims might be worthy
of consideration. Some Dutch pamphlets and laudatory poems
did indeed refer to them, but in England they were not mentioned. There any claims to his right to rule alone were based
on conquest or election rather than on his descent from Charles
I. What makes the question especially intriguing is not only

that William himself had a high opinion of his claims, but also that certain Englishmen had brought them up on several occasions during the reign of Charles II. Some of those who, at that time, had put his hereditary rights as a male over those of James's daughters were, it is true, on the lunatic fringe. But that cannot be said of the author of *Verbum Sapienti*, or of Henry Sidney and Godolphin who suggested in 1679 that William be brought over to England and seated in the House of Lords as a duke with definite recognition as "third son of England." [44] I venture to suggest two possible reasons why the claim was not made. One is that, even if recognized, it might have strengthened the idea of an elective monarchy, distasteful alike to William and to the greater number of the members of the Convention. The second is that William's interest was by now personal rather than dynastic. A crown matrimonial would be just as useful as any other. He would be king. It was already almost certain that he and Mary would have no children. The likelihood that he might survive her to remarry and have children by another wife seemed very slight indeed.

When the Convention met on January 22, representatives of all the above mentioned opinions were to be found in it. A detailed story of what went on during those days can be found in any number of other places. Here we are interested in events mainly in so far as they concern William. A brief sketch of what went on during the next two weeks will, however, be of help in later analysis. Very early it was obvious that in both houses the Orangists were the abler tacticians and that they were bent on controlling the assemblies. The first evidence of this came in the choice of the Speakers. In the Lords, Halifax, who had now become the leader of the Orangists, was chosen in preference to the Fabian Danby who had voiced a preference for the Princess. This was not particularly surprising as Halifax had been the leader of the peers' council ever since they began their informal deliberations in December. A more noteworthy upset occurred in the Commons where Sir Edward Seymour, who had been Speaker in 1678, expected the post again. He was, however, known to be opposed to the idea of making William king.

When the Commons met he heard them cry "No Seymour! No Seymour!" and soon after saw Powle elected to the position he had coveted for himself.

After they had elected their Speaker the Commons received a message from the Prince saying that

The dangerous condition of the Protestant Interest in Ireland requiring a large and speedy succour, and the present state of Things abroad oblige me to tell you that, next to the Danger of unseasonable Division amongst yourselves, nothing can be so fatal as too great delay in your Consultation.[45]

Almost immediately afterwards the Lords and Commons joined in an address to the Prince in which they thanked him for the care he had already taken in administering the government and asked him to continue with it. This was necessary in view of the fact that his first authorization had extended only up to this day. The next day the Prince answered that he would accept their request and once more urged them to make haste.

Nevertheless, on January 22, the Commons had voted to postpone debate on the state of the Nation until the following Monday, January 28, a step which may account for the terse, almost ungracious manner of the Prince's answer. Certainly their decision irritated Halifax[46] who knew how determined William was that everything should be settled with dispatch. But the Commons had some justification. Several of the counties and boroughs had not yet sent in members and it was not clear just who had authority to order them to do so. Moreover there were a good many contested seats that ought, if possible, to be decided upon before crucial decisions were made. Finally it is not strange that these men, convoked to settle problems of almost unprecedented magnitude, should have wanted time for informal discussion among themselves before they committed themselves to any resolutions.

Meanwhile the Lords, who could not act until Commons took the lead, contented themselves with appointing a committee of ten to examine the facts concerning the death of Essex. This was indeed flogging a dead horse, but it had its propaganda value. In a pamphlet that had appeared a few days before, James II had been accused of having been responsible. With Shrewsbury, Devonshire, Mordaunt, Lovelace, and Delamere on the committee[47] he was not likely to be whitewashed although subsequent investigations tended to support the verdict that Essex had been a suicide. Another committee was appointed to consider what would be done to prevent Catholics and reputed Catholics from remaining in the City, which must have embarrassed William although he was, as before, helpless.

On January 28 the great debate was finally held in Commons, culminating in the following resolution:

That King James the II, having endeavored to subvert the constitution of the Kingdom, by breaking the Original Contract between the King and the People; and by the Advice of the Jesuits, and other wicked persons, having violated the fundamental Laws, and having withdrawn himself out of the Kingdom; has abdicated the Government; and that the throne is thereby vacant.

On the next day two more resolutions were passed:

Resolved: that it hath been found by Experience to be inconsistent with the safety and welfare of the Protestant Kingdom, to be governed by a Papist Prince.

and

Resolved: that the House be moved to appoint a Committee to bring in general Heads of such Things as are absolutely necessary to be considered for the better securing our Religion, Laws, and Liberties.

The first of these resolutions together with the one which had been passed the day before were sent up to the Lords who immediately organized themselves into a committee of the whole to consider the latter. The first question that was put was whether or not, if the throne was vacant, a regency should be established. This was really the crucial vote of the whole period, involving both basic principle and immediate policy. It was of all possible decisions, the most serious threat to William's plans. But it was never more than a threat. The resolution was defeated by a margin of only two or three votes, the exact number being in dispute. The majority was so slight, however, that it has frequently been assumed that if Mulgrave, Huntingdon, and Churchill had been present the vote would have gone the other way, and that these men absented themselves purposely because, had they been present, they would have felt impelled to support the regency. That may be true, but Mulgrave and Huntingdon, although they were staunch Tories, consistently voted with the Court Party and it is pure conjecture that they would not have done so here.

On the next day the House of Lords, again in committee, proposed that the word "deserted" should be substituted for "abdicated." They then went on to consider the phrase of the Commons resolution which stated that "by breaking the Original Contract between the King and the People" James had endeavored to subvert the constitution. This they debated under two headings, the first being "whether or no there was an original contract between King and People." There seems to have been surprisingly little discussion on this question, although it struck at the very fundamentals of Whig-Tory differences. Not more than two or three hours can possibly have been devoted to it. Clarendon, who was present for at least part of the session, does not even mention that the subject was discussed. There was a division, and the question was decided in the affirmative by a vote of fifty-three to forty-six. The second heading was "Had James broken the contract?" Apparently no division was necessary on this. If one accepted the first proposition the second followed. We might remark in passing that the day was the anniversary of the execution of Charles I.

The next day the Lords turned to problems that were at once more immediate and concrete. The first question "Whether, instead of the throne is thereby vacant" should be inserted "the Prince and Princess of Orange be declared King and Queen" was defeated by five votes. The second met the same fate: "Whether to agree with the House of Commons in these words of the Vote, That the throne is thereby vacant." Several of the Lords entered formal dissent from this decision, among them all the Orangist standbys except Shrewsbury who must have been absent.

Friday appears to have been a dull day. The Lords could do nothing more until the Commons voted on their amendments. The chief discussion in the Lower House was the problem of a sermon that had been preached there two days earlier of which we shall hear more below. Saturday the Commons got down to consideration of two more important questions: the report of the committee authorized to see to the preservation of the laws and liberties; and the amendments of the Lords. On Monday they reported their refusal to accept the amendments, and the Lords reaffirmed their refusal to accept the wording of the Commons resolution. Again most of those lords who dissented made formal record of the fact. The names are almost identical to those which form the earlier list, with the addition of that of the Earl of Shrewsbury.

There seemed to be deadlock. The following day the Commons once more rejected the Lords' Amendments. This time we have a record of one of the votes: that which declared the throne vacant. It stood 282 for retaining the clause to 151 against.[48] On February 6, however, after a lengthy free conference with the Commons, the Lords voted again on whether or not to accept the version of the Lower House. This time the question was decided in the affirmative. Thirty-eight peers entered their dissent, including Nottingham, the Hydes, most of the bishops except London and St. Asaph, the Duke of Ormonde, and the sons of Charles II. Then the question was put

WHETHER THE PRINCE AND PRINCESS OF ORANGE SHALL BE DECLARED KING AND QUEEN OF ENGLAND AND ALL THE DOMINIONS THEREUNTO BELONGING.

The motion passed. Leave was given to the Lords to enter dissent but none did so.

The struggle was over, although the final act would not come until February 13. That is the story; let us now try to see what it means. It has been, I think, a mistake to try to analyze the events of these days on Whig-Tory lines, or even on what later came to be considered as the basic principles of the two parties. In the great free conference of February 5, the Earl of Nottingham said, arguing in support of the use of the word "deserted" rather than "abdicated," ". . . we have no words applicable to this case, because we never before had such a case; and we must not draw inferences of law in such a case that are not deducible from rules well known in our laws."[49] These words, it is true, were spoken with reference to a particular point, but they are applicable to the general situation. That situation was new, and such principles as the Whigs had formulated by this time could no more be advanced to deal with it than could those of the Tories. It is, of course, possible that if these men had had two months instead of two weeks in which to deliberate on their problems, clearer party lines might have emerged. Actually the time at their disposal was incredibly short — from Monday, January 28, when the Commons adopted their famous resolution, to Wednesday, February 6, when the Lords voted to accept it. Issues that would have taken more time to settle were evaded, thereby, ironically enough, earning for this assembly an unmerited reputation for "wise" willingness to compromise. But there is a vast difference between evading issues and compromising on them. The evasion grew out of pressure for time arising from the unsettled state of the country, especially with respect to trade; and from William's insistence upon an immediate settlement.

Such differences of opinion as there were do not indicate any strong desire among the members of the Convention to bring James back again. Messages that he sent stating terms were ignored. Why was this so? There are, of course, certain obvious reasons. James had not been a successful king. In the present situation his return was bound to mean that he had adopted the pro-French policy which he had resisted so long. It also would mean the establishment of a Catholic dynasty which, with or without the religious principle involved, was bound to create difficulties in a nation where Church and State were so closely related. But beyond that there are two further points to be considered. In both Lords and Commons there were too many men who at one point or another had worked with William closely enough so that, in the event of James's return, their political future would be very dark indeed even if an act of amnesty did save them from more dire consequences. This applies not only to the outright Orangists but also to many of the middle-of-the-roaders who, after all, turned the scale. Then there was the very real prospect of heavy financial loss to those who had loaned money to William both before and after his landing in England. Honor might call upon him to repay those debts, but, without the crown and its prerogatives he would lack the means of so doing. When one considers that some of the most important men in England had mortgaged their property to the hilt to back the expedition, and that others had contributed a large share of their ready cash, the financial debacle that would have occurred had William been put in a situation where he felt justified in repudiating his obligations is fascinating to contemplate!

On the other hand absence of an effective movement to recall James did not mean that there was a wholehearted and spontaneous desire to accept William in any of the various capacities that were being suggested. Quite the contrary. Witsen, the Amsterdam burgomaster who came to London with Dijkveld, noted and recorded several indications that William was far from popular.[50] The tone of the English who talked to him was dubious to say the least. Bentinck was criticized, and even Dijkveld, who was credited justifiably enough with having laid the groundwork for the present crisis, came in for his share of sharp remarks. Perhaps it was known among the English that Witsen had never favored his Stadholder's venture and that knowledge may have led some to express themselves more freely to him than they would have otherwise. Yet the impressions Witsen received were by no means restricted to remarks made in confidence. He noted that army officers drank to the confusion of the Prince, and he read a pamphlet being scattered widely about London that openly accused William of wishing to destroy the privileges and freedom of the English as he had those of the Dutch. Even from William himself Witsen had confirmation of the existence of unfavorable tension when the former, at the height of the Convention, requested him to make no mention of those controversies in his reports to the Estates of Holland.

Nor need Witsen have been alone in noting that William's standing in England was far from good. Throughout the country, especially in Newcastle, there were instances of bitter protest. Even in London, where the masses so generally favored the Prince, a man was arrested for threatening to kill him, and other voices were raised in dissent which, although less drastic, was still unmistakable. Such expressions seem to have reached their height on January 30 in sermons from three prominent members of the clergy. On this day, the fortieth anniversary of the execution of Charles I, Dr. Sharpe, rector of St. Margaret's, leading devotions for none other body than the House of Commons, prayed for King James and preached against deposition. Before the Mayor and court of aldermen of London, Dr. Lake, once Mary's tutor, also prayed for James and enlarged upon the sin of disobedience to higher powers. At St. Paul's, Dr. Sherlocke denounced the right of rebellion. "God keep us sober" was the additional prayer of one of those who recorded these events.[51]

With so much irrefutable evidence that William was fast losing whatever popularity he may have had among the English at the time of his arrival the question very naturally arises how he could have been made king even as a co-ruler with his wife. A statement attributed to Halifax, who is said to have told William on his arrival in London that "he might be what he pleased himself . . . for as nobody knew what to do with him, so nobody knew what to do without him"[52] sums up the situation about as well as anything. James was gone. William was present. Something had to be done for the country could not continue in a state of uncertainty. We see here also what can happen when a disorganized majority, united only on the common ground of disapproval of what is taking place, is faced by a well-organized minority which, however much it may be concealing dissension within itself, is united in its determination to reach an immediate objective. This minority had been able to gain control of the mechanism whereby that objective could be gained — the Convention. Observers and members of that Convention might note their uneasiness and apprehensive dislike of decisions being made,[53] pamphleteers might criticize, or clergymen denounce, but none of them was in a position to do anything constructive, or even obstructive. Another factor of importance was the presence in the country of a group which wanted to overthrow the monarchy entirely, the existence of which brought about a somewhat paradoxical situation which eventually worked toward William's benefit. The republicans had assisted in the Revolution hoping that the outcome might be victory for their point of view.

Once it was over, so far as the actual fighting was concerned, they very naturally turned against William. Never a serious menace, they were still of enough significance to provide a telling argument for the Orangists to convince their opponents that if William was rejected, or if, angered by continual controversy he carried out his threat to return to the Netherlands, a republic might be created to fill the political vacuum. Finally the importance of the time element cannot be too often repeated and emphasized. Not only was settlement imperative. The opposition, caught unprepared, did not have the time to organize, to sort out its own differences, and to reach an agreement upon any other solution than that which the Orangists offered.

Because the latter group controlled the Commons and were the most powerful single element among the Lords, the real debates in both Houses were upon procedure rather than upon objective, and were based on obscure legal points rather than upon fundamentals. The question of "abdicate" vs. "desert" involved the issue of whether or not James had acted voluntarily, for in principle abdication had to be voluntary. It was the fact that if "deserted this kingdom" were the chosen phrase a temporary aspect was given that finally turned the scale, for if James returned, or even tried to do so, he could no longer be said to have deserted. The word "vacancy" suggested a breach in the succession, a denial of the doctrine of indefeasible hereditary right. The issue involved here was much more serious than the other because it gave rise to the suggestion that the office of king was being made elective. When this point was forcibly advanced by the Lords we find 151 members of the Commons voting to drop the phrase. Most interesting is the fact that the doctrine of indefeasible hereditary right was far from being denied at this Convention in spite of later interpretations put upon its actions. Almost no one would admit even that what they were doing might create a precedent, and those who were willing to do so insisted that anything of an elective nature was for this time only. The contention was made that unless the throne was vacant with respect to James it could not be filled by anyone else; to the argument that it would be filled by his heir the old maxim of English law that a living man had no heir was advanced.

The real significance of the question lay in whether Mary alone, or William and Mary, should be raised to the throne. On the principle of immediate succession of the heir Mary would have had to be proclaimed and it was only by going through the fiction of a vacant throne that William could be considered unless the members of the Convention had been willing to pass over both daughters of James to adopt a modified Salic law of inheritance. In making their decision, however, the Convention was acting not so much as an elective or legislative body as in their old historic judicial capacity as a "High Court of Parliament." Their job was not to make an heir, since only God could do that, but to find out who was the heir.

All of William's followers in the Convention were very busy during the crucial week marshaling support and putting pressure on the wavering and on outright opponents. One of the busiest of all was Dijkveld. It was pointed out that a refusal to accept the Commons resolution would mean at worst a civil war and at best a continuation of the present unsettled conditions. When the important vote came up in the House of Lords on February 6, the country had been scoured to bring in all possible peers, as can be seen by the fact that the total number of votes cast, 109, is somewhat larger than on any of the previous decisions in spite of the fact that several of those who had usually voted against the Orangists found on that day urgent reasons why they could not attend the session.[54] Clarendon tells us that many who had attended few if any of the earlier meetings were on hand that day. The Earl of Carlisle hobbled in on crutches to vote with the Orangists, and the Earl of Lincoln appeared for the first time, stating that he "came to do whatever my Lord Shrewsbury and Lord Mordaunt would have him." [55]

As for William himself, he played a more direct part, once the Convention was assembled, than he had been doing for the past two or three weeks. His aims underwent a certain amount of modification for it soon became obvious that he could not have his way in his desire to rule alone when even such staunch supporters as Herbert were aghast at the idea. It was probably Dijkveld who influenced him here, by pointing out that insistence on the sole right to the crown would make him unpopular not only in England but also in the United Provinces and with Spain and the Emperor. William, however, was adamant in his refusal to consider Mary as sole ruler or to accept any kind of arrangement whereby his official position was contingent upon hers. That was not selfishness on his part, but merely common sense. No matter how sure he might be that she would survive him, he could not afford to run the risk involved. He knew that as Prince Consort he would be expected to undertake and carry out foreign policies and he could not take the chance of being left in mid-air on any of them by his wife's death. His diplomatic position would be intolerable. This, of course, involved coming to some agreement with Anne. The final arrangement — that he should have the crown jointly with Mary during his lifetime, but that any children of his by any other wife than Mary should be superceded by Anne and her heirs, seems to have been worked out in private some days before the public vote in the Convention.

Whatever arrangement there was had been worked out in the presence of only a small group. There remained the task of getting it accepted by the larger body. William spent the whole of Saturday, January 26, hunting and dining with Sir Robert Howard, one of his strongest and ablest supporters. Shortly after, in a speech before the Convention, Howard raised publicly the threat that if some attention were not paid to William's wishes he would go home again. At about this time a conference was held in Devonshire House at which Danby and Halifax came out clearly, the one for Mary alone, the other for William alone. Halifax, turning to one of the Dutchmen who were present, probably Dijkveld, asked the latter's opinion on William's views and received the answer that William would not like to be his wife's gentleman usher. Halifax may have been holding out for William alone in order to have a better bargaining position. Or he might have been acting as William's mouthpiece. It was clear, however, that some compromise would have to be made. The evening of February 2, after the Lords had refused to accept the Commons' version of the resolution, William and Halifax held a long conference.[56] On the following evening William called in Halifax once more and with him Shrewsbury, Mordaunt,

Winchester, and Danby.[57] He flatly refused to accept a position subordinate to Mary's but, by the very fact of doing so he let it be known that he would accept one which made them joint rulers. From then on the question was settled.

There remains only one further point: the Declaration of Rights, the conditional nature of which has been greatly overstressed. The origin and substance of this document are worthy on their own merits of an intensive study which cannot be accorded to them here. The demand for the declaration reflects the deep need of seventeenth-century England for clarification of many points of its laws. This was the logical time for such a clarification to be made. The Commons' resolution to draw up the declaration came the day after the one on which the resolution declaring the throne vacant was made. A committee appointed to draw up a first draft reported back to the whole House a few days later. During this period, at least up to February 7, the main issue confronting both Houses was the other resolution. Discussion on the two subjects, the declaration and the problem of the succession, went on concurrently in the Lower House, but the discussions were curiously unrelated to each other. Certainly at no time was the offer of the crown made directly or explicitly contingent upon acceptance of the declaration by William and Mary, and it is hard to find much indication of any implicit or indirect condition. In fact, the Declaration of Rights did not receive its final form nor was it adopted by Parliament and given the validity of royal approval until much later in the year, after William and Mary had been safely crowned for some months. A purely accidental circumstance seems to have given rise to the theory of the conditional nature of the declaration. Although the resolution to offer the crown to William and Mary had passed both houses by February 7, not until six days later was the offer formally made to them. In that interval certain differences in the tentative draft of the declaration were ironed out so that, by February 13, the document had been drawn up into what was to be substantially its final form. As far as can be discovered, however, the delay in making the formal offer was caused not by any problems concerned with the Declaration of Rights but simply by Mary's absence. She reached Westminster on Tuesday,

February 12. The next day she and her husband accepted the crown.

William was, it is true, somewhat upset at first by the suggestion of a declaration and is reputed to have said that he would not accept a crown with any strings attached to it. Here again Dijkveld is reported to have worked for moderation.[58] Yet a certain amount of moderating was done by the other side as well. All new points were carefully excluded so that the Declaration of Rights which William and Mary ultimately approved contained no limitations not already in existence. Nor was William accepting any theoretical principle that Parliament had an unlimited right of limitation. He agreed to rule according to the laws of England as every king had done who had ever worn the crown.

Conclusion

There remains the task of stating some evaluation of the significance of William's connection with the Revolution. That significance lies in the fact that the original combination of William with the Tories resulted in the end in what was actually nothing more than a palace revolution. William wanted the crown; the Tories the control of the chief offices of the realm. Next to the control of these offices the principal concern of the Tories was the Anglican Church, and the meager concessions of the Toleration Act attest to the hollowness of their glib promises to the Dissenters. To this combination of the Tories with William the Whigs brought some concern for the rights of Parliament, but they too were more interested in the Staff of the Treasury or in the Great Seal than in popular rights.

The Revolution of 1688 has been called a moral regeneration, a reaction from the corruption of the Restoration. Even if the truth of that statement is accepted it must be agreed that the regeneration was short-lived, for the political immorality of the century which succeeded the coronation of William and Mary makes the casual and inexpert looseness of the preceding three decades look very mild. But the statement cannot be accepted. Part of the difficulty in so doing lies in ascribing individual characteristics to a group. That there were people who felt a disinterested and sincere concern over James's mistakes there can be no doubt. Yet those men were, for the most part, not prime movers in the Revolution. Nottingham and, until the final weeks, Halifax are the outstanding examples of individuals who preferred a really constitutional settlement, while among the lesser men was old Sir John Bramston who refused to help James pack parliament, but stoutly condemned taking up arms against him. There were many like him. It is curious, but not too much

so, that of those to whom we may ascribe the deepest devotion
to constitutional government, many refused to accept William,
or did so with reservations. The fate of Mordaunt and Wildman
showed what could happen to those who expected real regeneration from the leadership of the Tories and the Shaftesbury
Whigs.

The very core of the whole problem, the reason for the immediate success of the Revolution as well as the explanation of
its failure to accomplish anything of lasting benefit, lies in the
point so often stressed in these pages: that men with varied
grievances and personal grudges were able to bury their differences for the moment in order to concentrate on the few
points on which there could be superficial and temporary agreement. Chief among these in the earlier stages had been the insistence
that the Test Act be maintained. With this to protect them Whig
and Tory alike hoped to be safe from the rivalry not only of
the Catholics but also of many of the Dissenters. Both sides
were willing to pay temporary lip service to condemnation of corruption in parliamentary elections: both were equally willing to
stoop to corruption for their own benefit. Neither actually wanted
to see the king deprived of the power to use the patronage in
obtaining a parliamentary majority, for each was quick to see
the tremendous advantage to themselves if the king could be
persuaded to use that power for its own party. Once the Revolution was over, neither side dared carry its differences with the
other too far for fear of pushing its opponents into the ranks
of the active Jacobites or, in some instances, of the even more
dreaded republicans. The result was compromise, but a compromise that grew out of fear and cynicism rather than out of
ethical considerations.

The only limitations which the Revolution, as embodied in
the legislation of the next few years, placed upon the king were
to deprive him of the already highly questionable right to
suspend the operation of laws, and to make it necessary for him,
through financial and other strictures, to call Parliament every
year. But, because Parliament must meet and because it could
control the purse, what happened was that the royal powers
which the king had hitherto been able to use in the interests of

whatever group he pleased, sometimes even — God save the mark — the common people, those powers now passed into the control of the landed aristocracy which could control Parliament. In that sense the long struggle that began at Runnymede turned once more in favor of the heirs of the baronial class and for a century and a half the country was more completely in their grip than ever before: the historic counterweight to them, the royal power, was ineffective. The view that the Revolution was essentially aristocratic has been attacked on the ground that the common people supported it. That this assertion cannot be accepted without rather strong qualifications has already been indicated in those parts of this study which deal not only with William's unpopularity but also with devices that were used in such places as York to trick an otherwise loyal populace into taking part in an uprising. Yet even if the assertion could stand unqualified, judgment should be based on results, not immediate participation. Of course many of the "mobile" as they are called in the letters and diaries of the leaders, were enthusiastic. Even if they had not been overmastered by anti-Catholic hysteria they still would have welcomed the prospect of improvement in their daily lives. But the benefits of the Revolution did not go to them.

If the Revolution was successful because stress could be laid on only one or two points, the person who made this tactic possible was William of Orange. Concentration of forces behind a supposedly disinterested leader gave the whole movement a superficial aura of altruism during the early and all-important days which saw the defeat and flight of King James. William, moreover, was able to make skillful and well-timed concessions to one group without letting the others know too much of what he was doing until he had led them all so far that they could not turn back. In the final and crucial weeks he, and he alone, was responsible for and in control of the military force which first assured the defeat of James and then made quibbling over points of difference seem just a little foolhardy. The Revolution was accomplished in part because of James's unerring and almost incredible ability to do the wrong thing, and in part because Whigs and Tories united against him. It would not have been accomplished at all if William of Orange had not accepted the leadership of the coalition and brought his brains and his army to its support.

The Revolution of 1688 has become a political myth and one that should be examined carefully for, while iconoclasm for its own sake is unimportant, the worship of false gods can be dangerous. This myth has enabled the Anglo-Saxon peoples for almost three centuries to uphold the right of revolution at the same time that they have gently deprecated the use of violence and the participation of a poverty stricken mass. Even in the United States we have tended to picture our own Revolution as the exclusive work of high-minded altruists and have been aghast at any suggestion that the Continental forces were a "rabble in arms." Apparently high-minded altruism and a rabble cannot coëxist. Reëxamination of the forces which brought about the flight of James II should bring a clearer perspective not only of that event but of many in our own time. This was in truth a *respectable* revolution, one in which the right people could and did take part. If the leaders of 1688 had found it necessary or desirable for the attainment of their goal to overthrow the whole political structure of their country, their task would have been more difficult. But their task was rather to preserve that structure intact for their own use and for protection against a group with truly revolutionary principles. This was as true of William as of those who worked with him. Hence the emphasis upon the rule of law. When, however, enacted law itself is a deterrent to success, when the needs of a people demand that the whole fabric must be destroyed rather than preserved, the task is not so easy. Such situations have existed and do exist. It is true that society must try to find a way of making progress by use of some means other than violence. But that cannot be done by reliance upon an inadequate and irrelevant example from the past.

Bibliography

The bibliography lists those works which have been most important for this study under the following headings:

I. Manuscript materials.

II. Printed sources: diaries, correspondence, memoirs, state papers, etc.

III. Secondary works.
   a. Published before 1850.
   b. Published after 1850.

In some instances the decision whether to place a work under "Printed sources" or "Secondary works published before 1850" has had to be arbitrary. The criterion has been whether a given work has been most useful for its secondary or for its primary material.

No attempt has been made to list individually the numerous pamphlets that appeared between 1685 and 1690 relative to the reign of James II and the Revolution of 1688. The principal collections of them which have been used are those in the British Museum, the Royal Library in The Hague, Widener Library at Harvard, and the New York City Public Library.

Unless otherwise noted, all references are to editions listed in this bibliography.

I. *Materials consulted in manuscript*

The British Museum, London

MacKintosh Collection, of which the most important was:
   Add. MS 34510. Letters of Aernout van Citters to the States General, 1688–1689.
Egerton MS 3361. "The Interregnum, or the Proceedings of the Lords of the Council and Others from the Withdrawing of King James II to the meeting of the Convention."

The Public Record Office, London

The contents of the collection known as King William's Chest were examined. Much of the material has been printed in one or more of the collections of printed sources listed below.

The State Papers, France, and the State Papers, Holland, for the appropriate years were also consulted.

The Bodleian Library, Oxford
Ballard MSS 45. f. 22 and f. 25.
Rawlinson MS D 1079.

The Rijks Archief, The Hague
A very rich collection of which the following were the most important:
St. Holland, *Register Saeken van Engelandt.*
Staten General, 2335, *Register Secrete Resolutions.*
Staten General, 2679, 2681, 2687, *Secrete Notulen.*
Staten General, 6335, *Secrete Brieven.*
Staten General, 6929 and 6930, *Engelandt.*
Staten General, 7335, 7336, *Secrete Brieven, Engelandt.*
Verbaal van de Heeren ex't Gedeputeerden in Engelandt; Witsen, Odijk, en Dijkvelt, 1689. Leg. 810.

Printed Sources

d'Avaux, J. A. de Mesmes, comte d'Avaux, *Negociations du Comte d'Avaux en Hollande*, 6 vols. Paris, 1752–53.

Bohun, Edward, *History of the Desertion* in State Tracts, William III, vol. I.

Burnet, Gilbert, *History of His Own Time*, 4 vols. London, 1766.

—— *A Supplement to Burnet's History of His Own Time, Derived from his original papers, his autobiography, his letters to Admiral Herbert, and his private meditations*, edited by H. C. Foxcroft, Oxford, 1902.

Dalrymple, Sir John, *Memoirs of Great Britain and Ireland*, 2 vols. second edition, London, 1773.

Ellis, *Ellis Correspondence*, edited by A. J. W. Ellis, (Baron Dover) 3 vols. London, 1831.

Grey, Anchitell, *Debates in the House of Commons, from the Year 1667 to the Year 1694*. 10 vols. London, 1769.

Heinsius, *Het Archief van den Raadpensionaris Antonie Heinsius*, edited by H. J. van der Heim, 3 vols., The Hague, 1867–1880.

Clarendon, *Correspondence of Henry Hyde, Earl of Clarendon, and of his brother, Laurence Hyde, Earl of Rochester*, 2 vols. edited by Samuel W. Singer, 1828.

Historical Manuscripts Commission Reports. Those which have been most useful are:
Denbigh MSS Seventh Report, Appendix, pp. 196–232.
Papers of Sir Richard Graham, viscount Preston, Seventh Report, Appendix, pp. 261–432.
Kenyon MSS Fourteenth Report, Appendix IV.

Leeds MSS Eleventh Report, Appendix, Pt. VII.

Le Fleming MSS Twelfth Report, Appendix, Part VI.

Lindsey MSS Fourteenth Report, Appendix IX.

Portland MSS Fourteenth Report, Appendix II, Portland III.

Huygens, "Journal van Constantijn Huygens den zoon, van 21 October, 1688 tot 2. September, 1696," vol. I, *Werken Uitgegeven door het Historisch Genootschap Gevestigt te Utrecht*, Nieuwe Reeks, no. 23.

Journal of the House of Commons.

Journal of the House of Lords.

Macpherson, James, editor, *Original Papers containing the Secret History of Great Britain from the Restoration to the Accession of the House of Hanover*. 2 vols. London, 1778.

Mary II, *Lettres et Mémoires de Marie, Reine d'Angleterre*, edited by Mechtild, Countess Bentinck, The Hague, 1880.

Parliamentary History of England edited by William Cobbett, 36 vols. London, 1806–1820.

Recueil des Instructions données aux Ambassadeurs et Ministers de France, depuis les traités de Westphalie jusqu'à la Révolution français, vols. XXI and XXII, Hollande, I and II, edited by Louis André and Emile Bourgeois, Paris, 1922; vols. XXIV and XXV, Angleterre (1649–1690) I and II, edited by J. J. Jusserand, Paris, 1929.

Reresby, *Memoirs of Sir John Reresby*, edited by James J. Cartwright, London, 1875.

Scheltema, Jacob, *Geschied- en Letter-Kundige Mengelwerke*, 6 vols. Utrecht, 1823.

Sheffield, John, Earl of Mulgrave, *Works*, 2 vols. fourth edition corrected, London, 1753.

Sidney, Henry, *Diary of the Time of Charles II, by the Honorable Henry Sidney, afterwards earl of Romney*, including his correspondence with the Countess of Sunderland and other distinguished persons at the English Court, edited by R. S. Blencowe, London, 1843.

Urkunden und Aktenstücke zur Geschichte des Kurfürsten Friedrich Wilhelm von Brandenburg, 21 vols. edited by Erdmansdorffer and others, Berlin, 1864–1915.

"Verbaal van de Buitengewone Ambassade van Jacob van Wassenaar-Duivenvoorde, Arnout van Citters, en Everard van Weede van Dijkveld naar Engelandt in 1685." *Werken uitgegeven door het Historisch Genootschaap*, Nieuwe Reeks, II.

Waldeck, *Wilhelm von Oranien Und Georg Friedrich von Waldeck,* 2 vols. edited by P. L. Müller, The Hague, 1873 and 1880.

William III, *Correspondentie van Willem III en Hans Willem Bentinck, eersten graaf van Portland,* 5 vols. edited by N. Japikse, The Hague, 1927–1935.

Secondary Works
a. Works published before 1850

MacKintosh, Sir James, *The Revolution in England of 1688,* 2 vols. Paris, 1834.

Mazure, F. A. J., *Histoire de la Révolution de 1688 en Angleterre,* 3 vols. Paris, 1825.

Oldmixon, John, *A History of England during the Reigns of the Royal House of Stuart,* London, 1730.

Orleans, Pierre Joseph d', *Histoire Des Révolutions D'Angleterre,* The Hague, 1729.

Ralph, James, *The History of England during the Reigns of King William, Queen Anne, and King George I,* 2 vols. London, 1744–1746.

de Thoyras, Rapin, *History of England,* 3 vols. London, 1737.

Wagenaar, Jan, *Vaderlandsche Historie,* 21 vols. Amsterdam 1749–1759.

b. Works published since 1850

Feiling, Keith, *A History of the Tory Party, 1640–1715,* Oxford, 1924.

Foxcroft, H. S., *The Life and Letters of Sir George Savile, First Marquis of Halifax,* 2 vols. London, 1898.

Japikse, N., *Prins Willem III, de Stadhouder Koning,* 2 vols. Amsterdam, 1930–1933.

Klopp, Onno, *Der Fall des Hauses Stuart und die Succession des Hauses Hannover,* 14 volumes, 1875–1888.

Macaulay, T. B., *The History of England from the Accession of James II,* 5 vols. Boston, n.d.

von Ranke, Leopold, *A History of England, Principally in the Seventeenth Century,* 6 vols. Oxford, 1875.

Notes

Abbreviations used in citations
The following abbreviations are used to indicate the location of manuscript materials:

Br. Mus. - - - British Museum, London.
PRO - - - - Public Record Office, London.
KWC - - - - King William's Chest, in the Public Record Office.
R.A. - - - - Rijks Archief, The Hague.
All other abbreviations are explained the first time they are used.

Chapter 1 THE LONG PROLOGUE

1. King James II to William III, Prince of Orange, February 6, O.S., 1685. Sir John Dalrymple, *Memoirs of Great Britain and Ireland* (Second edition; London: 1773), II, app., Part I, 114. (Hereafter cited as Dalrymple, *Memoirs*.) Author's Note: The only part of this introductory page which is conjectural is to be found in the second sentence. I do not *know* that James was tired but considering the circumstances it is highly probable that he was. As for the letter, if he signed any other personal, as distinguished from official, documents on that day, I have not been able to track them down.

2. William III, Prince of Orange, to the Prince of Nassau Dietz, February 19, N.S., 1685. Groen van Prinsterer, *Archives ou Correspondence Inedite de la Maison Orange Nassau* (Utrecht: 1861), V, 589. Translated by the author.

3. Keith Feiling, *History of the Tory Party, 1640–1715* (Oxford: 1924), p. 205.

4. J. S. Clarke, *The Life of James the Second* (London: 1816), vol. II, *passim*. Although parts of these memoirs are of doubtful authenticity the sections referred to probably give a reasonably accurate version of James's opinion.

5. J. A. de Mesmes, comte d'Avaux, *Négociations du comte d'Avaux en Hollande* (Paris: 1752–1753), *passim* for year 1685. (Hereafter cited as D'Avaux.)

6. See the letter of James, Duke of Monmouth to King James II, written after the former's arrest. It is printed in several places, notably in Clarke, *The Life of James the Second*, II, 32–33.

7. Bevil Skelton to the Earl of Sunderland, June 12, O.S., 1685. PRO, S. P. Holland, S.P. 84–220.

8. "Verbaal van de Buitengewone Ambassade van Jacob van Wassenaar-Duivenvoorde, Arnout van Citters, en Everard van Weede van Dijkveld

naar Engeland in 1685." *Werken uitgaven door het Historisch Genootschap,* Nieuwe Reeks, II.

9. Hans Willem Bentinck to the Prince of Orange, July 10, O.S., 1685. *Correspondentie van Willem III en Hans Willem Bentinck, eersten graaf van Portland* edited by N. Japikse (The Hague: Martinus Nijhoff; 1927–1935), first series, I, 23. (Hereafter cited as *Correspondentie.*)

10. For a discussion of this see F. C. Turner, *James II* (New York: Macmillan, 1948), pp. 253–256.

11. Onno Klopp, *Der Fall des Hauses Stuart und die Succession des Hauses Hannover* (Vienna: 1875–1888), III, 137.

12. G. Fagel to Heinsius, December 28, N.S., 1685. H. J. van der Heim, *Het Archief van den Raadpensionaris Antonie Heinsius* (The Hague: Martinus Nijhoff; 1867), I, xciv–xcv.

13. Feiling, *Tory Party,* p. 201.

14. Klopp, *Fall des Hauses Stuart,* III, 233. See also Historical Manuscripts Commission, 79th Report, *MSS of the Late Montague Bertie, Twelfth Earl of Lindsey,* pp. 270–272, "James, Earl of Abingdon's Discourse with King James II, November 18, 1687, from his own memorandum of it." The whole memorandum throws interesting light on James's attitude not only toward Louis XIV but also toward religious toleration.

15. Leopold von Ranke, *A History of England Principally in the Seventeenth Century* (Oxford: 1875), VI, 81.

16. John Sheffield, Earl of Mulgrave, *Works* (fourth edition, corrected; London: 1753), II, 90.

17. Gilbert Burnet, *History of His Own Time* (third edition; London: 1766), II, 392. "Upon the setting up of the Ecclesiastical Commission some from England pressed them (i.e. William and Mary) to write over against it. . ." Burnet is not always reliable but his conference with William in the summer of 1686 and the visits of Sidney and Mordaunt a little later give substance to his statement.

18. For William's conference with Burnet during this summer see Burnet, *History,* II, 387 ff. Burnet is vague on the number of these conferences and even more so on the exact time when they took place, but evidence on the latter point suggests July.

19. N. Japikse, *Prins Willem III, De Stadhouder Koning* (Amsterdam: J. M. Meulenhoff, 1930–1933), II, 218.

20. Burnet, *History,* II, 394–396.

21. *Ibid.*

22. Burnet, *History,* II, 492. Also Lord Mordaunt to Bentinck (?), October 12, O.S., 1686, *Correspondentie,* first series, II, 7–8; and van Citters to the Prince of Orange, October 8, O.S., 1686, *ibid.,* second series, II, 742.

23. E.g. S.P. Holland, S.P. 84–220; also unsigned dispatch, apparently to the Prince of Orange, June 1, O.S., 1686, KWC, S.P. 8–1. (Both in PRO.)

24. Burnet, *History,* II, 387–392.

25. H. C. Foxcroft, *The Life and Letters of Sir George Savile, First Marquis of Halifax* (London: 1898), I, 474–475.

26. R. A. St. Holland, *Register Saeken van Engelandt,* January 17, N.S., 1687.

27. The Dijkveld mission has been ably treated by James Muilenburg, "The Embassy of Everard van Weede, Lord of Dyckvelt, to England in 1687" (*University of Nebraska Studies*, XX, nos. 3 and 4, 1920). Muilenburg, however, is interested almost exclusively in the diplomatic aspects of the mission. He uses no sources which have not been carefully examined by the present writer, and has apparently not used some that have been consulted by her. Citations in the present discussion will, therefore, be to the sources rather than to the secondary accounts of Muilenburg and others.

28. Aernout van Citters to the Prince of Orange, July 23, N.S., 1686. *Correspondentie*, second series, II, 737.

29. D'Avaux, vol. VI, *passim*.

30. Burnet, *History*, II, 415–416.

31. *Ibid.*, p. 416.

32. D'Avaux, VI, 41–42.

33. Ellis, A. J. W. Agar (Baron Dover), ed. *Ellis Correspondence* (London: 1831), I, 242.

34. R.A. Staten General 6929 Public letter from Everard van Weede to the States General, March 4, N.S., 1687; and R.A. Staten General 6335 Secret letter from Everard van Weede to the Secretary of the States General, same date.

35. The Prince of Orange to Bentinck, March 15, N.S., 1687. *Correspondentie*, first series, I, 31.

36. Burnet, *History*, II, 418–419.

37. The Earl of Danby to the Prince of Orange, May 30, O.S., 1687. Dalrymple, *Memoirs*, II, app., Part I, 195.

38. Foxcroft, *Halifax*, I, 479.

39. Burnet, *History*, II, 421–422.

40. *Ibid.*, p. 422.

41. Dalrymple, *Memoirs*, II, app., Part I, 190–200.

42. *Ibid.*, p. 192.

43. Samuel W. Singer, editor, *Correspondence of Henry Hyde, Earl of Clarendon and of his Brother, Laurence Hyde, Earl of Rochester* (1828), II, 154, 165. (Hereafter cited as *Clar. Cor.*) The references cited from Clarendon's own diary prove conclusively that he had a pension of two thousand pounds and that it was promptly paid.

44. Halifax to the Prince of Orange, August 25, O.S., 1687. Dalrymple, *Memoirs*, II, app., Part I, 207.

45. Mordaunt to Bentinck, March 11, O.S., 1687. *Correspondentie*, first series, II, 10.

46. See biographical notes on Nottingham and Danby in William A. Aitken, editor, *The Conduct of the Earl of Nottingham* (New Haven: Yale, 1941).

47. Pierre Joseph d'Orleans, *Histoire des Révolutions d'Angleterre* (Nouvelle edition; The Hague: 1729), III, 1878.

48. Evidence for this assumption and for the nature of the plans is to be found in passages, too numerous for individual citation, in the correspondence of these men during 1687 and 1688. Specific references will be made later.

Chapter 2 THE ISSUES DEFINED

1. The original letter is in the Public Record Office, KWC, S.P. 8-1. It has been printed in Dalrymple's *Memoirs*, II, app., Part I, 187–190.

2. *Correspondentie*, first series, II, 597.

3. For Hume's letter and the *Memorial*, see *Correspondentie*, first series, II, 13–21.

4. T. B. Macaulay, *The History of England from the Accession of James II* (Boston: Aldine, n.d.), II, 198.

5. Many of these were printed and have been preserved in the various collections of pamphlets, tracts, and broadsheets in the British Museum and elsewhere.

6. For one of the many descriptions on this point see *Ellis Correspondence*, I, 285.

7. Burnet, *History*, II, 416. See also article on John Howe in the Dictionary of National Biography.

8. Halifax to the Prince of Orange, August 25, O.S., 1687. Dalrymple, *Memoirs*, II, app., Part I, 208.

9. For these letters see Dalrymple, *Memoirs*, II, app., Part I, 202–210.

10. *Ibid.*, 203.

11. Sir James MacKintosh, *The Revolution in England of 1688* (Paris: 1834), I, 342.

12. *Ibid.*, 342–343.

13. Historical Manuscripts Commission, Fourteenth Report, app., Part IV, *Manuscripts of Lord Kenyon*, p. 187.

14. Klopp, *Fall des Hauses Stuart*, III, 385–387.

15. Halifax to the Prince of Orange, April 12, O.S., 1687, KWC, S.P. 8-1. (PRO)

16. The Prince of Orange to Bentinck, September 27, N.S., 1687. *Correspondentie*, first series, I, 33–34.

17. *A Letter writ by Mijn Heer Fagel, pensioner of Holland to Mr. James Stewart, advocate, giving an account of the Prince and Princess of Orange's thoughts concerning the repeal of the test and the penal laws* (Amsterdam: 1688).

18. The Earl of Devonshire to the Prince of Orange, Dalrymple, *Memoirs*, II, app., Part I, 213.

19. The first letter from James to Mary is printed in *Lettres et Memoires de Marie, Reine D'Angleterre* (edited by Mechtild, Countess Bentinck, The Hague: 1880), pp. 4–9. Mary's replies of December 26, N.S., 1687 and February 17, N.S., 1688, are also printed there, pp. 10–24. For Mary's comments on these letters and others that were not printed see her memoir for 1688, *ibid.*, 57–65.

20. Burnet, *History*, II, 433–441.

21. *Lettres et Memoires de Marie*, p. 60.

22. For these varied devices see Bentinck to Sidney, December 5, 1687, *Correspondentie*, first series, II, 597–598; Bentinck to Joseph Rivers, December 9, 1687, *ibid.*, 598–599; MacKintosh Papers, Add. MS 34515 (Br. Mus.); and KWC, S.P. 8-1. (PRO)

23. KWC, S.P. 8-2. (PRO)

24. *Ibid.*

25. The Prince of Orange to the Emperor Leopold, n.d.; KWC, S.P. 8-2. (PRO) Printed in Dalrymple, *Memoirs*, II, app., Part I, 256-257.
26. *Miscellanies*, Philobiblion Society, vol. I. According to Japikse, *Willem de Deerde*, II, 241, this letter was written to the Marquis de Gastanaga, governor of the Spanish Netherlands.
27. P. L. Müller, *Wilhelm von Oranien Und Georg Friedrich von Waldeck* (The Hague: 1873-1880), vol. II, *passim*.
28. "Journal van Constantijn Huygens, den zoon, van 21 October, 1688 tot 2 September, 1696." *Werken Uitgegeven door het Historish Genootschap Gevestigt te Utrecht*, Nieuwe Reeks, no. 23 (hereafter cited as *Huygens*), I, 10.
29. See reports of interviews of Cramprich with Fagel and Pettecum, September 29, N.S., 1688, quoted in F. A. J. Mazure, *Histoire de la Revolution de 1688 en Angleterre* (Paris: 1825), III, 93-94.
30. Müller, *Wilhelm von Oranien*, letters from October 1688 to February 1689.
31. From Mazure, *Histoire*, III, 118: "The Spanish envoy (at The Hague) who had ordered prayers in his chapel for the Prince of Orange, gave a dinner to the principal members of the Estates, and gave a toast in these words 'To the Prince of Orange! May he, as King of England, enter Paris within a year with a hundred thousand men!'"
32. D'Avaux to Louis XIV, August 28, N.S., 1687. *Recueil des Instructions données aux Ambassadeurs, Les Pays Bas* (edited by Louis André and Emile Bourgeois, Paris: 1922), I, 394n. This reference is especially valuable because it comes from a letter written at the time rather than from memoirs compiled later. D'Avaux's *Negociations*, it is true, do at times show wisdom after the fact. By careful reading of them, however, it is usually possible to distinguish comments that he made on events some time after they occurred from opinions that he had when they were taking place.
33. D'Avaux, VI, 106-107.
34. Terriesis to the Grand Duke of Tuscany, October 10, O.S., 1685. Printed in Martin Haile, *Mary of Modena: Her Life and Letters* (London: 1905), p. 168.
35. Mazure, *Histoire*, III, 94.
36. *Huygens*, I, 8.
37. D'Albeville to Lord Preston. Historical Manuscripts Commission, app. to the Seventh Report, MSS of Lord Preston, p. 424.
38. Dalrymple, *Memoirs*, II, app., Part I, 337-338.
39. Extract from the Spencer House Journals, entry for December 30, 1688. Printed in Foxcroft, *Halifax*, II, 203-204.
40. Frederick III of Brandenburg to William III, February 27, O.S., 1689. Dalrymple, *Memoirs*, II, app., Part I, 254. I have not given any place here to the story that the Great Elector, when he heard of the death of Charles II, burst forth with the assertion that William should seize the throne immediately. If such a statement was indeed made by the Great Elector it is not evidence of William's intentions. Moreover I am not able to satisfy myself that the story is authentic.
41. Mazure, *Histoire*, II, 317.
42. Burnet, *History*, II, 453-454.

43. Bevil Skelton to the Earl of Sunderland, March 24, N.S., 1688. S. P. France, 1687-88, S.P. 78-151. (PRO)

44. The Earl of Winchester to the Prince of Orange, February 20, O.S., 1688. Dalrymple, *Memoirs*, II, app., Part I, 214-215. Similar letters are to be found in *Correspondentie*, second series, vol. III.

45. The Earl of Danby to the Prince of Orange, March 29, O.S., 1688. Dalrymple, *Memoirs*, II, app., Part I, 217.

46. Burnet, *History*, II, 469. Quoted in full to give basis of comparison with the way in which the conditions were actually carried out.

47. Dalrymple, *Memoirs*, II, app., Part I, 226-227.

48. *Ibid.*, pp. 227-228.

49. *Ibid.*

50. The "Invitation" and Sidney's letter are printed in Dalrymple, *Memoirs*, II, app., Part I, 228-232. (Originals in KWC.)

51. The date of this conference is clearly indicated in a letter from William to Bentinck (*Correspondentie*, first series, I, 36), dated April 29, N.S., 1688, in which we find the words "Mr. Herbert and the two Russells have been here. I do not wish to tell you what they have said to me, since it would be much better to do so by word of mouth."

52. G. N. Clark, *The Later Stuarts* (Oxford: 1934), p. 121.

53. *Correspondentie*, first series, II, 603.

54. *Lettres et Mémoires de Marie*, pp. 62-63.

55. Dalrymple, *Memoirs*, II, app., Part I, 305-306.

56. *Lettres et Mémoires de Marie*, pp. 75-76.

57. Dalrymple, *Memoirs*, II, app., Part I, 238.

58. Halifax to the Prince of Orange, July 25, O.S., 1688. *Ibid.*, p. 236.

59. Nottingham to the Prince of Orange, July 27, O.S., 1688. *Ibid.*, p. 237.

60. The Prince of Orange to Bentinck, August 29, N.S., 1688. *Correspondentie*, first series, I, 49.

61. *Ibid.*

Chapter 3 THE DIPLOMATIC BACKGROUND

1. C. F. N. Rousset, *Histoire de Louvois* (1862-63), IV, 107. Quoting from Montesquieu.

2. On this see the correspondence between Louis XIV and Barillon, especially during the first year of James's reign. Letters of that year are printed in C. J. Fox, *History of the Early Part of the Reign of James II* (London: 1808), app. I. For 1685 and earlier see also Dalrymple, *Memoirs*, vol. II.

3. Instructions to the Imperial ambassador, Martinitz, for his embassy to England, May 19, N.S., 1685. Quoted in Klopp, *Fall des Hauses Stuart*, III, 48.

4. Gaspar Fagel to Anton Heinsius, December 28, N.S., 1685. Heim, *Het Archief van den Raadpensionaris Antonie Heinsius*, I, xciv-xcv.

5. Rousset, *Histoire*, III, 417 ff. Also *Recueil des Instructions données aux Ambassadeurs, Angleterre* (edited by J. J. Jusserand; Paris: 1929), II, 323 ff. especially pp. 326-336, "Instructie pour le sr. de Bonrepaux," December 30, 1685.

THE DIPLOMATIC BACKGROUND 251

6. Gaspar Fagel to Anton Heinsius, February 4, N.S., 1686. Heim, *Archief*, I, xcvii.

7. This is brought out again and again in the diplomatic correspondence of the time.

8. See, for example, Louis's instructions to D'Avaux in 1678 and 1679, *Recueil des Instructions données aux Ambassadeurs, Les Pays Bas*, I, 382–384.

9. See letters of Aernout van Citters to the Prince of Orange, December 16 and 19, O.S., 1684. *Correspondentie*, second series, II, 677, 689.

10. MacKintosh, *The Revolution*, p. 428.

11. Klopp, *Fall des Hauses Stuart*, III, 19–20.

12. Middleton to the Prince of Orange, March 17, O.S., 1685. *Correspondentie*, second series, II, 698. Rochester to the Prince of Orange, March 24, O.S., 1685. *Ibid.*, pp. 699–700.

13. Louis XIV to Barillon, August, 1685. Fox, *History*, app. I, cxvi.

14. Heemskerk to the Prince of Orange, from Madrid, August 30, N.S., 1685. *Correspondentie*, second series, II, 710–712.

15. Instructions to Fuchs, May 8, O.S., 1685. *Urkunden und Aktenstücke zur Geschichte des Kurfürsten Friedrich Wilhelm von Brandenburg* (edited by Erdmansdorffer and others; Berlin: 1864–1915), XXI, 86. (Hereafter cited as *Urk. & Akt.*)

16. Fuchs to the Great Elector, June 2, O.S., 1685. *Ibid.*, p. 92.

17. Text of Hoffman's report, March 11, 1686. Klopp, *Fall des Hauses Stuart*, III, 188–190.

18. D'Avaux, IV, 288.

19. The Earl of Rochester to the Prince of Orange, March 24, O.S., 1685. *Correspondentie*, second series, II, 700.

20. King James II to the Prince of Orange, February 2, O.S., 1686. Dalrymple, *Memoirs*, II, app., Part I, 162–163.

21. *Ibid.*

22. Anton Heinsius to Gaspar Fagel, February 19, O.S., 1686. Heim, *Archief*, I, cv. Heinsius to Fagel, February 26, O.S., 1686. Heim, *Archief*, I, cv. Also reports of Aernout van Citters, March 8, N.S., 1686. R.A. Staten General 7335, *Secrete Brieven*, Engelandt, 1686.

23. Klopp, *Fall des Hauses Stuart*, III, 229.

24. *Ellis Correspondence*, I, 89.

25. Aernout van Citters to the Prince of Orange, July 23, O.S., 1686. *Correspondentie*, second series, II, 737.

26. Aernout van Citters to the States General, August 2, N.S., 1686. R.A. Staten General 7335, *Secrete Brieven*, Engelandt, 1686.

27. Van Citters to States General, August 16, N.S., 1686. *Ibid.*

28. Van Citters to States General, August 27, N.S., 1686. *Ibid.*

29. See D'Avaux, VI, 1–20; and R.A. Staten General 2679, *Secrete Notulen*, October–December, 1686.

30. Klopp, *Fall des Hauses Stuart*, III, 243.

31. *Ibid.*

32. Pufendorf, *Friederich Wilhelm der Grosse Churfürsten zu Brandenburg, Leben und Thaten* (Berlin: 1710), p. 1222.

33. Von Ranke, *History of England*, IV, 408.

34. "Kurbrandenburgische Gedanken in puncto einer Zusammensetzung wider Frankreich," May 22, O.S., 1686. *Urk. & Akt.* XIV (2), 1293–1294.

35. Report of Cramprich, September 12, N.S., 1686. Klopp, *Fall des Hauses Stuart*, III, 245.

36. *Ibid.*, III, 343.

37. R.A. Staten General 2681, *Secrete Notulen*, April, May, and June, 1687.

38. Berichte von Jacob von Hop. *Urk. & Akt.*, III, 784–801.

39. The Prince of Orange to Simon von Pettecum, July 21, N.S., 1687. *Correspondentie*, second series, vol. II, 756–757.

40. Prince of Orange to von Pettecum, November 28, N.S., 1687. *Ibid.* p. 770. ". . . et vous en revenir icy, prenant vostre chemain par Cell et Hanover, afin de pouvoir m'informer de quels sentiment ms. les Ducs sont, qui sans doubt vous donneront reponse sur le lettres que je leurs ay escrit par vous, et sur les propositions que vous leurs avait fait de ma part."

41. Marshal Schomberg to Henry Sidney, September 25, N.S., 1687. R. W. Blencowe, ed., *Diary of the Time of Charles II, by the Honorable Henry Sidney* (London: 1843), II, 265–267.

42. Pettecum to the Prince of Orange, January 21, N.S., 1688. *Correspondentie*, second series, III, 1–3.

43. *Ibid.*

44. The Great Elector to the Prince of Orange, January 26, O.S., 1688. *Urk. & Akt.*, XXI, 133.

45. For Bentinck's mission to Berlin see letters of the Prince of Orange to Bentinck from May 22 to June 15, 1688. *Correspondentie*, first series, I, 36–42. As in the case of Pettecum, information about Bentinck's reports must be derived from references to them in William's letters, for the reports themselves are missing.

46. Prince of Orange to Bentinck, June 4, N.S., 1688. *Correspondentie*, first series, I, 40.

47. The Prince of Orange to Bentinck, June 15, N.S., 1688. *Ibid.*, p. 43.

48. For the negotiations of Amerongen with the Elector of Saxony between May 26 and June 8, see *Correspondentie*, second series, vol. III, 14–29.

49. Bentinck to E. Danckelmann, June 22, N.S., 1688. *Correspondentie*, first series, II, 124.

50. E. Danckelmann to Bentinck, June 27, O.S., 1688. *Correspondentie*, first series, II, 128.

51. Marshal Schomberg to Bentinck, June 13, and June 17, O.S., 1688. *Ibid.*, pp. 152–153.

52. Waldeck to Bentinck, June 16, and June 24, N.S., 1688; Waldeck to the Prince of Orange, June 21, N.S., 1688. *Correspondentie*, first series, II, 142–147.

53. R.A. Casa Lit. C. Log. Q. no. 222.

54. The Duke of Hanover to the Prince of Orange, August 4, N.S., 1688. *Correspondentie*, second series, III, 35–36.

55. Report of Fuchs, July 27, O.S., 1688. Printed in von Ranke, *History of England*, VI, 90–99.

56. Blancard to the Prince of Orange, January, 1687. Klopp, *Fall des Hauses Stuart*, III, 277.

57. Instructions to Fuchs, July 21, O.S., 1688. Printed in von Ranke, *History*, VI, 88–90.

58. R.A. Casa Lit. C. Log. Q. no. 222 (Hesse-Cassel), 223 (Würtemberg), 224 (Celle–Wolfenbüttel), 225–226 (Brandenburg).
59. Waldeck to Bentinck, August 16, N.S., 1688. *Correspondentie,* first series, II, 147.
60. Waldeck to Bentinck, June 16, N.S., 1688. *Ibid.,* 143.
61. Waldeck to the Prince of Orange, December and January, 1688–89. Müller, *Wilhelm von Oranien,* II, 121–132.
62. The Prince of Orange to Bentinck, September 2, N.S., 1688. *Correspondentie,* first series, I, 53.
63. John Ham to Bentinck, September 25, N.S., 1688. *Correspondentie,* first series, II, 135–137. Also Danckelmann to Bentinck, end of September, 1688. *Ibid.,* pp. 139–140.
64. *Ibid.*
65. R.A. Staten General 2687, *Secrete Notulen,* October-November, 1688.
66. R.A. Casa Lit. C. Log. Q. no. 227.

Chapter 4   WAITING FOR THE PROTESTANT WIND

1. Historical Manuscripts Commission, Fourteenth Report, app. II, Portland MSS, III, 410.
2. For specific references see next chapter.
3. Historical Manuscripts Commission, Twelfth Report, app. VII, Le Fleming MSS, p. 213.
4. *Clar. Cor.,* II, 194.
5. James J. Cartwright, editor, *Memoirs of Sir John Reresby* (London: 1875), p. 407. (Hereafter cited as Reresby, *Memoirs.)*
6. Burnet, *History,* II, 573.
7. Job de Wilde to Bentinck, October, 1688. *Correspondentie,* first series, II, 618.
8. Jan Wagenaar, *Vaderlandsche Historie* (Amsterdam: 1756), XV, 466–467.
9. *Huygens,* I, 21.
10. The Earl to the Countess of Danby, October 2, O.S., 1688. Historical Manuscripts Commission, Fourteenth Report, app. IX, Lindsey MSS, p. 447.
11. See, for example, "A letter from Colonel Ambrose Norton," J. Macpherson, editor, *Original Papers containing the secret history of Great Britain* (London: 1778), I, 287–293.
12. Report of Jacob van Leeuwen to Bentinck. *Correspondentie,* first series, II, 607–610.
13. *Huygens,* I, 5–11, *passim.*
14. *Ibid.,* I, 9.
15. Report of Jacob van Leeuwen to Bentinck. *Correspondentie,* first series, II, 607–610.
16. Mazure, *Histoire,* III, 119.
17. Peregrine Bertie to the Earl of Danby, September 25, O.S., 1688. Historical Manuscripts Commission, Eleventh Report, app. VII, Leeds MSS, p. 25.
18. Mazure, *Histoire,* III, 120. Mazure says that "the son of the Marquis

of Halifax went at the same time." This, however, is open to question. See Foxcroft, *Halifax*, II, 1-2n.

19. This account has been summarized and parts of it quoted in full in Wagenaar, *Vaderlandsche Historie*, XV, 426-431. Unfortunately the original has been lost.

20. The Prince of Orange to Bentinck, August 25, N.S., 1688. *Correspondentie*, first series, I, 45. Prince of Orange to Bentinck, August 29, N.S., 1688. *Ibid.*, p. 48.

21. R.A. Staten Holland, *Reg. Saeken van Engelandt*, 1688.

22. R.A. Staten General 2686, *Secrete Notulen*, July-September, 1688. September 20, N.S., 1688.

23. R.A. Staten General 2335, *Reg. Sec. Res.* 1687-88, October 8, N.S., 1688.

24. Wagenaar, *Vaderlandsche Historie*, XV, 467.

25. "Instructie by Sijne Hoogheit gegeven aen den Heer Arthur Herbert, sijnen aengestelden Lieutenant Admiral-General, omme benevens den Lieutenant-Admiral Evertse te commandeeren een vloot scheepen van oorlogh tot executie van de ordres hiernaer volgende," October 6, N.S., 1688. *Correspondentie*, first series, II, 613-616.

26. *Ibid.*, first series, I, 59-60.

27. *Huygens*, I, 19.

28. Memorial of Admiral Herbert, *Correspondentie*, first series, II, 612-613.

29. William had received this information in van Leeuwen's report. *Correspondentie*, first series, II, 607-610.

30. Edward Bohun, "History of the Desertion" in *State Tracts, William III*, I, 59.

31. For an account of the storm and its effect upon the members of the expedition, including the Prince, see *Huygens*, I, 5-12.

32. *Huygens*, I, 11. On the accuracy of these figures see also E. B. Powley, *The English Navy in the Revolution of 1688* (Cambridge: University Press, 1928), pp. 35-36.

Chapter 5 THE MARCH TO LONDON

N.B. In Chapters 5 and 6 all dates in the text or in citations are in Old Style unless otherwise noted.

1. *Huygens*, I, 19.

2. *Ibid.*, I, 17-21.

3. Burnet, *History*, II, 531-532. But Burnet himself ascribes the length of the stay in Exeter to the need for transportation. See Burnet to Herbert, November 16, 1688. Foxcroft, ed. *A Supplement to Burnet's History of His Own Time* (Oxford: 1902), p. 530.

4. The Prince of Orange to Admiral Herbert, November 10/20, 1688. *Correspondentie*, second series, III, 55.

5. Japikse, *Willem de Deerde*, II, 261.

6. Newsletter of November 13, 1688; Historical Manuscripts Commission, Fourteenth Report, app. IV, MSS of Lord Kenyon, p. 207; and another newsletter, same date; Historical Manuscripts Commission, Twelfth Report, app. VII, Le Fleming MSS, p. 219.

7. *Huygens*, I, 21.

8. *Ibid.*

9. *Ibid.*, p. 18.

10. *Ibid.*, p. 19.

11. Historical Manuscripts Commission, Eighth Report, app. I, p. 416.

12. Bentinck to Admiral Herbert, November 21/December 1, 1688. *Correspondentie*, second series, III, 65.

13. Historical Manuscripts Commission, app. to Seventh Report, MSS of Lord Preston, p. 414. Also *Ellis Correspondence*, III, 288.

14. *Huygens*, I, 17, 21.

15. *Ibid.*, p. 24.

16. Gilbert Burnet "Expedition of His Highness the Prince of Orange for England (In a letter to a person of Quality)," *Harleian Miscellany* (T. Parks, ed.; London: 1808–1813), I, 45.

17. *Huygens*, I, 21.

18. *Ibid.*

19. Bohun, "History," 77.

20. For fuller accounts of the incident see "A letter from Colonel Ambrose Norton" in Macpherson, *Original Papers*, I, 287–293; Bohun, "History," 62; and "Relation du Voyage d'Angleterre," Historical Manuscripts Commission, app. to Seventh Report, Denbigh MSS, p. 226.

21. Earl of Devonshire to Earl of Danby, n.d. Historical Manuscripts Commission, Ninth Report, app. II, Morrison MSS, p. 460.

22. Danby to the Prince of Orange, December 10, 1688. Historical Manuscripts Commission, Fourteenth Report, app. IX, Lindsey MSS, p. 453.

23. Bentinck to Admiral Herbert, November 23/December 3, 1688. *Correspondentie*, second series, III, 66.

24. Historical Manuscripts Commission, Fourteenth Report, app. IV, MSS of Lord Kenyon, p. 199.

25. *Ibid.*, pp. 201–208.

26. Sir John Reresby to Lord Preston, November 13, 1688. Historical Manuscripts Commission, appendix to Seventh Report, MSS of Lord Preston, p. 415.

27. Reresby, *Memoirs*, p. 415.

28. *Ibid.*, pp. 413–416.

29. *Ibid.*, p. 417.

30. Historical Manuscripts Commission, Eleventh Report, app. VII, Leeds MSS, p. 27.

31. *Huygens*, I, 4.

32. *Ibid.*

33. *Ibid.*, p. 19.

34. *Ibid.*, p. 17.

35. Memorandum in Bentinck's hand, November 12, 1688. *Correspondentie*, first series, II, 639.

36. "Speech of the Prince of Orange to some of the Principal Gentlemen of Somerset and Dorset on their coming to join His Highness at Exeter." November 15, 1688. (Pamphlet, Br. Mus.)

37. *Huygens*, I, 22.

38. Historical Manuscripts Commission, Eleventh Report, app. VII, Leeds

MSS, p. 30. Also "Diary of Sir John Knatchbull," Br. Mus. Add. MS 33, 923; entries for December 8 and December 11, 1688.

39. W. Cobbett, ed. *Parliamentary History* (London: 1806-1820), V, 17.

40. Bohun, "History," 83.

41. *Huygens*, I, 24.

42. Bohun, "History," 57.

43. Henry Compton, Bishop of London, to the Earl of Danby, c. December 10, 1688. Historical Manuscripts Commission, Ninth Report, app. II, Morrison MSS, p. 460.

44. St. Asaph to Bentinck (?) December 17, 1688. Dalrymple, *Memoirs*, app., Part I, 326.

45. *Huygens*, I, 31.

46. *Ibid.*, p. 33.

47. *Ibid.*, p. 35.

48. *Ibid.*

49. Unsigned, undated letter, KWC, S.P. 8-2 (PRO). See Foxcroft, *Halifax*, II, 20, n. 3 for method by which date and writer were determined.

50. Foxcroft, *Halifax*, II, 208.

51. *Huygens*, I, 49.

52. *Correspondentie*, first series, I, 24.

53. Historical Manuscripts Commission, Fourteenth Report, app. IV, MSS of Lord Kenyon, p. 207.

54. From report of Commissioners to the Earl of Middleton, December 8, 1688. Printed in Foxcroft, *Halifax*, II, 24-26.

55. Newsletter, Historical Manuscripts Commission, Twelfth Report, app. VII, Le Fleming MSS, p. 225.

56. *Huygens*, I, 35.

57. *Clar. Cor.*, II, 215-217.

58. *Ibid.*, p. 216.

59. *Ibid.*, p. 222.

60. *Ibid.*

61. Bentinck to Admiral Herbert, December 10/20, 1688. *Correspondentie*, second series, III, 80.

62. Burnet, *History*, II, 538.

63. It is possible that Bishop Compton had told William of the statement made by James before the peers that he might "fly beyond the sea." (Compton to Danby, Historical Manuscripts Commission, Ninth Report, app. II, Morrison MSS, p. 460.) William received a letter from Compton at about this time that must have been written about the same day that the bishop sent Danby the above information, and, although his letter to William is known only through references to it in William's reply (William to Henry Compton, Bishop of London, December 5, 1688), its content may have been similar to that of the other.

64. William to Danby, December 12, 1688. Historical Manuscripts Commission, Ninth Report, app. II, Morrison MSS, p. 461. Also William to Danby, same date. J. H. Plumb and Alan Simpson, "A letter of William, Prince of Orange, to Danby on the Flight of James II," *Cambridge Historical Journal*, 1935.

65. Feversham to the Prince of Orange from Uxbridge. KWC S.P. 8-2 (PRO).

66. *Correspondentie*, second series, III, 82–83.
67. *Ibid.*, p. 83.
68. *Huygens*, I, 45.
69. Address of the Lieutenancy of London, December 11, 1688. *Correspondentie*, second series, III, 81.
70. See Br. Mus. Egerton MS 3361, "The Interregnum – or the Proceedings of the Lords of the Council and Others from the withdrawing of King James to the meeting of the Convention."
71. Foxcroft, *Halifax*, II, 58.
72. *Huygens*, I, 45, 48.
73. *Ibid.*, p. 47.
74. Burnet, *History*, II, 545.
75. *Clar. Cor.*, II, 229.

Chapter 6　THE INTERREGNUM

1. Macaulay, *History of England*, II, 541.
2. See especially the Prince of Orange to Waldeck, December 25/January 4, 1688–89. Müller, *Wilhelm von Oranien*, II, 126.
3. Rapin de Thoyras, *The History of England* (London: 1737), III, 293.
4. Historical Manuscripts Commission, Fourteenth Report, app. IX, Lindsey Papers, 456.
5. Ballard MS, 45 f. 22 (Bodleian Library, Oxford).
6. *Ibid.*
7. Burnet, *History* (Oxford edition of 1852), III, 341. Onslow's note.
8. Van Citters to the States General, December 25, 1688. R.A. Staten General 6930, *Engelandt*.
9. *Clar. Cor.*, II, 235.
10. Van Citters to the States General, December 25, 1688. R.A. Staten General 6930, *Engelandt*.
11. Ballard MS, 45 f. 22 (Bodleian Library, Oxford).
12. Sheffield, *Works*, II, 85.
13. Burnet to Herbert, December 25, 1688. Foxcroft, *Supplement to Burnet's History*, p. 535.
14. E.g. John Oldmixon, *A History of England During the Reign of the Royal House of Stuart* (London: 1730), II, 765.
15. Van Citters, December 28, 1688. R.A. Advuysen uit Engelandt.
16. Van Citters to the States General, January 11, 1689. R.A. Staten General 6930, *Engelandt*. Van Citters mentions the sum of 200,000 pounds. Other accounts vary slightly from this.
17. E.g. Historical Manuscripts Commission, Twelfth Report, app. VII, Le Fleming MSS, p. 230.
18. Laurence Echard, *The History of England* (third edition; London: 1720), II, 1138.
19. Historical Manuscripts Commission, Twelfth Report, app. VII, Le Fleming MSS, p. 230.
20. Echard, *History*, II, 1138. Also "A Speech of a Fellow Commoner of England," *Harleian Miscellany*, V, 353.
21. "A Declaration for the Better Quartering of Troops" (Broadsheet, Br. Mus.).

22. "Declaration of His Highness, the Prince of Orange," January 16, 1688 (Broadsheet, Br. Mus.).
23. Müller, *Wilhelm von Oranien*, II, 122–131, *passim*. Also *Correspondentie*, second series, III, 92–93.
24. Müller, *Wilhelm von Oranien;* and report of the special embassy of Dijkveld, Odyck, and Witsen, January 15/25, 1689. R.A. Staten General 7336, *Secrete Brieven*, Engelandt.
25. See text, p. 95.
26. J. Ralph, *The History of England during the Reigns of King William, Queen Anne, and King George I* (London: 1744–1746), II, 11.
27. Waldeck to the Prince of Orange, December 14/24, 1688. Müller, *Wilhelm von Oranien*, II, 121.
28. Klopp, *Fall des Hauses Stuart*, IV, 308.
29. Sheffield, *Works*, II, 75.
30. *Ibid.*
31. Klopp, *Fall des Hauses Stuart*, IV, 309, quoting Hoffman's report.
32. The Prince of Orange to the King of Spain, January 15, 1689. Historial Manuscripts Commission, Fifteenth Report, app. II, MSS, of J. Eliot Hodgkin, pp. 77–78.
33. *Huygens*, I, 67.
34. Foxcroft, *Halifax*, II, 203–204. Extract from the Spencer House Journals.
35. *Huygens*, I, 58.
36. Journals of the House of Commons, X, 8.
37. J. H. Plumb, "The Elections to the Convention Parliament of 1689," *Cambridge Historical Journal*, 1937.
38. Historical Manuscripts Commission, app. to Seventh Report, Denbigh MSS, p. 234.
39. For information on this point see the Journals of the House of Commons, vol. X, for January and February, 1689; reports on contested elections.
40. "Diary of Sir John Knatchbull," Br. Mus. Add. MS 33923.
41. Historical Manuscripts Commission, Fourteenth Report, app. II, Portland MSS III, p. 422.
42. Sheffield, *Works*, II, 86.
43. *Huygens*, I, 68. Dijkveld says "mousenest."
44. Blencowe, ed. *Diary of the Time of Charles II*, I, 35.
45. Journals of the House of Commons, X, 9.
46. *Clar. Cor.*, II, 253.
47. Unless otherwise noted authority for the material in the next few pages is to be found in the Journals of the House of Lords and the Journals of the House of Commons for the days covered by this action.
48. Feiling, *Tory Party*, p. 257.
49. Cobbett, *Parliamentary History*, V, 77.
50. Jacob Scheltema, *Geschied-en Letter-kundige Mengelworke* (Utrecht: 1823), III, 135–141.
51. Ballard MS, 45 f. 25 (Bodleian Library, Oxford).
53. Interesting instances of this can be found in Rawlinson MS D 1079
53. Interesting instances of this can be found in Rawlinson MSS D 1079 and in Ballard MS, 45 f. 25 (Both, Bodleian Library, Oxford).

54. *Clar. Cor.*, II, 261.

55. *Ibid.*

56. Reresby, *Memoirs*, pp. 432–433.

57. *Huygens*, I, 81, tells us that, on the evening of February 3, the Prince had a long conference with "seven or nine" (sic) lords, including Halifax, Winchester, and Mordaunt. Burnet, *History*, II, 574–575, mentions a conference and names Halifax, Shrewsbury, and Danby, but, as usual, gives no date. The probability is that both are speaking of the same conference, and that from the two accounts we can gather the names of at least five of the men who were present.

58. Wagenaar, *Vaderlandsche Historie*, XV, 507.

Index

cision, 207, 208. *See also* Convention Parliament
Compton, Bishop, 72; on James II's intended flight, 256
Conventicle and Five Mile Acts, 22–23
Conventiclers, 26
Convention Parliament, William administers until meeting of, 210; elections for and purpose of, 220–223; resolutions and debate on vacant throne, 225–233; Declaration of Rights, 234
Cornbury, Lord (son of Earl of Clarendon), a leader of deserters, 160, 180, 183
Cornwall, England, 151
Council of Peers, James II calls, 181; decree against Catholics, 215
Court of Ecclesiastical Commission, formed by James II, 14–15; William and Mary attitude on, 246
Covenanters, 11
Cramprich, imperial envoy, 103, 106
Cromwell, Oliver, 80

D'Adda, Papal nuncio, 27
D'Albeville, Marquis, mission to William, 28–29, 30; Fagel correspondence on Catholic issue, 54, 55; informer to James, 60, 140; questioned extensive arming, 140, 142, 144
Dalrymple, Sir John, *Memoirs of Great Britain and Iceland*, 33, 93, 93fn., 95fn., 245
Danby (Thomas Osborne), Earl of, 4, 23, 24, 157, 198, 218; Dijkveld interview with, 31; Shrewsbury House group, 33, 35; letter of the "immortal seven," 66; expedition advice, 72; position on political crisis, 134, 135; subversion activities in army, 136, 139, 140; invasion preparations, 139, 140; raising troops, 150; York incident, 165, 166; aid to Orangist cause, 167; on choice of succession, 222, 223, 233, 234; William's conference with, 259

Danckelmann, Minden meeting, 123–124
Dartmouth, Earl of, James II's adviser, 132
D'Avaux, Comte, French ambassador at The Hague, 7, 29, 62, 97, 203; anticipated William's plans for throne, 59; effort to win over United Provinces, 94; informer to James II, 140; questioned extensive arming, 142
Declaration (William's Invasion), drawn up by Fagel, 73; objectives, 146, 147, 169, 203, 216; purpose of second, 147; distribution and James's action toward, 177–178
Declaration of Indulgence, consternation over, 43–44; reception of a new, 64
Declaration of Rights, 234–235
Declarations (associations), 173–175. *See also* Exeter Association
De Gastanaga, Marquis, Spanish Netherlands governor, 58
Delamere, Lord, 133, 135; Orangist movement, 163; Earl of Derby squabble, 164; order to James II on Whitehall departure, 199
Denmark, 109
Denmark, Prince of, 218
De Platen and von Grote, conference of von Pettecum with, 111
Derby, Earl, Lord Delamere squabble, 135, 164
Desertions, 185; among officers, 138, 180
Devon, 151, 152
Devonshire, Earl of, Dijkveld interview with, 31, 36; in opposition to crown, 36; letter of the "immortal seven," 66
Devonshire, England, early adherents of William at, 174
De Witt, John, 79
Dijkveld (Everard van Weede), Lord, missions to England, 27–30, 33, 98, 100; advises Witsen of necessity of invasion, 141; Orangist cause, 220, 232; advice to William, 222, 235
Dissenters, contest for support of,

25; William's promises to, 31, 43,
51–52; effect of Declaration of
Indulgence on, 43–44; William's
public stand on, 53–54; effect of
prince's birth on, 68–69
Divine Right, 12
Dover, Straits of, 151
Dover, Treaty of, 146
Dumblaine, Lord, liaison officer be-
tween England and William, 139
Dutch, English rivalry with, 127;
support for invasion secured, 147
Dutch Government, invested in in-
vasion, 137. *See also* United
Provinces *and* Netherlands
Dutch naval yards, activity, 127
Dutch traders, 144

East Indies, 87
Ecclesiastical Commission, Court of,
James II's formation of, 14–15;
William and Mary on, 246
Edict of Nantes, Louis XIV's revo-
cation of, 10, 13, 44, 88
Edict of Toleration (Scotland), 26
Elections, Parliamentary, Orangists'
attempt to manipulate, 132
Emperor (Leopold), William's letter
on purpose of invasion, 57; uneasy over purpose, 58; Turkish
conflicts, 78, 107; policy toward
England, 84–85; difficulties with
Spain and France, 96; League of
Augsburg, 103; treaties with United Provinces, 124
England, tensions under James II,
7–12, 26–28; relations with Netherlands, 27–33; William's plans for
invasion, 56, 57; strained relations
with United Provinces, 62, 86–87;
relations with France, 77; wars
with United Provinces, 78; unreliability in international affairs,
78–82, 84, 85; imperial possessions,
79; uninspired military record, 80;
policy toward France, 86, 87; and
Dutch claims, 87; shift in French
policy toward, 87–88; religious
issue, 89; William's personal and
official relation with, 92–95; weakness of, 96–97, 139; colonial dif-

ferences with Dutch, 101; confusion and frustration over James,
135, 221, 230–231; fleet outnumbered by William's, 139; William's
agents in, 139; propaganda in favor
of invasion, 140, 144–146; feeling
against France, 145; need of sovereignty during interregnum, 204;
Council of Peers decree against
Catholics, 215. *See also various
entries under* Anglo-
England, Church of. *See* Anglicans
and Church of England
English refugees (in Netherlands),
attitude on William, 42
Essex, Earl of, death of, 224–225
Essex, England, 149
Europe, diplomatic background, 76–
91
Exclusion Controversy, 5, 6, 83
Exclusionists, 36; Monmouth supporters, 148
Exe River, William's forces on, 153
Exeter, England, landing of expeditionary forces at, 152, 153–154;
William addressed newcomers,
171–172; length of stay at, 254
Exeter Association, 172–173, 209
Exeter Cathedral, William's orders
to clergy of, 170
Expedition of William, invading
England, letters from William on
objectives, 56, 57; William's real
purpose in, 59–60, 73, 75; careful
preparations, 61, 137; William's
timing of, 88, 117; delay in, 113;
aid from Germans solicited, 114–
115; William's determination to
make, 126; conditions in England
determined by imminence of, 139–
140; military preparations for,
137–140; sailing from Netherlands,
150–151; conjectures on planned
landing place, 151–152; actual
landing, 153–154; financial difficulties after landing, 154–155; recruits for, 158, 159, 160, 161;
William's Exeter speech on objectives, 172

Fagel, Gaspar (pensioner of Hol-

Archbishop of Cologne, 117;
turns against Louis, 117
Popery, English masses' fear of, 14
Popish Plot, 6
Portman, Sir William, 133, 156
Powle, Sir Henry, 209, 224
Presbyterians, 11; Edict of Toler-
ation (Scotland) effect on, 26
Prince of Wales, 136, 170; legiti-
macy maintained by James, 178
Proclamations, William's demand
that James recall, 192
Propaganda, William stresses in
England, 146; people under in-
fluence of, 142–144, 145, 167–168
Protestant Religion, William's de-
fense of, 172, 173
Protestants, effect of birth of prince
on, 69; Hapsburg hostile policy
toward, 88; in opposition group,
131–132
Protestantism, William's open stand
on, 51–52
Public Record Office (London),
Invitation and Sidney letter in, 67

Quakers, Edict of Toleration (Scotland) effect on, 26

Ratisbon, Twenty Years Truce of, 77
Recruits, William's call in England
for, 158, 159, 160
*Reflections on the Letter of Mr.
Fagel*, 70
Refugees (Netherlands), 42; Wil-
liam's need of support from, 43;
plotting for an attack, 59; from
the Rebellion, 99
Regency, considered at Convention,
225
Regiments, William's raising in
England for expedition, 170
Religious issue, use as a propaganda
weapon of Revolution, 88–89; dur-
ing interregnum, 215–216
Religious toleration, William's at-
titude, 22; terms of a major issue,
45; William's open stand on, 51–52;
William's public stand on, 53–54

Republicanism, 12
Reresby, York incident, 165, 166
Revenue, William's demands of
James for, 193
Revolution of 1688, contention on
immediate inception of, 19, 20fn.;
plans for carefully concealed, 38;
effect of prince's birth on success
of, 69, 70; importance of timing
of, 75–76, 88; religious issue used
as a propaganda weapon, 88–89;
William's plans for insurrection
and desertion under control, 157;
basic principle of, 191; evaluation
of results, 237–238; contributary
forces to success, 238–239; becomes political myth and impli-
cations thereof, 239
Rochester, Earl of (Laurence Hyde),
23, 24, 26, 51, 98, 180
Rock-a-bye baby, folk song, 69
Ronquillo, Don Pedro (Spanish
envoy in London), 215, 216;
uneasy over purpose of William's
invasion, 57
Royal prerogative, Stuarts' use of,
12
Russell, Admiral, Dijkveld interview
with, 31; in opposition to crown,
36; urged William to act, 63–64;
letter of the "immortal seven,"
66; feared all was lost, 151; in
William's expedition in England,
161
Rye House Plot, 42, 64

Salisbury, James II at, 180; William
in, 183
Sawyer, Sir Robert, 209
Saxony, Elector of, 116
Schomberg, Marshal, 104, 111, 149;
leader of Dutch army, 208

Scots, in conspiracy against crown,
37; uninterested in expedition, 160
Scottish refugees (in Netherlands),
42
Scottish regiments, ready to submit
to William, 195

103–104; meeting with Great Elector, 104–106; confusing sentiment on Turk defeat, 107; support to rumors of French attack, 108, 143; reëntry into German affairs, 109–110; reasons for delaying expedition, 113; negotiations in Germany for aid, 114–115; interview with Elector postponed, 114–115, 117–118; missions to German states, 118; plans unknown to States General and German states, 121, 122; Minden meeting, 123–124; intentions unknown to England, 127–129; personal fortune staked on invasion, 137; well informed of English plans for resistance, 139, 149; pretext for reasons for military preparations, 140, 142; in touch with English state of mind, 141–142; explanations to States General on his plans, 142–143, 149; Declaration to English people, 146–147; Second Declaration drawn up, 147; his three previous trips to England, 148; false moves and final start, 149–150; landing of expedition and march into Exeter, 152–154; pressing problems attending the landing, 154–155; claim of representing lawful sovereign power in England, 169, 170; civil appointments in local governments, 175; as a sickly man, 175; success in expedition, 182; characteristics, 185; planned actions carefully, 186; first meetings with King's Commissioners, 186–188; confers with gentry on terms tö King, 189–190; policies formed toward his opponents, 191–192; demands submitted to James through commissioners, 192–193; welcome to

London, 195–196, 200; reluctance to assume crown, 203, 204–206; call of members of Charles II's Parliament, 207, 208–209; consented to take over until Convention, 210; administrative problems, 210–214, 215; religious issue in England during Interregnum, 215–216; heavy duties during Interregnum, 217–220; constant control over English political developments, 219–220; hereditary claim to throne, 220–223; joint monarchy declared, 227; unpopularity in England, 229–230; modification of aims, and agreement with Anne, 232–233; offer of crown on joint basis, 234–235; on Declaration of Rights, 235; supposed disinterestedness, 238

William and Mary, on repeal of Test and Penal laws, 248
Winchester, Marquis of, 36–37, 234, 259
Windsor, William in, 196
Witsen, 140, 141, 229–230
Wolfenbüttel, Duke, 115; treaty for aid to William, 118; William's alliance with, 121
Württemberg, Duke, treaty for William's aid, 118; William's alliance with, 121

York, Duke of (James II), popularity of, 6. *See also* James II
York incident, 165–166

Zell (*sic*), 115
Zuylestein, Count, special envoy to England and mission, 49, 50, 52; effort to win Opposition, 65; sent to find James II, 197